PRECIPITOUS CITY

THE STORY OF LITERARY EDINBURGH

PRECIPITOUS CITY

TREVOR ROYLE

MAINSTREAM PUBLISHING
EDINBURGH
·
TAPLINGER PUBLISHING
NEW YORK

This edition published by
MAINSTREAM PUBLISHING COMPANY (EDINBURGH) LTD.
28 Barony Street
Edinburgh EH3 6NY

ISBN 0 906391 09 1

Reproduced from copy supplied
printed and bound in Great Britain
by Billing and Sons Limited
Guildford, London, Oxford, Worcester

I saw rain falling and the rainbow drawn
On Lammermuir. Hearkening I heard again
In my precipitous city beaten bells
Winnow the keen sea wind. And here afar
Intent on my own race and place I wrote.

Robert Louis Stevenson

CONTENTS

Preface

"I trust that among the many *literateurs* of Edinburgh there will
ere long be found some person to compose a full and detailed
history of this city, considered as a great mart of literature."

So wrote Peter Morris to his Welsh relative, the Rev. David
Williams, in that treasure trove of nineteenth-century literary
gossip, John Gibson Lockhart's *Peter's Letters to his Kinsfolk*. To pick
up that particular gauntlet was my intention but, inevitably, in
writing such a book choices had to be made: some names had to be
omitted for reasons of space, others have been emphasised to a
greater or lesser degree for reasons of choice. It was not my intention
to write a book of literary criticism, yet some judgments have been
made; neither have I set out to tell the tale of Edinburgh, although it
was impossible to ignore the political and social background; nor
have I been able to forget what was happening elsewhere, outside the
city's walls. It is, simply, the story of literary Edinburgh from its
beginnings to the middle of the twentieth century.

I owe a formal debt to the many writers who have celebrated
Edinburgh, none greater than to David Daiches, the doyen of "the
heavenly city of philosophers", and no book about Edinburgh could
be attempted without the assistance of the city's excellent public
libraries: the Edinburgh Room of the Central Library remains the
real guardian of the city's traditions.

Friends have made the task of research easier by offering advice
and snippets of useful information and Bill Campbell suggested the
idea for the book in the first place, on a winter's evening in the Cafe
Royal, with, I have come to suspect, the shades of many long dead
Edinburgh writers chuckling in the background.

Trevor Royle
Edinburgh
December 1979

Introduction

Edinburgh is one of the most beautiful of cities. No one who has climbed up Waverley Steps for the first time from the depths of the romantically named railway station and has stood astonished at the splendour of the craggy skyline in Princes Street can doubt that it is an entrance to another world. For here are brought together two entirely different settings. To the south, the castle on its rock, crouching like an ancient beast on its lair, with the towering tenements and spires of the Royal Mile within its protection; to the north, the cool elegance of Georgian architecture blessed by the smile of Reason. From whichever aspect the first time traveller beholds Edinburgh, the enchantment remains the same. From distant Soutra Hill on the old road to England, the hills neatly enfold the city giving it an orderly compactness; from the west, leafy Corstorphine Hill with the backdrop of Arthur's Seat and the Castle Rock amazes the eye, while from the sea to the north Edinburgh remains Auld Reekie, the hazy, smoky town which used to announce dinner time to its neighbours across the Forth estuary by the billowing smoke from its countless chimneys.

It is a city steeped in history and legend. Far beneath the foundations of the castle lie the fossilised remains of the first encampment where a shaggy-headed group of men took refuge, decided to stay and prospered, later pushing down the scarpment of the volcanic rock to form the beginnings of the original town. No one can be certain of the exact date in history when Edinburgh was founded, but gradually, because of its position, the settlement began to assume a strategic importance and it grew. The men who founded the city were not slow to realise its defensive potential and the rock burgeoned a fortress which became the strong first line of defence for the fledgeling township. Within its protective walls sprang up

1

the medieval town, the remains of which stand to this day around its central thoroughfare, the Royal Mile, which leads down from the castle to the Abbey of the Holy Rood. By the middle of the sixteenth century, despite occasional sackings by invading English armies, Edinburgh was an organised city inhabited by busy merchants and craftsmen. The Stewarts made Edinburgh their home and until 1603 it was the Royal capital, a title it keeps to this day.

The remains of its long history are all around. The Royal city of Scottish kings, the ordered world of the church and learning, the symmetry of the Enlightenment when Edinburgh was at home to European thought, the expanding Victorian city, and older, less happy memories of a tumultuous past. It is a city which lends itself to extravagant praise and to lavish description and hardly a decade passes without a new book adding to the chorus of adulation. The city, too, has been the setting for countless poems and many novels and it has won the admiration of visiting writers over the centuries. In all the books about Edinburgh, from R. L. Stevenson's deliciously anecdotal *Edinburgh: Picturesque Notes* to David Daiches' cool and scholarly *Edinburgh* there has been one common strand: hardly a page turns without reference to, or description by, a poet or a writer.

As Allan Ramsay, one of Edinburgh's favoured poets, reminds us, Edinburgh was from the outset a safe haven and fertile refuge for the literary imagination:

> The chiels of London, Cam and Ox,
>   Ha'e raised up great poetick stocks
> Of Rapes, of Buckets, Sarks and Locks,
>   While we neglect
> To shaw their betters, This provokes
>   Me to reflect
>
> On the lear'd days of Gawn Dunkell.
> Our country then a tale cou'd tell,
> Europe had nane mair snack and snell
>   At verse or prose;
> Our kings were poets too themsell,
>   Bauld and jocose.

Although it might have lacked the bohemian gayness of Paris, the

2

INTRODUCTION

metropolitan helter-skelter of London or the eccentric charm of Dublin, Edinburgh was, above all else, a literary city. There may be those of sterner temperament who would argue for the Law or for the Church as its principal claim to fame but a glance at Scotland's literary history confirms the city's tastes. Dunbar and Douglas, Drummond of Hawthornden, Ramsay and Fergusson, Hogg and Burns, Scott and Cockburn, Robert Louis Stevenson, Muriel Spark, Sydney Goodsir Smith: the list reads like a litany of all that is good in Scottish writing. The city was also once a centre of publishing and bookselling, rivalling London in the nineteenth century, and it should not be forgotten that the *Encyclopaedia Britannica* first saw the light of day within its walls.

Wherever one looks Edinburgh's literary past is seen in the landmarks that remain to this day: Fergusson's Cowgate, the Royal Mile which so delighted Boswell, Blackwood's saloon in George Street, the town house of Sir Walter Scott, Stevenson's Swanston Village, the literary pubs — the Cafe Royal and Abbotsford Bar — of the Scots Renaissance. The signs for the determined are not hard to find, and still, in city howffs the tradition of debate and discussion continues for those who have ears to hear:

> The Cafe Royal and Abbotsford
> are filled wi orra folk
> whaes stock-in-trade's the scrievit word,
> or twice scrievit joke.
> Brains, weak or strang, in heavy beer,
> or ordinary, soak.
> Quo yin: this yill is aafie dear,
> I hae nae clinks in poke,
> nor faulden money,
> In Embro to the ploy.

There is, though, another side to Edinburgh and Robert Garioch's poem, *Embro to the Ploy* is a clue to it. Far removed from its historical splendour or from the Georgian drawing rooms of the New Town and the respectable villas of the suburbs, there existed a world of violence, brutality, neglect and licence and it was to this world that the writer was able to turn. For there was, and continues to be, a duality of attitude in Edinburgh which allows prim gentility to exist

3

alongside excess and coarse high spirits. It is no accident that William Dunbar, who is regarded as the quintessential poet of medieval Edinburgh, pointed out in disgust to the city fathers that the "stink of haddockis and of scattis" in the streets had become well-nigh intolerable. For around the high tenement buildings that flanked the streets of the old town — the Royal Mile, the Lawnmarket, the Grassmarket and the Cowgate — medieval glamour gave way to filth, disease and stench and in their midst to the drinking clubs where social equality reigned supreme. There, Law Lords rubbed shoulders with clerks and carriers and strong drink, especially port and claret on which no tax was paid, was drunk in great quantities, Lord Cockburn remarking in his *Memorials* that it was not considered particularly monstrous for a gentleman to drink five pints of claret at a sitting.

The howffs, like Lucky Middlemasses in the Cowgate, were also the haunt of the writer and the poet. Three hundred years after Dunbar's complaint, another Edinburgh poet, poor Robert Fergusson, who was to die at the tragically early age of twenty-four, celebrated with gusto and delight the same colourful city of writers, lawyers, merchants and craftsmen. Allan Ramsay, a near contemporary, also proclaimed the city's low life and Robert Burns who came to Edinburgh in 1787 riding high on the success of the Kilmarnock edition of his poems was able to straddle the world of the tavern and the polite discretion of the drawing room with particular ease. The end of the eighteenth century marked the high watermark of Edinburgh's rumbustious literary life, but the Old Order was changing more rapidly than could ever have been realised. The gradual effects of the Union of the Parliaments in 1707 and the steady deracination of Scottish culture and decline of Scots speech, with its attendant conformity and emphasis on gentility and good manners, made it impossible for those wild, lusty, all-night drinking sessions to take place.

There was, though, the great, glorious late flowering of this golden period when from 1802 until 1832, Edinburgh was, and ever will be, the Edinburgh of Sir Walter Scott. All things and persons that were contained in the city of those thirty years are generally considered to have had their being and shelter under the presidency of that one over-arching personality: Henry Mackenzie, Dugald Stewart, Lady Nairne, James Hogg, J. G. Lockhart, Christopher

4

INTRODUCTION

North, William Blackwood, D. M. Moir, Susan Ferrier, Thomas Carlyle, Robert Chambers, Lord Cockburn, Francis Jeffrey. Scott acted as a kind of genial literary patron over their company and cast an eye over all that passed in his "own romantic town". If he developed a tendency to rewrite its history in fantastic terms he was also prepared to take a part in its everyday realities: befriending his fellow Borderer, James Hogg, The Ettrick Shepherd; writing for Jeffrey's Whig *Edinburgh Review*, while taking a hand in the establishment of its Tory rival, *Blackwood's Magazine*; masterminding a Royal visit; making and losing a fortune; and making and breaking a publisher.

The poet James Hogg, the Ettrick Shepherd, was a link between the older Edinburgh and its modern Athenian outlook, the connection with the city of Burns and Fergusson, and he is a good example, too, of the ambivalent attitudes towards the writer held by the new middle classes. Born and brought up a shepherd in the Scottish Border country, his country directness and honesty initially delighted his patrons but as time wore on he became an embarrassment to "polite" society, and though some of his friends such as the editor of *Blackwood's Magazine*, Christopher North, kept up a pretence of friendship, they were in fact exploiting him behind his back. Hogg's world of the tavern and of the common country people had to be kept strictly apart from the ambience of the literary salon and what were originally seen as his virtues were used in print to crucify him.

Little wonder that later on in the century Stevenson, with all his senses alive, was to turn against the city he loved, to reject it for its stiff morality, its lack of spirit and for its dour, chill, windy weather. Although he grew to hate Edinburgh's false morality and his restless spirit was to take him to the ends of the earth, he has left us with the most complete and loving evocation of the gulf that exists between the old Edinburgh that he was drawn to and had grown to love and the modern Edinburgh which he felt was stultifying the vigour of past years. And like Fergusson before him, it was the city's underworld which attracted him most.

> I love night in the city,
> The lighted streets and the swinging gait of harlots.
> I love cool pale morning

5

PRECIPITOUS CITY

In the empty bye-streets,
With only here and there a female figure,
A slavey with lifted dress and key in her hand,
A girl or two at play in a corner of waste-land
Tumbling and showing their legs and crying out to me loosely.

Probably no other writer celebrated Edinburgh as Robert Louis Stevenson did: it informs and shines through his poetry and the city's variety gives delight in his novels. Even in distant Samoa his beloved city was not far away from his mind's eye.

Apart from Stevenson's subtle genius, the latter half of the nineteenth century saw a general ossification of the literary scene, not only in Edinburgh, but also in the rest of Scotland. The influence of the once great magazines waned and novelists who stayed at home turned to quaint, sentimentally homespun stories of a never-never land where the triumph of rural virtue was always assured. Edinburgh as a centre of taste was being rapidly eclipsed by London and to achieve any sort of distinction writers found that they either had to write for a British market or for the inanities of a tartan-based tourist trade. For, as travel became easier and more convenient, so also did the first tourists begin to descend each summer to admire the visual delights of Scotland's capital. The city, too, was changing its character, pushing south to the Pentland Hills and westwards towards Queensferry on the Forth estuary, and in its expansion, inevitably it began to shake off the remaining sights and sounds of its tempestuous past.

Today, Edinburgh remains on the one hand a busy, cosmopolitan city and on the other a curiously provincial town unsure of its place in the world. A quaintly divided and schizophrenic city in its attitudes, it has never been certain in recent years what it wants of itself and has too often taken the easier option and plumped for prim respectability. It is still a city of contrasts where social and economic differences are not only visible area by area but also street by street, and the unwary visitor can still turn the corner from the quiet of a Georgian lane to the hustle and bustle of a busy shopping thoroughfare, or in the course of a five minute walk leave open rural spaces for the canyons of high tenement buildings.

The twentieth century has seen a revival of letters in Edinburgh and there is present in the work of poets like Robert Garioch,

INTRODUCTION

Norman MacCaig and Sydney Goodsir Smith a fondness for the city which is more critical and more reminiscent of their forbears Ramsay and Fergusson. Novelists such as Eric Linklater and Muriel Spark have evoked Edinburgh with a sense of brightness and understanding and there are today within the city a host of writers of all kinds and ages quietly adding to the city's story. The theatre, long in a moribund state, is reawakening and publishing, too, is enjoying something of a renaissance. The signs in the territory suggest that the city is re-establishing itself as a centre of literary taste and that, however modestly, the writers within its walls have retrieved the garland given to the city by the poets of the past.

But let Sydney Goodsir Smith, a poet of the twentieth century whose work spans the centuries, have the last word in this introduction:

> And shall she get the richts o' it
> A diadem for the brou?
> Shall Scotland croun her ain again,
> This ancient capital? —
> Or sell the thing for scrap?
> Or some yankee museum maybe?
> I'll be here bidin the answer . . . . . .
> Here I be and here I drink,
> This is mine, Kynd Kittock's land
> For ever and aye while stane shall stand —
> For ever and aye till the World's End.

Chapter One

The Golden Age of Scots Poetry

The beginnings of the city of Edinburgh lie buried in ancient history. There is no mention of a township there during the Roman occupation of Scotland in A.D.80 and the first reference to dwellers in the Forth valley comes from Ptolemy's *Geography* of A.D.160 where a race of people, the Votadini or Goddodin gave the town its first name of Dunedin or Edinburgh. Both John Stow and Andrew of Wyntoun, who were early chroniclers of Scottish history, placed an exact date on the city's foundation when a mythical king called Ebrauke (who was supposed to have had twenty-one wives, twenty sons and thirty daughters) established a "Maidens Castle" on the castle rock in 989 B.C.

> His sone Ebrawce in hys stede
> Regnyd, quhen that he wes dede;
> He fwndyd Yhork that gret Cyte,
> And Kayrbroye it callyd he;
> He byggyd Edynburgh wytht-alle,
> And gert thaim Allynclowd it calle
> De Mayden castell, in sum plas
> De Sorowful Hil, it callyd was.

Whatever the merits of that piece of mythology we know for certain that the tribes in the Forth valley were overrun in 638 by the Northumbrian kingdom of King Edwin, giving rise to the erroneous belief that Edwin gave his name to the city. Centuries later the city was recaptured by the Scots, a race from Ireland who had occupied present-day Argyll and who had united with, or defeated, the Picts, a Celtic people who had occupied most of the Highlands.

The first mention of Edinburgh as a centre of importance came in the reign of Malcolm Canmore (1058-1093) who had married

Margaret, the sister of Edward of Wessex. Although Malcolm chose to keep his Royal court at Dunfermline in Fife he used the Castle Rock to build a lodge for his hunting expeditions to the forest which lay to the south. The forest was not so much woodland but more a game reserve which played an important part in the economy of Malcolm's Scotland. As it was important to hunt frequently the Royal settlement grew and Margaret, who was devoutly concerned with the re-organisation of the Church in Scotland, had built for her a chapel on the Castle Rock, a building which stands to this day and which is supposed to be the oldest in the city.

Malcolm Canmore spent much of his reign harrying the north of England and interfering with English politics. On his fifth invasion he was killed while besieging Alnwick and, three days after his death, Margaret died of grief on 16th November, 1093. John of Fordun, another early historian, noted the miraculous escape of her retinue from Edinburgh after her death.

When the Queen, who had before been racked with many infirmities, almost unto death, heard this — or, rather, foreknew it through the Holy Ghost — she shrived, and devoutly took the Communion in church; and commending herself unto God in prayer, she gave back her saintly soul to heaven, in the Castle of Maidens, on the 16th of November, the fourth day after the king. Whereupon, while the holy Queen's body was still in the castle where her happy soul had passed away to Christ, whom she had always loved, Donald the Red, or Donald Bane, the king's brother, having heard of her death, invaded the kingdom, at the head of a numerous band, and in hostile-wise besieged the aforesaid castle, where he knew the king's rightful and lawful heirs were. But, forasmuch, as that spot is in itself strongly fortified by nature, he thought that the gates only should be guarded, because it was not easy to see any other entrance or outlet. But those who were within understood this, being taught of God, through the merits, we believe, of the holy Queen, they brought down her holy body by a postern on the western side. Some, indeed, tell us that, during the whole of that journey, a cloudy mist was round about all this family, and miraculously sheltered them from the gaze of any of their foes, so that nothing hindered them as they journeyed by land or by sea; but they brought her away, as she had herself before bidden them, and prosperously reached the place they wished — namely, the church of Dunfermline, where she

now rests in Christ.
(translation by F.J.H. Skene)

Their son David expanded the city, building the Abbey of Holy Rood for the Augustinians and granting a charter to them to set up markets for trade. Edinburgh was by then firmly placed on the map.

The city grew and prospered, despite being the object of raiding English armies for much of the fourteenth century, an English report in 1295 stating the blunt facts of an invasion: "The Wednesdaie to Edenbrough the abbey, and causid ther to be set up iij engyns castyng into the Castell day and nyght; and the Vth daie thei spake of pees." In 1329 the city was granted a Royal Charter by Robert 1 and it was beginning to assume the pattern that determines the shape of the present Old Town. To the west stands the Castle on its rock, to the east the Abbey (and Palace) of Holy Rood. Both are joined together by a long, narrow street, the Royal Mile (which is made up of Castlehill, the Lawnmarket, the High Street, the Canongate and the Abbey Strand), the spine of the old town from which run the many wynds and closes where stood the towering tenements or "lands". It was a crowded, bustling city which by the fifteenth century was starting to assume the dignity of the capital of the country as the Stewart kings came to make their Royal residence the Castle, and like other medieval princes, to foster the arts and sciences.

There was, however, another, darker side to the picture. Although Edinburgh was described by the historian Hector Boece as surpassing other cities in "polese, reparation, wisdome and riches", it was also a poverty-stricken, disease-ridden, stinking den. Most of the houses were built of wood with thatched roofs, they lacked even the most basic sanitation and all the household refuse was thrown into the street by the front door. At the end of the fifteenth century Edinburgh was hit by successive outbreaks of plague and although the city council finally made some attempt in 1505 to remove the waste from the streets, the situation was exacerbated by using the burial ground as a public midden for all manner of unwanted refuse from the city.

The gulf between rich and poor was enormous and although the Court and the merchants enjoyed a style of life which kept them

11

apart from the horrors of everyday life, for the commoners it was a
short-lived and miserable existence. William Dunbar, who may be
considered to be Edinburgh's first poet, was also the first of many
writers to take the city to task for its money-grubbing attitudes.

> Quhy will ye merchantis of renoun,
> Lat Edinburgh, your nobil toun,
> For laik of reformatioun
> The commone proffeitt tyine and fame?
>   Think ye not schame,
> That onie uther regioun
> Sall with dishonour hurt your name!
>
> May nane pas throw your principall gaittis
> For stink of haddockis and of scattis,
> For cryis of carlingis and debaittis,
> For fensum flyttingis of defame;
>   Think ye not schame,
> Before strangeris of all estaittis
> That sic dishonour hurt your name!

It was not a pleasant picture. The city smells horribly, poverty is
rife, merchants swindle honest men, the citizens fall pray to violence
and crime and even the town's minstrels have fallen on such a
poverty of ideas that they can only sing two songs. At the end of this
long complaint, where the word "schame" becomes a recurring
litany against the evils perpetrated by mankind, Dunbar calls on the
city council and the Court of Session to find a remedy for the city's
ills.

> Sen for the Court and the Sessioun,
> The great repair of this regioun
> Is in your burgh, thairfoir be boun
> To mend all faultis that ar to blame,
>   And eschew schame;
> Gif thai pas to ane uther toun
> Ye will decay, and your great name!
>
> Thairfoir strangeris and leigis treit,
> Tak not ouer meikle for thair meit,
> And gar your merchandis be discreit,

That na extortiounes be proclame
  All fraud and schame:
Keip ordour, and poore nighbouris beit,
That ye may gett ane bettir name!

Very little of certainty is known about William Dunbar's life except that he was perhaps the most "professional" poet to flourish during the reign of James IV. It has been suggested that he was born and brought up in East Lothian and then sent to the University of St Andrews, where he became a priest. Certainly his poetry rings with a knowledge of the Church and he himself confessed to a childhood ambition to reach high orders in the Church.

I wes in youthe, on nureice kne
Cald dandillie, bischop, dandillie,

Like many other learned men of his day he depended on Court patronage. As a prebendary of the Church he was paid a pension of £10 a year but this was increased, probably because of his literary and diplomatic services to the Court, to £20 in 1507 and three years later to £80. In addition he was entitled to an annual gift of clothing, the neglect of which in one sad year gave rise to one of his best bitter-sweet satires, *The Petition of the Gray Horse, Auld Dunbar*, a remarkable and imaginative comparison of the forgotten poet with a tired, old work-horse. After a long life of devoted service the old horse asks the King for mercy and kindness — the poet Dunbar asks for his gift of clothing — which is granted in the final *Respontio Regis*.

Efter our wrettingis, thesaurer,
Tak in this gray horse, Auld Dunbar,
Quhilk in my aucht with service trew
In lyart changeit is in hew.
Gar hows him now aganis this Yuill,
And busk him lyk and bischopis muill,
For with my hand I have indost
To pay quhatevir his trappouris cost.

Dunbar, in fact, spent much of his time and energy in vain attempts to be granted a benefice by the King. Although this period is known as the "Golden Age" it was only golden in the quality of poetry written. Despite James IV's accomplishments and his interest in science, Scotland was a fairly wretched place as far as the arts were concerned and those without means, like Dunbar, felt keenly the absence of a decent income. In his *Complaint to the King* he bemoans the Court's preference for all manner of charlatans, cowards, rascals and "mismad mandragis of mastris strynd" (mis-shapen mandrakes of mastiff strain) instead of for noble men of virtue.

Although Edinburgh was the centre of government during the reign of James IV the King spent parts of the year away from the capital. He brought some cohesion to Highland society, he busied himself in the construction of a navy — half of Fife's forests being cleared for the construction of the *Great Michael* — he interested himself in such diverse subjects as surgery and languages and he used the Church as a means of governing his country. Pedro de Ayala, a visiting Spanish nobleman, commented on the monarch's generosity and gayness and on the geniality of Court life, but he also noted James's impatient and impulsive character, traits which were later to cost him his life. He was also a religious man, consumed with guilt over his father's murder, and it was while the King was in religious retreat in Stirling that Dunbar wrote another complaint, *The Dregy of Dunbar*. This time Dunbar was in comic mood, making his poem a travesty of the mass for the dead and comparing the worldly joys of Edinburgh to the purgatory of life as a hermit in Stirling.

> We that ar heir in hevins glory,
> To yow that ar in purgatory,
> Commendis us on our hairtly wyis;
> I mene we folk in parradyis,
> In Edinburgh with all mirrines,
> To you of Strivilling in distres,
> Quhair nowdir plesance nor delyt is,
> For pety this epistell wrytis.

It was perhaps due to this kind of ridicule of the Church that James denied Dunbar the rewards he felt to be his due. The Church was a powerful force in the land and in Edinburgh, in addition to the Abbey of Holy Rood, the church of St Giles had become a collegiate church and there were two other churches of importance within the city — the Church of Holy Trinity (demolished in 1848 to make way for Waverley Station) and St Marys-in-the-Fields which stood to the south of the High Street and which was destroyed during the Reformation.

Despite the emergence of Edinburgh as a religious centre, the Church was a hotbed of oppression, corruption and neglect and Dunbar was not slow to satirise its excesses in the city. When the law courts were in session the city became a busier place as plaintiffs jostled for a fair deal. In *Tydingis frae the Sessioun* Dunbar mocks the whole legal set-up, smiling grimly at the dance which allowed lawlessness to flourish in the streets while the judges tried previous offences. To the teeming streets came monks and priests determined to father a new generation of religious men.

> Religious men of divers placis
> Cumis thair to wow and se fair facis;
> Baith Carmeleitis and Cordilleris
> Cumis thair to genner and get ma freiris,
> And ar unmyndfull of thair professioun;
> The yungar at the eldar leiris:
> Sic tydingis hard I at the Sessioun.
>
> Thair cumis yung monkis of he complexioun,
> Of devoit mynd, luve and affectioun,
> And in the courte thair hait flesche dantis,
> Full faderlyk, with pechis and pantis;
> Thay ar so humill of intercessioun,
> All mercyfull wemen thair eirandis grantis:
> Sic tydingis hard I at the Sessioun.

Dunbar was never a man to pull his punches, especially when he was in argument and he has left us with the best example of a 'flyting' — a battle of words with a fellow poet. This literary form has a long and honourable history amongst Scottish poets, but the insults hurled by Dunbar and his opponent Walter Kennedy have a uniquely vituperative flavour and have been unequalled by any other poet, even in recent times.

> Conspiratour, cursit cocatrice, hell caa,
>   Turk, trumpour, traitour, tyran intemperate;
> Thow irefull attircop, Pilote apostata,

15

Judas, jow, juglour, Lollard laureate;
Sarazene, symonyte provit, Pagan pronunciate,
Machomete, manesuourne, bugrist abhominable,
Devill, dampnit dog, sodomyte insatiable,
With Gog and Magog grete glorificate.

In the *Flyting of Dunbar and Kennedy* as in other poems Dunbar was very much a man of his times. All round him Edinburgh was growing but not all the changes he noticed were for the better. Feudalism was giving way to a new form of capitalism with the rise of the merchants who came to be an important class in the city, dominating both its politics and its financing and thus deciding the city's ultimate physical shape. Later writers, especially in the early nineteenth century looked back at the city in its "golden" medieval period and fondly imagined a society rich with the birth of learning and bathed in material comfort which wanted for nothing. In his long poem *The Queen's Wake* James Hogg, friend of Sir Walter Scott, imagined a city that could have come out of a Bellini painting.

See yon hamlet, o'ershadow'd with smoke;
See yon hoary battlement throned on the rock;
Even there shall a city in spendour break forth,
The haughty Dun-Edin, the Queen of the North;
There learning shall flourish, and liberty smile,
The awe of this world, and the pride of the isle.

The reality was much harsher and Dunbar was fully aware not only of the gulfs that existed in society but also of the duality of his own vision: he was capable of joyous praise, but he knew, too, the depths of despair when James's hand was turned against him. As we shall see, Edinburgh was to give birth to many writers and poets who were to display that same schizoid attitude towards the city they chose to live in. On the one hand was the splendour of the Court and the wealth of the merchants and on the other the stench of rotting haddocks and skates.

James's reign came to an abrupt end in 1513 when European political monoeuvering put Scotland once again into conflict with her neighbour England. In 1502 a treaty had been signed between the two countries pledging peace with the marriage of James to

Margaret, eldest daughter of Henry VII. But the Scots were also in treaty with France — the Auld Alliance — and when the Pope set up the Holy League to keep France out of Italy, England joined it, leaving France to call on her treaty obligations with Scotland. In the summer of 1513 James raised a Scottish army to invade England and set off for the Border where he met an English army under the command of Thomas Howard, Earl of Surrey. On 9th September the two armies fought at Flodden Field and James, betraying all the impetuosity remarked on by de Ayala, not only surrendered a superior tactical position but also rushed headlong into battle with his troops.

He was killed early in the battle along with many of Scotland's leading nobility and churchmen and several thousand troops. It was an unparalleled disaster, and fearful of an invasion, the city council in distant Edinburgh hurriedly built a defensive wall which ran from the south-east corner of the Castle, skirted the area south of the Grassmarket and ended at the east end of the Nor Loch. The anticipated attack never happened but the shock of grief at the loss of James IV and his retinue reverberated throughout the land. In another century, Jean Elliot (1727-1805) wrote one of Scotland's most haunting songs about the disaster, *The Flowers of the Forest*.

> Dule and wae for the order sent our lads to the Border;
>   The English for ance, by guile wan the day;
> The Flowers of the Forest, that foucht aye the foremost,
>   The prime o' our land are cauld in the clay.
>
> We'll hear nae mair lilting at our yowe-milking,
>   Women and bairns are heartless and wae;
> Sighing and moaning on ilka green loaning:
>   'The Flowers of the Forest are a' wede away.'

Others writers of later times were also grimly attracted to the tragedy and wrote about it eloquently, even if the facts were more than somewhat cavalierly treated. Examples were William Edmonstoune Aytoun's *Lays of the Scottish Cavaliers* and Walter Scott's *Marmion*, which also gives a highly romanticised view of Edinburgh in the sixteenth century, especially in the famous description of the city as seen from Blackford Hill.

Still on the spot Lord Marmion stay'd,
For fairer scene he ne'er survey'd.
When sated with the martial show
That peopled all the plain below,
The wandering eye could o'er it go,
And mark the distant city glow
  With gloomy splendour red;
For on the smoke-wreaths, huge and slow,
That round her sable turrets flow,
  The morning beams were shed,
  And tinged them with a lustre proud,
  Like that which streaks a thunder-cloud.
Such dusky grandeur clothed the height,
Where the huge Castle holds its state,
  And all the steep slope down,
Whose ridgy back heaves to the sky,
Piled deep and massy, close and high,
  Mine own romantic town!
But northward far, with purer blaze,
On Ochil mountains fell the rays,
And as each heathy top they kiss'd,
It gleamed a purple amethyst.
Yonder the shores of Fife you saw;
Here Preston-Bay, and Berwick Law;
  And broad between them roll'd,
The gallant Frith the eye might note,
Whose islands on its bosom float,
  Like emeralds chased in gold.
Fitz-Eustace' heart felt closely pent;
As if to give his nature vent,
The spur he to his charger lent,
  And raised his bridle hand,
And making demi-volte in air,
Cried, "Where's the coward that would not dare
  To fight for such a land!"

The death of his patron on Flodden Field also marks the end of Dunbar's career as a Court poet. Although there is no record of his death, his name disappears from the Royal Accounts in 1513 when payment ceased to be made to him.

Although during the reign of James IV Scotland had remained a poor country in comparison with Burgundy or the wealthy Italian states, some cultural advancements were made during the early sixteenth century. Chepman and Myller set up the first printing press in Edinburgh in 1507 with machines brought over from France, and they had been responsible for printing some of Dunbar's poems. The advent of printing in the city was very much a double-edged sword: it could be used as a powerful tool of education to spread knowledge and learning, but there were those Churchmen who felt that printing could undermine their power and influence over the population. It was to be a long time before printing became a fully established craft within the city and most writers had to look to Paris to have their work produced with the kind of sophistication that was becoming widespread throughout Europe. The historians Hector Boece and John Major had their work printed at the press of Jodocus Badius Ascensius in Paris. Both wrote in Latin because they thought of their work — especially Boece's *Vitae* and Major's *Historia Majoris Britanniae* — as being written for a European audience.

One writer who eschewed the use of printing techniques was the other great poet of James IV's reign, Gavin Douglas, Bishop of Dunkeld. In his translation of the *Aeneid* he explains to the reader that his work would be copied by other writers.

> The writaris all, and gentill redaris eyk,
> Offendis nocht my volum, I beseik,
> Bot redis leill, and tak gud tent in tyme.
> The nother maggill nor mysmetyr my ryme.

Unlike his fellow poets, Douglas's life is reasonably well documented, probably because he was the scion of a wealthy and influential family. He was the third son of Archibald, fifth Earl of Angus who carried with him the ominous nickname of "Bell the Cat", because like other members of the tempestuous Douglas family he was not afraid of challenging authority. Gavin Douglas was probably born in Tantallon Castle in East Lothian and educated at the University of St Andrews at the end of the fifteenth century. He entered the Church, becoming a dean of Dunkeld and winning for himself the kind of benefices from the King that befitted the younger son of a noble family. In 1503 he was appointed Provost of the Church of St Giles in Edinburgh, a post which gave him considerable spiritual and temporal power as his influence at James's Court began to grow. The stability of his life is in stark contrast with the pleadings of his contemporary William Dunbar for a small church in the heather.

It was during this period that he embarked on his translation of Virgil's *Aeneid* into Middle Scots. Like many other translators of his day Douglas did not feel the need to render an exact translation of the Latin, rather he wrote in a way that his contemporaries would understand. Thus the characters in the poem behave like fifteenth-century knights and often the background is more Edinburgh and the grey North Sea than the colourful panoply of the Mediterranean. Douglas also doubted if it was in fact possible to write in Scots: Latin had a long pedigree whereas his own tongue did not. This was not a rejection of Scots, nor indeed of English its close relation, but rather an acknowledgement that in a changing European society, vernacular languages were beginning to supplant the centuries old use of Latin.

That Douglas had a firm grasp of Scots as a living language and was not afraid to take risks with it can be seen to good effect in the Prologue to Book VII of the *Eneados* which contains a description of winter in Edinburgh so accurate and representative that it could have been written yesterday.

Bewte was lost, and barrand schew the landis,
With frostis hair ourfret the feldis standis,
Seir bittir bubbis and the schowris snell
Semyt on the sward a symylitude of hell,
Reducyng to our mynd, in every sted,
Gousty scaddois of eild and grisly ded.
Thik drumly skuggis dyrknyt so the hevyn,
Dym skyis oft furth warpit feirfull levyn,
Flaggis of fire, and mony felloun flaw,
Scharpe soppys of sleit and of the snypand snaw.
The dolly dichis war all donk and wait,
The law valle flodderit all with spait,
The plane stretis and every hie way
Full of floschis, dubbis, myre and clay.
Laggerit leyis wallowit farnys schew,
Browne muris kythit thar wysnyt mossy hew,

Brank, bra and boddum blanchit wolx and bar.
For gurl weddir growit bestis hair.
The wynd maid waif the red wed on the dyke,
Bedowyn in dinkis deip was every sike.
Our craggis and the front of rochis seir,
Hang gret ische schoulis lang as ony speir.
The grond stud barrant, widderit, dosk or gray,
Herbis, floweris and gersis wallowyt away.
Woddis, forrestis, with nakyt bewis blowt,
Stude stripyt of their weid in every howt.

Even if the language is difficult to the modern ear, the use of harsh,
onomatopoeic words fully suggests a bitter wind rattling around the
chimney pots and a hard frost holding the countryside in its vice-like
grip. To redress the balance later in the poem there is also a view of a
Scottish spring time, which although it may resemble the wealth and
beauty of medieval tapestries nevertheless is a fondly observed
picture of the reawakening of the year in a rural community. Even
though the description of the weather comes more from the
imagination than from seasonal facts, Douglas's fondness for young
animals in May would have been instantly recognised by his fellow
townsmen with the countryside lying just outside the city walls.

Under the bewys beyn in lusty valys,
Within the fremans and parkis cloys of palys,
The bustuus bukkis rakis furth on raw;
Heyrdis of hertis throw the thyk wod schaw,
Baith the brokkettis, and with braid burnyst tyndis,
The sprutlyt calvys sowkand the red hyndis,
The young fownis followand the dun days,
Kyddis skippand throw ronnys efter rays;
In lyssouris and on leys litill lammys
Full tayt and tryg socht bletand to thar dammys,
Tydy ky lowys, veilys by thame rynnys;
All snog and sleikit worth their bestis skynnys.

After the completion of the *Eneados*, Douglas was made a burgess
or freeman of the city of Edinburgh. The date was the 30th
September 1513 — in the grim days following the Battle of Flodden
— and for Douglas it was a turning point in his life. His other major

21

work of poetry had been *The Palice of Honour*, a medieval dream allegory, but after becoming a freeman he stopped writing poetry as his family's fortunes changed again with the marriage of his nephew to the king's widow, Margaret Tudor. This action created a political crisis as James's successor, his eighteen-month-old son, required protection and his mother's re-marriage was considered by her opponents to be tantamount to a forfeiture of the Regency. To this position was appointed the Duke of Albany, the exiled brother of James III, who ruled Scotland between 1515 and 1524 when James V achieved his majority at the age of twelve.

For Douglas it was a period of heavy involvement in Scottish affairs. As a loyal member of the Queen's party he was rewarded for his services by being created Bishop of Dunkeld in 1515, having failed earlier to secure the influential archbishopric of St Andrews. But his family loyalty cost him dear later that year when he was imprisoned by Albany in "the wyndy and richt unplesant castell and royk of Edinburgh". He later made his peace with Albany and acted as an ambassador in France but during the whole period suspicions of the Douglas family ran high and in 1521, while on a mission to Cardinal Wolsey in London, he was found guilty of high treason and exiled in England. He died in the September of the following year and was buried at the Hospital Church of the Savoy beneath a plaque which states, *Gavanus Dowglas, natione Scotus, Dunkellensis praesul, patria sua exul.*

Douglas had enjoyed a life of comparative ease and luxury and during his period as Provost of St Giles and as Bishop of Dunkeld (he had a palace in Edinburgh) he was a well-known figure in the High Street. There is no formal evidence that he knew his older contemporary William Dunbar but they must have met at Court and certainly they knew one another's work. In *The Palice of Honour*, the dreamer is summoned before a Court of Poetry where,

> Great Kennedie, and Dunbar yet undeid,
> And Quintine with ane huttock on his heid.

Quintine is probably Quintyn Shaw, the cousin of Walter Kennedy who fought the poetic battle with William Dunbar.

The political upheavels of the early sixteenth century, though, had removed much power and influence from Edinburgh. The young

James V had spent most of his childhood at Stirling Castle where he had been surrounded by the familiar faces of the Royal household whose Master was Sir David Lyndsay of the Mount and who in later years reminded the King of his services to him when a child.

> How, as ane chapman bears his pack,
> I bore thy Grace upon my back,
> And sumtymes, stridlings on my neck,
> Dansand with mony bend and beck.
> The first syllabis that thou did mute
> Was PA, DA LYN. Upon the lute
> Then playit I twenty springs, perqueir,
> Whilk wes gret piete for to hear.

Lyndsay remained a close friend of the king's and went on to write a play which gave pleasure not just to the court but also to a wide range of Scottish society, *Ane Satyre of the Thrie Estaitis*, a castigation of the complete lack of spiritual values held by the Church. He had been born in 1488 near Cupar in Fife and was educated at the University of St Andrews, taking up a minor post at the Court of James IV, serving his son and ending up as Lord Lyon King of Arms in 1538. He wrote several pleasing verses celebrating the monarchy, using much of it for political and religious propaganda, but it is in the *Satyre* that he achieves his greatest triumph.

Drama was not new to Scotland. The main religious centres of Perth, St Andrews, Haddington, Glasgow and Edinburgh had staged Passion and Nativity plays and guild processions were an accepted part of the religious calendar. Tableaux were also popular at Court where the King's patronage extended to music and courtly song, and on a lower scale, guisings and festivals for May Day and other holidays were enjoyed by all in the city's streets. In Edinburgh the Master of Ceremonies, or Lord of Misrule, was called Robin Hood and some idea of the lusty wildness over which he ruled can be seen from a city council edict later in the century expelling the roisterers from the city: "all menstrallis, pyperis, fidleris, common sangsteris, and specially of badrie and filthie sangs, and siclyke all vagabounds and maisterless persons quha hes na service nor honest industrie to leif be".

Lyndsay, then, was brought up in a society where dramatic form was all around him, from the stateliness of Holyrood Palace to the noise and bluster of the High Street on public holidays, scenes which would have doubtless influenced the creation of the *Satyre*. The play opens with Rex Humanitas under the influence of the deadly sins, but Divine Correctioun calls on the Parliament of the Thrie Estaitis to bring about the reforms advocated by John the Common-weill. These are carried through despite the opposition of the first estate, the clergy (the second being the nobility and the third the merchants) who see too many of their interests such as the ownership of vast tracts of land being taken away from them. Beneath that moral outline, though, lies a play rich with dramatic tension and a sharp but lyrical use of Scots which reaches its heights in the sustained argumentative speeches of the main characters.

The play was first performed in front of James V on Twelth Night 1540 in the Great Hall of Linlithgow Palace which lies some twenty miles to the west of Edinburgh. Later it was shown at Lyndsay's native town of Cupar and again in August 1554 at the Greenside fields in Edinburgh, below Calton Hill (where the Playhouse now stands at the top of Leith Walk) in front of Marie of Guise who watched it from a Royal pavilion decorated with flowers and branches of birch. At that last, contemporary performance — the play was not to be resurrected until the Edinburgh International Festival of 1948 — Lyndsay was able to introduce allusions to local social conditions, such as thieving merchants, dishonest farmers and the pest of all manner of beggars and rogues.

> This bebe against the strang beggers,
> Fidlers, pypers and pardoners:
> Thir Iugglars, Iestars, and idill cuitchours,
> Thir carriers and thir quintacensours:
> Thir babil-beirers and thir bairds,
> Thir sweir swyngeours with Lords and Lairds
> Ma then thair rentis may susteine,
> Or to thair profeit neidfull bene,
> Quhilk bene ay blythest of discords,
> And deidly feid amang thar Lords.
> For then they sleutchers man be treatit,
> Or else thair querrels vndebaitit.
> This bene against thir great fat Freiris,
> Augustenes, Carmeleits and Cordeleirs:

And all vthers that in cowls bene clad,
Quhilk labours nocht laborand Spirituallie,
Nor for thair living corporallie:
Lyand in dennis lyke idill doggis
I them compair to weil-fed hoggis.

The play is also rich in earthly humour suggesting that all the
social classes went to, and enjoyed, the play and that Lyndsay
himself was aware of the need to nod at the differences in his
audience. At the end of the first act he gives some practical,
down-to-earth advice to those watching the play, proposals which
would no doubt have been approved by his fellow poet of another
century, Robert Burns. Not unnaturally it is given by Gvde
Covnsall.

And als I mak yow exhortatioun,
Sen ye haif heard the first pairt of our play:
Go tak ane drink, and mak Collatioun,
Ilk man drink till his marrow, I yow pray.
Tarie nocht lang, it is lait in the day,
Let sum drink Ayle and sum drink Claret wine:
Be great Doctors of Physick I heare say,
That michtie drink comforts the dull ingine.
And ye Ladies that list to pisch,
Lift up your taill, plat in ane disch:
And gif that your mawkine cryis quhisch,
    Stop in ane wusp of stray.
Let nocht your bladder burst I pray yow,
For that war euin aneuch to slay yow:
For yit thair is to cum, I say yow,
    The best pairt of our Play.

Lyndsay was a Court poet and he acted as a kind of poet laureate,
celebrating the events of the city. In 1537 James V had married
Madeleine, daughter of Francois I, King of France and the Auld
Alliance was cemented once more. Her arrival in Scotland in May
that year was an occasion for official rejoicing and Lyndsay was on
hand to record the scene.

Thief! saw thow nocht the greit preparatyis
Of Edinburgh, the nobill famous town;

Thow saw the peple, labouring for thair lyvis,
  To mak triumphe, with trump, and clarioun;
  Sic plesour was never, in to this regioun,
As suld have bene the day of hir entrace;
With greit propynis, gevin ti hir Grace.

Thow saw makand rycht costlie scaffalding
  Depayntit weill, with gold, and asure fine,
Reddie preparit for the upsetting,
  With fontanis, flowing watter cleir and wyne,
  Disgysit folkis, lyke creaturis divyne,
On ilk scaffold, to play ane syndrie storie,
Bot, all in greiting turnit thow that glorie.

Thow saw mony ane lustie fresche galland,
  Weill ordourit for resaving of thait Quene:
Ilk cratisman, with bent bow in his hand,
  Full galyeantlie in schort clething of grene:
  The honest Burges, cled thow suld have sene,
Sum in scarlot, and sum in claith of grane,
For til have met thair Lady Soverane.

Provest, Baillies, and Lordis of the town,
  The Senatouris, in order consequent,
Cled into silk or pupure, blak and broun;
  Syne the greit Lordis of the Parliament,
  With mony knychtlie Barroun and Banrent,
In silk, and gold, and colouris confortable;
Bot thow, allace! all turnit into sable.

As the poem suggests, unfortunately Madeleine died seven weeks after her triumphant entrance into Edinburgh, but nothing daunted, the Auld Alliance was kept in being when Francois gave his son-in-law the hand of Marie of Guise, the widow of the Duc de Longueville. This last period of James's reign was one of continuing hostility from the nobility he had spent time and energy trying to tame, a policy which won him the love and respect of his poorer subjects. No less popular was his custom of dressing up as a beggar and moving amongst his subjects incognito. "The Gudeman o' Ballengeich", as he was known, passed into Scottish folklore as

26

being synonomous with the king as did the many stories of drunken
nights spent with beggars and tinkers and his seduction of servant
girls, for as Pierre de Ronsard, the French poet who came to
Scotland in 1537, noted, James was a fine figure of a man.

> His bearing was regal, his glance was eloquent
> Of honour in war, skill in love's tournament;
> Sweetness and strength together in his face
> Showed Mars and Venus both had lent him grace.

Like his earlier Stewart ancestors James was also a poet and to him
has been attributed *Christ's Kirk on the Green* which is full of rich
humour about country folk and their celebrations. He also enriched
the Palace of Holyrood with trappings from France and upheld the
Catholic faith at a time when Lollardry and Calvinism were making
swift inroads into the country and building up the seeds of
confrontation later in the century.

The connection with France brought the Stewart family into
conflict in 1541, once again with England, but James's nobles, many
of whom had become Protestants, were unwilling to risk a
repetition of the disaster at Flodden and a half-hearted attempt to
prevent the English army entering Scotland was made at Solway
Moss when the Scots were routed by an inferior English force. James
died of grief a few months later, leaving his country in the Regency
of his wife, the mother of their young daughter, Mary, who was to
become Queen of Scots.

His capital city became the subject of numerous attacks upon it by
the English and in 1544 the Port of Leith and the Abbey and Palace of
Holyrood were razed by an English army under the command of the
Earl of Hertford. Only the old town within the walls was
unmolested and its inhabitants left reasonably safe. In the nineteenth
century, David Masson, Professor of English at the University of
Edinburgh, wrote a telling description of the Edinburgh of the
mid-sixteenth century, based on that extraordinary and anonymous
documentation of the period, the *Diurnall of Occurrents in Scotland*.

A belated traveller passing through the hamlets that once
straggled on the grounds of the present New Town, and arriving
at the edge of the North Loch in what is now the valley of Princes

27

Street Gardens, must have looked up across the Loch to much the same twinkling embankment of the High Street and its closes, and to much the same serrated sky-line, lowering itself eastward from the shadowy mass of the Castle Rock. If the traveller desired admission into the town, he could not have it on this side at all, but would have to go round to some of the ports in the town-wall from its commencement at the east end of the North Loch. He might try them all in succession — Leith Wynd Port, the Nether Bow Port, the Cowgate Port, the Kirk of Field Port, Greyfriars Port and the West Port — with the chance of finding that he was too late for entrance at any, and so of being brought back to his first station, and obliged to seek lodging till the morning in some hamlet there, or else in the Canongate. He could perform the whole circuit of the walls, however, in less than an hour, and might have the solace, at some points of his walk, of night views down into the luminous hollows of the town, very different from his first view upward from the North Loch. While the belated traveller was thus shut out, the inhabitants within might be passing their hours till bed-time comfortably enough, whether in the privacy of their domiciles, or in the less noisy loitering and locomotion among the streets and wynds. If it were clear moonlight or starlight, the wynds and especially the stately length of the High Street, would be radiantly distinct, and locomotion in them would be easy. But even in the darkest nights the townsmen were not reduced to actual groping through their town, if *ennui*, or whim, or business, or neighbourly conviviality determined them to be out of doors. Not only would they carry torches and lanterns with them for their own behoof, especially if they had to find their way down narrow closes to their homes; not only were there gratuitous oil-lights or candle-lights from the windows of the fore-tenements in the streets and wynds, sending down some glimmer into the streets and wynds themselves; but, by public regulation, the tenants of the fore-stair houses in the principal thoroughfares were bound to hang out, during certain hours of the evening, lamps for the guidance of those that might be passing. One has to remember, however, that people in those days kept very early hours. By ten o' clock every night Auld Reikie was mostly asleep. By that hour, accordingly, the house-lights, with some exceptions, had ceased to twinkle; and from that hour, save for bands of late roysterers here and there at close-mouths, and for the appointed night watches on guard at the different ports, or making an occasional round with drum and whistle, silence reigned till dawn.

28

The population of Edinburgh at James's death was about 30,000 souls crammed into the narrow area of the High Street, the Canongate and the lands to the south of the Grassmarket. This excluded the numberless beggars who crowded into the narrow streets to display gross deformities and injuries in their quest for money or shelter. The city council tried unsuccessfully on many occasions to rid the town of these living examples of an uncaring society, as they also tried to keep the streets clear of all manner of filth and rubbish. It was a coarse, brutal, disease and poverty ridden age and of its poets only Dunbar was prepared to hold up a mirror to the society of his "nobill toun".

But in spite of the desperate inequalities, the city's compact shape gave it a sense of togetherness in the tenements which lined the main street. Here, all classes lived together, the poor on street level, the merchants and craftsmen higher up and the nobility on the top floors where they could breath the fresher, clearer air. Here too, were the taverns and the shops, and connected to the Old Tolbooth by St Giles stood the Luckenbooths — or locked booths — seven timber-fronted tenements of six storeys, which was a kind of shopping arcade. They lasted until 1815 when they were finally pulled down, because, "the paradise of childhood" remembered by Lord Cockburn had become too dangerous and verminous, but, in their day, although they reduced the width of the High Street to fifteen feet at St Giles, they were an important focal point of trade within the city.

During the reigns of James IV and V Edinburgh, because it housed the Court, became a literary centre, attracting both poets and scholars to live within its walls. Printing had gained a tenuous foothold but ahead lay tempestuous times which would threaten the whole fabric of the new found poetic imagination.

Chapter Two

Reformation

Shortly before his death in December 1542, James V received a further affliction when he learned that his wife had given birth to a baby daughter who would eventually succeed him as monarch of Scotland. When the messenger from Linlithgow passed the news to him, he is supposed to have said, "Adieu, farewell, it came with a lass, it will pass with a lass." During the consequent struggle for power, Henry VIII of England attempted to gain influence in Scottish affairs by arranging a marriage between his son and the future Scottish queen, Mary, but he overplayed his hand by invading Scotland, in the grimly named "Rough Wooing" which led not only to French intervention in Scotland but also to the removal of Mary to France and marriage to the Dauphine.

The Queen Mother, Mary of Guise, encouraged this French involvement, French troops were stationed in Leith and she spent much of her time interfering in Church politics. As William Dunbar and Sir David Lyndsay had pointed out so caustically in their work, the Church was in need of reform and this came from Europe in the doctrines of Luther and Calvin whose ideas quickly gained a foothold in the main religious centre, St Andrews, and later in Edinburgh. By 1560 the Protestant church was triumphant in Scotland, a Confession of Faith was passed by parliament, the authority of the Pope was abolished and the celebration of Mass was made a punishable offence. Most importantly of all for the country's future, an ambitious plan was launched, through the reformed church, for the provision of universal education for all classes in Scotland.

There is a telling contemporary description of the conflicts between the ruling Catholics and the new clergy in John Leslie's *History of Scotland* which was published in 1571.

REFORMATION

In this meinetyme the tumult incressed dalie within the realme of Scotland, quhill at last the precheours begouth to preche opinlie in divers partis, and principallie within sum housis of the toun of Edinburgh; and sindre Inglis buikis, ballettis and treateis was gevin furth be thame amangis the people, to move thame to seditione. The Quene regent perceaving the tumult incres, past all the rest of that winter in sumpteous and magnificque banqueting, quhilk sho caused the lordis make severalie in Edinburgh, thinking be that and siclike familiar intertenement to have stayed all thair interprices; bot nothing culd stay thame from the same.

The man who stood behind the reform movement was John Knox, who had been born in Haddington, East Lothian, in 1514 and who had worked in his home area as a priest until 1545 when he met the visionary reformer, George Wishart. After the murder of Cardinal Beaton in St Andrews and the capture of the town's castle by the Protestants, Knox became a prisoner of the French and spent some time as a galley slave for his beliefs. After a period in Geneva he returned to Edinburgh and on the completion of the Reformation settlement became a minister in Edinburgh, where he wrote his *History of the Reformation in Scotland*. The following year, 1561, the Dauphine's death brought Mary back to Scotland, as Catholic queen of a Protestant country.

She arrived in Edinburgh on 19th August on a warm day which had been preceded by several days of heavy mist in the Forth estuary, unseasonal weather which was seen by many as an ill omen. Included among those was Knox, who took time in his *History* to prophesy bleakly on his country's future.

The verray face of heavin, the time of hir arryvall, did manifestlie speak what confort was brought into this cuntrey with hir, to wit, sorow, dolour, darknes, and all impietie; for in the memorie of man, that day of the year, was never seyn a more dolorous face of the heavin, then was at hir arryvall, which two days after did so contineu; for besides the surfett weat, and corruptioun of the air, the myst was so thick and so dark, that skairse mycht any man espy ane other the lenth of two pair of buttis. The sun was not seyn to schyne two dais befoir, nor two dayis after. That foir warning gave God unto us; but allace, the most pairt war blynd.

31

Edinburgh was taken aback by her arrival but the warmth of her triumphant procession from Leith to the Palace of Holyrood has been captured in the poem of welcome written by Sir Richard Maitland.

> Excellent Princes! potent and preclair,
>   Prudent, peerless in bontie and bewtie!
> Maist nobil Quein of bluid under the air!
> With all my hairt, and micht, I welcum the
>   Hame to thy native pepill, and cuntrie.
> Beseikand God to gif the grace to haive
>   Of thy leigis the hairtis faythfullie,
> And thame in luife, and favour to receave.
>
> Now sen thow art arryvit in this land,
>   Our native Princes, and illuster Queine!
> I traist to God this regioune sall stand
> Ane auld frie land, as it long tyme has bein.
>   Quharin, richt schoone, thair sall be hard and seine
> Grit joy, justice, gude peax, and policie:
>   All cair, and cummer, baneist quyte and clein;
> And ilk man leif in guid tranquillitie.

Sadly, during the "dolorous" reign of Mary, Queen of Scots, Maitland's pious hopes were to die stillborn. The whole country was about to enter a period of strife again as the nobles jostled with one another to build up their positions of power, but on that first night at the Palace of Holyrood, such cares were banished as the people of Edinburgh welcomed their new monarch with a homespun mixture of psalms and ballads played on fiddles and rebecks — a stringed instrument played with a bow. John Knox was even able to note approvingly, for once, that "the melodye, as she alledged, lyked her weill, and she willed the same to be continewed some nightis after", but a young poet in the Queen's retinue, Pierre de Bourdeilles, better known as Sieur de Brantome, told a different and probably more truthful story.

> There came under her window five or six hundred rascals of the town to serenade her with vile fiddles and rebecks, such as they do not lack in that country, setting themselves to sing psalms, and

singing so ill and in such bad accord that there could be nothing
worse. Ah! what music, and what a lullaby for the night!

Scottish links (even if they were not of a musical kind) were strong
with France and Mary would have been well acquainted with
Scottish visitors at the Court of Francois, she would have known of
the many scholars who looked on Paris as their centre of classical
studies and trade, too, was a well-established and flourishing affair.
Doubtless, also, she would have heard of her country's fighting
instinct — many Scots served in the army of France — and there
would be a sombre recognition of a darker side that gave rise to the
French phrase, *poignarder a l'ecossais* — to give a victim a thorough,
and usually violently executed, stabbing.

To her native country, so full of contradictions, and to her
adopted Court which had known both her father's and her
grandfather's love of learning and coarse revelry, Mary brought a
number of innovations. She shared the Stewarts' love of hunting and
the Park of Holyrood became populated again with wild deer;
colour was brought to Edinburgh with the numerous pageants and
processions; and, despite the Church's abhorrence of music, she
introduced more gentle instruments to play within the Palace and at
the Masses which she was still allowed to celebrate in her private
chapel. Under her patronage the Royal library grew to include
books from all over Europe, especially new texts in Latin which
were read to her by George Buchanan, her formidable tutor who
enjoyed a European reputation for his classical studies. Later he was
to turn against Mary and attack her savagely and unfairly, but in the
early days of her reign he wrote lyrical poems and short, pithy
maxims in honour of the Queen and her ladies in waiting. Even
before her arrival in Scotland he had composed an elegant
epithalamium on the marriage to the Dauphine of France.

George Buchanan was born in Stirlingshire in 1506 and had spent
much of his time studying in Paris and in other parts of France where
he had developed a Renaissance fondness for writing in Latin.
Although his career in Scotland is inexorably bound up with St
Andrews and its University and with his zeal for the reformed
church, Buchanan's relationship with Mary was initially good.
However, her marital entanglements and her involvement in affairs
of state alienated him from the Court, and when Mary appeared to

contrive at the murder of her foolish young husband, the Earl of Darnley, Buchanan was so convinced of her guilt that he wrote a Latin indictment proclaiming to the English Court a tragic but largely untrue story. Even its title gives the modern reader an idea of the seriousness of his accusations and of the hectoring language with which he made them — *De Maria Scotorum Regina, totaque eius contra Regem conjuratione, foedo cum Bothuelio adulterio, nefaria in maritum crudelitate et rabie, horrendo insuper et deterrimo eiusdem parridio, plena et tragica plane Historia*. Some idea of the fierceness of Buchanan's addiction to the new church could be seen in his portrait which until recently appeared each month on the front cover of *Blackwood's Magazine* — there is a story that when William Blackwood founded his Edinburgh magazine in 1817 thrift overcame typographical sensibilities and he used an old block of a picture of George Buchanan to fill the space.

Although the Protestant religion preached sobriety and lack of excess in all things, including the arts, poetry continued to flourish on a number of different levels. At Mary's Court encouragement was given to the poet Alexander Scott who has left us with a handful of delicately beautiful love lyrics like *Up Heilsum Hairt, Returne The, Hairt* and *A Rondel of Luve*. He also wrote a praise-poem for Mary on her first year in Scotland in which he tells her what the people expect of her and of what they deserve at her hands. In so doing he takes a side-swipe at the rapacity of the Church, condemns idolatry, and asks her "to punisch Papistes". Whatever she thought of those sentiments, Mary was presented with an accurate picture of the evils in the Church in Scotland, because like Lyndsay, Scott was not afraid of pointing a stern finger at the wickedness he saw flourishing around him.

> Bot wyte the wickit pastouris wald not mend
> Thair vitious living all the world prescryvis;
> Thai tuke na tent thair traik sould turne till end,
> Thai wer sa proud in thair preroga tyvis;
> For wantonnes thay wald not wed na wyvis,
> Nor yit leif chaste, but chop and change thair cheir;
> Now, to reforme thair fylthy licherous lyvis,
> God gife the grace aganis this guid new year.
> Thai brocht thair bastardis wt the skrife thai skraip,

REFORMATION

To bland thair blude wt barrownis be ambitioun;
Thai purchist pithlis pardnis fra the Paip,
To caus fond folis confyde he hes fruitioun,
As God, to gif for synnis full remissioun,
And saulis to saif frome suffering sorowis seir;
To sett asyde sic sortis of superstitioun,
God gife the grace aganis this guid new year.

It was typical of the period that Scott's poem, *Ane New Year Gift to Quene Mary* should contain so much practical and sound advice. Poetry as a means of improving the body politic existed at another level in the publication of numerous broadsides in Edinburgh attacking the Catholic church and the rule of Mary. Chief amongst her detractors in this field was Robert Sempill, a bluff soldier who used all his considerable wit in damning the Queen and in praising Knox. Although biographical details about Sempill are scarce, from the satires he published we can be certain that he knew Edinburgh intimately. His world was that of the shops and Luckenbooths of the High Street where the crowd was quick to denounce any breach of propriety they knew, or imagined, to be taking place at the Palace of Holyrood. Their information came from the type of scurrilous verse produced by Sempill and his cronies and from the production of giant placards which lampooned Court life. After Mary's marriage to Bothwell, the most infamous of these posters appeared, depicting Mary as a mermaid and Bothwell as a hare, both creatures being motifs of libidinous and lewd behaviour. Not that Sempill was a sea-green incorruptible — some of his poems resound with a coarse, but good-humoured, eroticism such as his *Ballat maid upoun Margret Fleming, Callit the Flemyng Bark in Edinburght* where maritime metaphors abound with a sexuality in the best tradition of Scottish folk poetry.

With evin keill befoir the wind
Scho is richt fairdy with a saill
Bot at ane lufe scho lyis behind;
Gar heiss hir quhill hir howbands skaill,
Draw weill the takill to hir taill,
Scho will nocht miss to lay your mast,
To pomp als oft as ye may haill,
Yeill nevir hald hir watterfast.

35

The traumatic nature of Mary's reign was an ideal breeding ground for a war of words and assaults on the Queen were met with equally virulent onslaughts on Knox and his fellow reformers. Most of the printers in Edinburgh were in the hands of the Protestants who granted licences for the production of broadsheets and religious tracts. Of their trade the best known was Robert Lekprevik who published most of Sempill's work and who enjoyed the care and protection of the church. "The Kirk having respect to his (Lekprevick's) povertie, the great expenses he hes made in buying of printing yrnes, and the great zeale and love he beares to serve the Kirk at all tymes, hes assignit to him fiftie punds to be yearlie payit out of the thrids of the Kirk."

But this support did not prevent Catholic propagandists like Ninian Winzet from denouncing Knox in print and from scoring telling points against the reformer's earnestness and what Winzet saw as his hypocrisy. A schoolmaster in Linlithgow, Winzet was eventually expelled from Edinburgh in 1562 and spent the rest of his life in Europe, but before he left he enjoyed some success in outwitting the authorities, as John Leslie, his fellow Catholic, recounted in a story where Winzet "chaiped" or escaped from the "haereticks" to their "luiche" or discomfort.

> This mater maid Mr Ninian verie inviet with the haereticks, and verie saire; quhairfore, quhen tha hard that he was busie with the prenter in setting furth a buik, quhairby he thocht to compleine of Knox to the Nobilitie for falsing his promis (by this onlie way, he thocht, he mycht provoik thame til answer) thay consult to hinder his labour, to tak Mr Ninian, to permise the prenter. The magistratis with the suddartis brak in upon the prenter, quhen of al his gudes spoyled him tha had, tha cloised him in prisone; bot Mr Ninian, quhom with sa gude wil tha wold have had, mett the magistrat in the yett, bot becaus tha knew him nocht tha mist him and sa he chaiped; the haereticks war wae, the Catholickis luiche.

Despite the warring religious factions, Mary's first four years on the throne were reasonably successful. With the help of Lord James Stewart, later the Earl of Moray, she kept the dissident nobles in check and allowed the reformed church to have a share of Catholic

revenues. Her refusal to ratify the Treaty of Edinburgh which had
ended French domination of Scotland, left her as a claimant to the
throne of England. (The Pope had not recognised the marriage of
Henry VIII to Anne Boleyn and in all Catholic eyes Mary was the
true heiress.) Scotland became the political axis of Europe — Mary
had close links with France, and at one time a marriage between her
and Don Carlos of Spain was mooted, and relations with Elizabeth
and the English Court were cautiously maintained. But Mary
needed a husband and in 1565 she married her cousin, the vapid,
weak-willed young Earl of Darnley, in the full rites of the Catholic
Church. His mother, the Countess Lady Margaret Douglas had long
contrived at the marriage and had schooled her son in the courtly
virtues of song, dance and poetry, encouraging him to write at
Mary's court in Edinburgh a conventional verse, *To the Queen*.

> Be to rebellis strong as lyoun eik,
> Be ferce to follow thame quhair evir thay found,
> Be to thy liegeman bayth soft and meik,
> Be thair succour and help thame haill and sound,
> Be knaw thy cure and caus quhy throw was cround,
> Be besye evir that justice be nocht smord,
> Be blyith in hart, thir wordis oft expound,
> Be bowsum aye to knaw thy God and Lord.

Darnley, though, could not act out his good intentions and he
quickly became a slave to sex and the bottle. By November 1566 he
had been banished from Edinburgh and Mary had agreed that her
marriage must be ended. In consultation with the Earls of Moray,
Argyll and Bothwell at Craigmillar Castle in Edinburgh she plotted
for an "outgait" to the unhappy affair. The following year saw
Darnley weak and ill in Glasgow and supposedly to ease his suffering
he was brought back to Edinburgh where he died a horribly violent
death at the House of Kirk O'Field which stood about a mile away
from the Palace of Holyrood in the quadrangle of the collegiate
church of St Mary-in-the-Field. Mary's purported part in the
murder and her hasty marriage to Bothwell ended her honeymoon
period with the Scottish people.

Thair remanit ane Thing, quhilk na les vexit the Quene then offendit the Pepill; that is to say, hir companying with Bothwell, not altogidder sa oppinly as scho wald fane have had it; and yit not sa secreitly bot the pepill persuauit it, for that all Mennis Eyis wer gasing upon thame. For quhairas Bothwell had ane Wyfe of his awin, and to tary for ane Divorce was thocht ane over lang Delay, and in the meane tyme, the Quene culd nouther oppinly avow to have him, nor secreitly enjoy him, and yit in na wise culd be without him, sum Schift, thocht not ane honest ane, yit ane Schift forsuith must be devysit; and quhen they culd not think upon ane better, it seemit thame ane mervellous fyne Inventioun, God wait, that Bothwell suld ravische and tak away the Quene be Force, and sa saif hir Honour. Sa within a few Dayis eftir, as the Quene was returning from Striviling, Bothwell forceabillie tuk hir be the Way, and caryit hir to Dunbar, quhidder with hir Will, or aganis his Will, everie Man may esilie persaif be hir awin Letteris that scho wrait to him be the Way as scho was in her journay.

George Buchanan was only one of many who saw the Queen as an evil influence on the realm and the birth to her of a young son in the summer of 1566 had given the opposing nobility the chance they had been seeking. After a hasty, undignified and sparsely supported struggle, the Queen was forced to abdicate and the infant prince was crowned King James VI of Scotland. Mary was brought to Edinburgh where the Scottish nobles, under the Earl of Moray, held her in captivity in the house of Sir Symoun Prestoun of Craigmillar which belonged to him while he was the Lord Provost. As she was taken through the streets the same Edinburgh mob who had welcomed her triumphant return to Scotland six years previously, roared out their disgust, "Burn her, burn the whore, she is not worthy to live. Kill her! Drown Her!" (These were not idle threats: Knox had preached tyrannicide.) Later she was imprisoned in the island fortress of Loch Leven before escaping to England, to imprisonment and to eventual execution at Fotheringhay at the hands of her cousin, Elizabeth of England.

> I was the Queen o' bonnie France,
>   Where happy I hae been;
> Fu' lightly rase I on the morn,
>   As blythe lay down at e'en:
> And I'm the sovereign of Scotland

REFORMATION

And mony a traitor there;
Yet here I lie in foreign bands
And never ending care.

But as for thee, thou false woman,
  My sister and my fae
Grim vengeance yet, shall whet a sword
  That thro' thy soul shall gae:
The weeping blood in woman's breast
  Was never known to thee;
Nor th' balm that draps on wounds of woe
  Frae woman's pitying e'e.

Robert Burns, writing in the eighteenth century, was one of many later writers who immortalised Mary and her tragic plight: in years to come her memory was to arouse as conflicting emotions as her life had done.

During Mary's reign, many changes had come to Edinburgh. The reformers had banned carnivals and processions in the streets, thus helping to stultify the progress of drama in Scotland for years to come. Attempts were also made to outlaw prostitution and drunkenness, edicts were passed to forbid the dumping of filth in the city's streets and leper houses were set up to combat disease and pestilence. The repitition of these thundering proclamations from the city council suggests, though, that however much the reformers may have raged against excess in society, human nature generally managed to remain triumphant.

Despite the troublesome times of the Regencies — James was still too young to rule — education prospered in the city. The council caused a High School to be built in 1578 near Blackfriars Chapel and four years later the "Tounis College" was founded as an institute of higher learning that later became the University of Edinburgh. All this activity was in keeping with the admirable enjoinder of the reformed church that education was the best way of improving the stature of the country, and the twin centres of learning in Edinburgh were to become fertile breeding grounds for generations of writers and scholars. If there was any regret for the passing of a Catholic Scotland it was felt, as was so often to become the case, in the nation's literature where a fondness for a romantic past was to become one of the touchstones of Scottish letters. Sir Richard

Maitland, an Edinburgh judge, was no exception in his *Satire on the Age*.

> Quhair is the blythnes that hes bein
> Bayth in burgh and landwart sein,
> Amang lordis and ladyis schein
> Daunsing, singing, game and play?
> Bot now I wait nocht quhat thai mein,
> All mirrines is worne away.
>
> For now I heir na wourde of yule
> In kirk, on cassay nor in scule,
> Lordis lattis thair kitchings cule
> And draws thame to the abbay
> And scant hes ane to keip thair mule,
> All houshaldaris is worne away.
>
> I saw no gysaris all this yeir
> Bot kirkmen cled lyk men of weir,
> That never cummis in the queir;
> Lyk ruffyanis is thair array,
> To preiche and teiche that will nocht leir,
> The kirk gudis thai waist away.
>
> Kirkmen affoir war gude of lyf,
> Preichit, teichit and stanchit stryf,
> Thai feirit nother swerd nor knyf;
> For luif of god the suyth to say,
> All honorit thame bayth man and wyf,
> Devotioun was nocht away.
>
> Our faderis wyse was and discreit,
> Thay had bayth honor, men and meit,
> With luif thai did thair tennents treit
> And had aneuche to poiss to lay,
> Thay wantit nother malt nor quheit
> And mirriness was nocht away.

The Highlands remained Catholic, but that was a different matter. For the most part Scotland either accepted or rejected, at different levels, the new form of religion. Although the church of Calvin preached a narrow conformism where God was to be feared rather than loved, it also produced a people strong in faith and patient in the discipline of their beliefs. The new found delight in education led to an increasing importance being placed in rational argument and the emergence of a confined humanism where shrewdness was a virtue and happiness was looked on askance. The Reformation, though, did not have an immediate effect on the nation's literature — James VI practised and encouraged the Renaissance arts — but there were uneasy straws in the wind.

In Edinburgh printers were a suspect race, unless like Lekprevik they chose to support the Church. Popular poetry was also held to be dangerously corrupting and the Church was anxious to see it, if not exterminated then at least brought under control. The publication in 1567 of *The Gude and Godlie Ballatis* was the first blast against the vibrant, naturally expressive nature of Scots folk poetry, for here was gathered together a strange collection indeed. Popular songs, bowdlerised to proclaim the new gospel appeared alongside psalms and the catechism. Although many songs were lost in this way — despite their forbidding nature, the *Ballatis* were popular — the folk tradition remained strong in Scotland. Today, we owe the survival of many of those songs to the industry of George Bannatyne a wealthy Edinburgh merchant. When plague struck the city in 1568 Bannatyne returned to his native Newtyle near Forfar where he amused himself by copying out the work of poets and songwriters whose work appealed to him. The Bannatyne Manuscript was an invaluable source book to later poets and it was edited in the eighteenth century by an equally remarkable Edinburgh man, Lord Kames. The upsurge in printed matter did have another positive effect: people became used to seeing Scots in print.

In 1572 John Knox died. During his lifetime he had helped to introduce the Protestant religion to Scotland, he had harried and hectored its Catholic Queen and yet for all his faith he too had played a part in betraying his country. For many of the changes he had advocated had helped Scotland turn from her past and her traditions towards what was happening south of the Border, and there was a gradual shift away from Europe and its influence. His fellow theorist, George Buchanan, died in an Edinburgh lodging house in 1582, having finally completed the proofs of his Latin History of Scotland.

That September in tym of vacans, my uncle Mr Andro, Mr Thomas Buchanan and I, hering that Mr George Buchanan was weik, and his Historie under the presse, past over to Edinbruck annes errand to visit him and see the work. Quhen we came to his chalmer we found him sytting in his chair, teaching his young man that servit him in his chalmer to spell a, ab, and e, e, b, eb, etc. Eftir salutation Mr Andro sayes, "I sie, sir, yow are not idle." — "Better this." quoth he, "nor stealing sheep — or sitting idle quhilk is as ill." Thereafter he shew us the Epistle Dedicatorie to the King, the quhilk quhen Mr Andro had red he told him that it wes obscure in sum places and wantit certan wordes to perfyte the sentens. Sayes he, "I may do na mair for thinking on anither matter." — "Quhot is that?" sayes Mr Andro. "To die," quoth he; "but I leave that and monie maur things for yow to help."

We went fro him to the printer's workhouse quhom we found at the end of the 17 buik of his Cornicle at a place quhilk we thocht verie hard for the tyme, quhilk micht be an occasioun for staying the haill work, anent the buriall of Davie, Therefore staying the printer from procedding, we came to Mr George again, and fand him bedfast by his custom and asking him how he did. "Ever going the way of weilfare," sayes he. Mr Thomas, his cousin shawes him of the hardness of that part of his Storie, that the King would be offendit with it, and it micht stay all the work. "Tell me, man," sayes he, "gif I have told the truth?" — "Yes," sayes Mr Thomas, "Sir, I think so." — "I will bide his feud and all his kin's then," quoth he. "Pray, pray to God for me, and lat him direct all." So by the printing of his Cornicle was endit, that maist leraned, wyse, and godly man endit this mortal lyf.

James Melville, a Professor at St Andrews, who had left a detailed, if biased, diary of the period, was one of the many minor writers who visited Edinburgh during the inter-regnum. During that period there was no real interruption in the scholarly and literary activity within the city. It may have become more austere and partisan in outlook, but as David Masson, himself no mean chronicler of the city, pointed out in the nineteenth century, "the torch that had been kindled in Scotland was passed there most nimbly and brilliantly from hand to hand".

Chapter Three

The Castalian Band

James, sixth of Scotland, and first of Great Britain has not always been looked on with kindness by history. Henry IV of France, forgetting the Auld Alliance for once, called him "the wisest fool in Christendom", and his fellow countryman, Sir Walter Scott, has also left us with a disparaging and incomplete picture in his novel, *The Fortunes of Nigel.*

> The king's dress was of green velvet, quilted so full as to be dagger-proof — which gave him the appearance of clumsy and ungainly protuberance; while its being buttoned awry, communicated to his figure an air of distortion. Over his green doublet he wore a sad-coloured nightgown, out of the pocket of which peeped his hunting-horn. His high-crowned grey hat lay on the floor, covered with dust, but encircled by a carcanet of large balas rubies; and he wore a blue velvet nightcap, in the front of which was placed the plume of a heron, which had been struck down by a favourite hawk in some critical moment of the flight, in remembrance of which the king wore this highly honoured feather.
>
> But such inconsistencies in dress and appointments were mere outward types of those which existed in the royal character, rendering it a subject of doubt amongst his contemporaries, and bequeathing it as a problem to future historians. He was deeply learned, without possessing useful knowledge; sagacious in many individual cases, without having real wisdom; fond of his power, and desirous to maintain and augment it, yet willing to resign the direction of that, and of himself, to the most unworthy of favourites; a big and bold asserter of his rights in words, yet one who tamely saw them trampled on in deeds; a lover of negotiations, in which he was always outwitted; and one who feared war, where conquest might have been easy. He was fond of his dignity, while he was perpetually degrading it by undue familiarity; capable of much public labour, yet often neglecting it

43

for the meanest amusement; a wit, though a pedant; and a scholar, though fond of the conversation of the ignorant and uneducated. Even his timidity of temper was not uniform; and there were moments in his life and those critical, in which he showed the spirit of his ancestors. He was laborious in trifles, and a trifler where serious labour was required; devout in his sentiments, and yet too often profane in his language; just and beneficient by nature he yet gave way to the iniquities and oppression of others. He was penurious respecting money which he had to give from his own hand, yet inconsiderately and unboundedly profuse of that which he did not see.

Scott was, of course, a notoriously selective historian and, for all his faults, James hardly deserved the description of a poltroon. Unlike his Stewart forebears he had an uncanny knack for self preservation which was desperately essential in the Scotland of the late sixteenth century, and his love of poetry became his true metier in what was fast becoming a deeply anti-intellectual age. He was frequently accused of physical cowardice but the reason for that may run deep, to a horrific spectacle which his mother Mary had to endure three months before his birth on a cold, early Spring, Edinburgh evening in 1566.

While Mary was dining alone with her entourage, Darnley entered her room in the palace of Holyrood. He was followed by the ghastly spectre of the dying Lord Ruthven dressed in full armour beneath a dirty white nightgown. Other conspirators quickly entered the room with murder in their hearts — their target was David Riccio, Mary's secretary who dealt with her French correspondence, and something of a favourite and confidant at court. Despite his multi-lingual terror, "Justizia! Justizia, Madame! Save ma vie! Save ma vie!", the Queen was powerless to save him (she was kept at pistol point) and Riccio was brutally murdered — *poignarder a l'ecossais* — by the conspirators who took care to implicate the wretched Darnley.

George Buchanan, who had by then little love left in his heart for the Queen, started the quite unjustifiable rumour that the reason for Riccio's assassination was that Mary had become pregnant by her secretary and that there were grave doubts about the future king's paternity.

These things were spoken openly, but in private men went further
in their mutterings, as is commonly the case in matters not very
credible; yet the King would never be persuaded to believe it,
unless he saw it with his own eyes; so that, one time hearing that
Rizzio was gone into the Queen's bedchamber, he came to a little
door, the key of which he always carried about him, and found it
bolted in the inside which it never used to be. He knocked, but no
one answered; upon which, conceiving great wrath and indignation in his heart, he could hardly sleep a wink that night.

This gave rise in later years to the taunt that James was "the son of
Seigneur Davie", and when James was complimented as the "British
Solomon", his detractors would snigger behind his back that the
new Solomon was also the son of David. The real reason for the
murder was more prosaic: Darnley had been denied the Crown
Matrimonial which Moray and his supporters wanted so that they
could exert their authority on the Queen through her feeble
husband. Although Mary was able to turn the plot to her own
advantage, and as we have seen to have extricated herself from her
marriage, it is not difficult to believe that the terror of that night and
the consequent turbulent period of her confinement would have had
a dire effect on her still unborn child.

After James's birth and baptism he was kept in Stirling under the
guardianship of the Erskine family and most of his early years were
spent in the grim fortress where his tutor was the equally grim
George Buchanan. Some idea of the old man's hopes for the young
prince may be seen in his *Epigram* to Thomas Randolph.

In chief I would have him a lover of true piety, deeming himself the
veritable image of highest God. He must love peace, yet be ever
ready for war. To the vanquished he must be merciful; and when
he lays down his arms he must lay aside his hate. I should wish him
to be neither a niggard nor a spendthrift, for each, I must think
works equal harm to his people. He must believe that as king he
exists for his subjects and not for himself, and that he is, in truth,
the common father of the state. When expediency demands that he
shall punish with a stern hand, let it appear that he has no pleasure
in his own severity. He will ever be lenient if it is consistent with
the welfare of his people. His life must be the pattern of every

citizen, his countenance the terror of evil doers, the delight of those that do well. His mind he must cultivate with sedulous care, his body as reason demands. Good sense and good taste must keep in check luxurious excess.

His other tutor, Peter Young was more sparing in his moral stance, but James's early learning was heavily influenced by a thorough study of Latin and Greek and a grounding in Old Testament history and Calvinistic theology. He was also taught the gentle art of golf, he was given a gentleman's training in the martial arts and he shared his family's love of the hunt, so that during the long period of the Regencies he was being gradually groomed for the Scottish throne.

In 1578, the waning powers of the Regent Morton, James's second cousin, led him to proclaim his young kinsman King of Scots. His childhood in Stirling was over, and the following year, at the age of thirteen, he set out to make a triumphal entry to Edinburgh, to take up residence again in his country's capital city. Although it is dated some twenty years later, there is a good description of the city during his reign in the diary of Fynes Moryson, an English traveller.

This City is high seated, in a fruitful soil, and wholesome air, and it is adorned with many noblemen's towers lying about it, and abounds with many springs of sweet waters. At the end towards the east is the king's palace joining to the monastery of the Holy Cross, which King David the first built, over which, in a park of hares, conies, and deer, a high mountain hangs, called the chair of Arthur (of Arthur, the Prince of Britons, whose monuments, famous among all ballad-makers, are for the most part to be found on these borders of England and Scotland). From the King's palace at the east the city rises higher and higher towards the west, and consists especially of one broad and very fair street (which is the greatest part and sole ornament thereof), the rest of the side streets and alleys being of poor building and inhabited with very poor people, and this length from the east to the west is about a mile, whereas the breadth of the city from the north to the south is narrow, and cannot be half a mile. At the farthest end towards the west is a very strong castle which the Scots hold expugnable . . . . and from the castle towards the west, is a most steep rock pointed on the highest top, out of which this castle is cut: but on the north and south sides without the walls, lie plain and fruitful fields of corn. In the midst of the foresaid fair street, the Cathedral church is built, which is large and lightsome, but little stately for the building, and nothing at all for beauty and ornament . . . .

To do the young King honour, the city council made arrangements for Edinburgh to be given a face-lift: rubbish was cleared from the steeets and autumn flowers were strewn in their place, the West Port was bedecked in purple, pageants were organised by young people, great open-air stalls were set up to serve food and drink, and a poet, Alexander Montgomerie, was on hand to celebrate the occasion.

> Haill bravest burgeon brekking to the rose,
> The deu of grace thy leivis mot inclose
> The stalk of treuth mot grant the nurishing
> The air of faith support thy florishing.

It must have been a heady day (the city council provided over three hundred gallons of wine) even for the wordly wise adolescent that James had become. But other forces were at play in his world: he was in love and writing poetry.

> Even so all women are of nature vaine,
> and can not keip no secret unreveild,
> and quhair as once thay do conccave disdaine,
> Thay are unable to be reonceild,
> fulfillid with talk and clatteris but respect,
> and oftentymes of small or none effect.
>
> Ambitious all without regaird or schame,
> but any mesure gevin to greid of geir,
> desyring ever for to winn a name
> with flattering all that will thaime not forbeir,
> sum craft thay have, yit foolish are indeid,
> with liying quhyles esteiming best to speid.

Without a mother's love, and brought up in a household which was not only devoid of female company but which also encouraged him to despise his mother, it is not surprising that James's first love should have been his cousin, the strikingly handsome Esme Stuart d'Aubigny, whom James came to characterise as the phoenix in his love poems to him. Anxious to honour his lover in other ways, James created him Duke of Lennox and amongst other secular titles, Lord Chamberlain of Scotland. Into this tight little group came the poet Alexander Montgomerie who served the Duke of Lennox, and James's court in Edinburgh began to become a centre of literary patronage. As in other Renaissance courts, the King became the centre of its everyday life around whom all artistic life existed. The Castalian Band of Poets, as they came to be known, occupied an important place at court, and James was quick to extend invitations to other poets to join him.

James was learning in other ways too. Under Lennox's tutelage he began to take a hand in his country's affairs, but there his knowledge of *realpolitik* was decidedly inferior to his skill in verse. The execution of Morton for his alleged part in Darnley's murder put Lennox at the centre of Scottish politics, and afraid of his influence on the King, the Earl of Gowrie took James captive at his castle in Ruthven in Perthshire and demanded that the King give up his favourite. In December 1582 Lennox left Scotland for ever: there was to be no rising again from the ashes of James's torment.

> And thou, O Phoenix, why was thow so moved
> Thou foule of light, be enemies to thee,
> For to forget thy heavenly hewes, whilkis loved
> Were baith by men and fowlis that did them see?
> And syne in hew of ashe that they sould bee
> Converted all: and that thy goodly shape
> In Chaos sould, and noght the fyre escape?

Montgomerie shared his master's downfall and there is a pathetic and remorseful lament to his brother poet Robert Hudson about the indignities he had to face while absent from court in Edinburgh.

> My best belovit brother of the band,
> I grein to sie the silly smiddy smeik.
> This is no lyfe that I live upaland
> On raw rid herring reistit in the reik,
> Syn I am subject somtyme to be seik,
> And daylie deing of my auld diseis.
> Eit bread, ill aill, and all things are ane eik;

This barme and blaidry buists up all my bees.
Ye knaw ill guyding genders mony gees,
And specially in poets. For example,
Ye can pen out twa cuple, and ye pleis;
Yourself and I, old Scot and Robert Semple.
Let Christian Lyndesay wryt our epitaphis.

If Montomerie was the most versatile and imaginative of the Castalians, he was also the most singular in his views. A soldier who had fought in Europe, he was a devout Catholic and was linked through his mother to the Royal family. He was born in mid-sixteenth century and died about 1611, dates which make him a near contemporary of Shakespeare's. Much of his time was spent at court in Edinburgh and after the Ruthven Raid he became again a trusted, if not altogether sympathetic, member of James's entourage. It is possible that Montgomerie's mastery of poetic technique (which has caused critics to compare him with Dunbar) and the brilliance of his imagination may have led him to quarrel with the brittle King; certainly James took him to task in his *Admonition* where he warns "Sanders" not to be boastful, "lest he not onlie slander himselfe; bot also the whole professours of the art".

In 1585 Montgomerie was in Europe again and closely identified with Catholic plots to overthrow the Protestant dynasty in Scotland. Shortly before he left Scotland, on that occasion for ever, he composed his glorious allegory *The Cherrie and the Slae* for which he is best remembered. The poem's complex rhyming stanzas and elaborate structure seem to suggest that originally it was set to music. In fact, much of the Castalian poetry was arranged to be sung and this "musik fyne" became an important decorative feature of James's court.

There were other poets of the Castalian Band whose reputations have survived intact: John Stewart of Baldynneis, a distant cousin of Montgomerie's; William Fowler, the son of a wealthy Edinburgh lawyer; and Sir Robert Ayton who was to become secretary to James's future wife. Although the band orbitted around James's central role both as monarch and as author of the *Reulis and Cautelis*, an essay on poetry, the members were prepared to disagree with each other. Montgomerie took part in a flyting with Polwarth, and like his predecessor Dunbar, he was not afraid of speaking his mind.

PRECIPITOUS CITY

Polwart, ye peip like a mouse amongest thornes;
Na cunning ye keip; Polwart, ye peip;
Ye luik lyk a sheipe and ye had two hornes;
Polwart, ye peip like a mouse amongest thornes.

It is interesting to compare, too, the differing attitudes to the newly discovered narcotic weed, tobacco. Sir Robert Aytoun's poem *Upone Tabacco* could almost be a present day advertisement with its images of contemplation beside a roaring fire with a good pipe going.

Forsaken of all comforts but these two,
My faggott and my Pipe, I sitt and Muse
On all my crosses, and almost accuse
The heavens for dealing with me as they doe.
Then hope steps in and with a smyling brow
Such chearfull expectations doth infuse
As makes me think ere long I cannot chuse
But be some Grandie, whatsoever I'm now.
But having spent my pype, I then perceive
That hopes and dreames are Couzens, both deceive.
Then make I this conclusion in my mind,
Its all one thing, both tends unto one Scope
To live upon Tobacco and on hope
The ones but smoake, the other is but winde.

Whereas his monarch's *Counterblaste to Tobacco* is and ideal model for the most dedicated of abolitionists.

And for the vanities committed in this filthy custome, is it nt both great vanitie and uncleannesse, that at the table, a place of respect, of cleanlinesse, of modestie, men should not be ashamed, to sit tossing of tobacco pipes and puffing of smoke and tobacco one to another, making the filthy smoke and stinke thereof, to exhale athwart the dishes and infect the aire, when very often, men that abhorre it are at their repast? Surely smoke becomes a kitchin farre better then a dining chamber and yet it makes a kitchin also oftentimes in the inward parts of men, soyling and infecting them, with an unctuous and oily kind of soote, as hath bene found in some great tobacco takers, that after their death were opened.

By 1589 James had come reluctantly to the conclusion that however pleasant were the delights of literary debate, the time had come to take a wife and to ensure the Stewart succession. The choice lay between Catherine of Navarre who was older than James and Ann of Denmark who was eight years his junior. After careful consideration he chose Ann, much to the delight of the Edinburgh merchants who saw in the marriage an opportunity to increase their trade with Scandinavia. That same year James set sail for Oslo to marry Ann and he wintered with the Danish Royal family in Kronborg before returning to Edinburgh in April the following year.

The Royal couple landed at Leith on 1st May and they were lodged at the King's Wark (a building which still stands at the corner of the Shore and Bernard Street) before being taken to Holyrood in a silver carriage which had been brought with them from Denmark. Two weeks later Ann was crowned Queen of Scots in a service that managed to combine Calvinistic prudence with Catholic splendour. John Burrell, an Edinburgh merchant, wrote admiringly of the spectacle which included mass bands of musicians, daily banquets and splendid decorations of taffeta and silk. Other burgesses were not so amused: the city council had to bear most of the costs of the celebrations.

Problems of finance loomed large, too, over the newly established Tounis College which depended on the generosity of the King and of the city for its funding. Robert Rollock, who had been appointed the first principal of the college, was a strict presbyterian who shared his fellow ministers' belief in universal education, and he was fully aware of the need to build up a staff of "regents" to teach the classics and theology, thus giving the college an early leaning towards speculative thinking in the Humanities. Rollock was also much aided by the gift of a library of three hundred books which were bequeathed by Clement Little to form the basis of the present university library. Edinburgh owed much to both men and it is interesting to note that in the late nineteenth century it was the habit of Professor Masson to give an introductory lecture to his English Literature Class on Robert Rollock and the beginnings of the University of Edinburgh, in which he described the founder as "the first president of one of the most important institutions in the Scottish nation".

PRECIPITOUS CITY

Although the foundation of a university within the city and the creation of a school of poetry at court had lifted the city's intellectual atmosphere there were still dark thoughts harboured in people's minds about the power of witchcraft and the supernatural and James's return to Scotland marked a new fervour for witch-hunting. James was convinced that the storms which had accompanied his North Sea passage had been caused by malevolent spells being cast against him. In particular he accused a group of women in North Berwick of using witchcraft against him in collusion with his cousin Francis Stewart, fifth Earl of Bothwell. Although his easy French manners had originally endeared him to the King, the other side of his character, his unpredictable, psychopathic nature, had alienated him from court — on one occasion he had raided Holyrood late at night, almost terrifying James out of his wits. Eventually the career of terrorism of the Wizard Earl led to his exile, but it awakened in James an irrational delight and interest in witchcraft which led him to write *Daemonologie* a learned, if turgid, tome on the subject.

Another shameful episode in the latter part of James's reign in Scotland was the sordid murder of the Earl of Moray at the hands of his rival, the Earl of Huntly. In an effort to heal the breach between the men James ordered Moray to come south to his castle in Fife, but there, Huntly took the opportunity of murdering him in cold blood. James was thought popularly to have arranged the murder because Moray was in love with Ann and a haunting ballad grew up around an affair which was more to do with inter-family warfare than any romantic attachment with the throne of Scotland.

> Nou wae be tae ye, Huntly,
> And wharfore did ye sae?
> I bade ye bring him wi ye,
> But forbad ye him to slay.
>
> He was a braw callant,
> And he played at the gluve,
> And the bonnie Earl o Moray,
> He wes the queen's true-love.

For running alongside the high culture of Castalian poetry was the directness of the folk tradition which manifested itself in the great

52

ballads of the Borders and the North East of Scotland. The tradition
of the Scottish ballads has greatly enriched the country's literature
with its mixture of oral poetry and song and a stylised set of rules
governing their form. The subject matter ranged from the
supernatural to the historical event, such as Moray's murder, and in
most of the ballads these happenings, real or imagined, are
heightened to give them a powerfully dramatic effect which makes
them eminently listenable to. Although the great ballads were
generally confined to the peripheries of Scotland where cultures
intermingled, some, like *The Laird o' Logie*, were set in Edinburgh,
with the dramatic escape of Wemyss of Logie after he had been
sentenced to death for trafficking in witchcraft with Bothwell. It
seems that Logie was saved by his lover, Margaret Twynstoun, who
tricked the guards and let him escape from confinement in the
Tolbooth.

> May Margaret turned her round about;
> I wot a loud lauch lauchit she:
> 'The eggis chippit; the bird is flown;
> Ye'll see nae mair o' young Logie.'

> The tane is shippit at the pier o' Leith,
> The tother at the Queen's Ferrie;
> And now the lady has gotten her luve,
> The winsome young Laird o' Logie.

The folk tradition continued to play an important part in
Edinburgh's history and came, in later years, to be used to good
effect by the city's poets.

   Although James gave Scotland a period of much needed peace,
there were qualms about his leanings towards episcopacy, feelings
which reached fever pitch in 1597 when he imprisoned David Black,
a minister from St Andrews, for denouncing Elizabeth of England as
an atheist. Enflamed by this move, which they saw as evidence of
popery, the Edinburgh crowd took to the streets in a riot of such
violent proportions that James was forced to flee to the neighbour-
ing Royal palace of Linlithgow. The king's retaliation was swift and
effective: he threatened to remove the Royal court and the courts of
law from Edinburgh. Such a move would have had a dire effect on

the city's economy and the merchants, scared of losing their trade and profits, apologised abjectly to their king and the city was reprieved.

But, by then, James's mind was already turning to the English throne. As the senior descendant of Henry VII James had always held the best claim to the English crown and he had determined at an early age that he should be the first King of Great Britain. All that was required of him was to await the death of his kinswoman Elizabeth who, he once complained, looked like outliving the sun and the moon. In the early morning of 24th March 1603 her strength finally did wane and Sir Robert Carey, who, years earlier, had broken the news of Mary's execution to her son, now rode north, in three days of hard riding, to bring more welcome news to James. The drama of his arrival at Holyrood on Saturday, 26th March, in the late evening, is taken up by David Masson.

> All is dull and sleepy within the Palace, the King and Queen having retired after supper, and the lights in the apartments now going out one by one. Suddenly, hark! what noise is that without? There is first a battering at the gate, and then the sound of a horse's hoofs in the courtyard, and of the bustling of the Palace servants round some late arriver. It is the English Sir Robert Carey, brother of Lord Hunsdoun. He had left London between nine and ten o'clock in the forenoon of the 24th; he had ridden as never man rode before, spur and gallop, spur and gallop, all the way through that day and the next and the next, the two intervening nights hardly excepted; and here he is at Holyrood on the evening of the third day — an incredible ride! His horse, the last he has been on, is taken from him all a-foam; and he himself, his head bloody with a wound received by a fall and a kick from the horse in the last portion of his journey, makes his way staggeringly, under escort, into the aroused King's presence. Throwing himself on his knees before his half-dressed Majesty, he can but pant out, in his fatigue and excitement, these words in explanation of the cause of his being there so unceremoniously: "Queen Elizabeth is dead, and your Majesty is King of England."

The thirty-seven-year-old James had to await several days for confirmation from the Privy Council but that evening was the proudest moment of his life. Preparations were put in hand immediately for the transfer of the Royal court to London and on 3rd April James said farewell to his Scottish subjects in a sermon delivered at the Church of St Giles.

It was a speech intended to console them for their grievous loss. "There is no more difference," he said, "betwixt London and Edinburgh, yea, not so much, as betwixt Inverness or Aberdeen; for all our marches are dry and there be no ferries betwixt them"; and after dilating somewhat further on the undeniable fact of the geographical continuity of his new kingdom with his old, he mentioned one of its probable consequences. "Ye mist not doubt," he said in conclusion, "but, as I have a body as able as any king in Europe, whereby I am able to travel, so I sall visit you every three year at the least, or ofter as I sall have occasion."

Chapter Four

Dark Ages

James soon found it impossible to keep his promise to visit Scotland every three years. Affairs of state forced him to stay in London where he had to come to terms with an English Parliament which was beginning to show signs of opposition to the authority of the Crown. In Scotland he set up a Privy Council but the country, to all intents and purposes, was governed by letter from London. Opening the English Parliament on 31st March 1607, James chided them with the reproachful words: "This I must say for Scotland, and may truly vaunt it, here I sit and govern with my pen; I write and it is done; and by a clerk of the council I govern Scotland now — which my ancestors could not do by the sword."

Fourteen years passed before James visited Edinburgh again, and to his surprise on his only visit in 1617, he found that many changes had taken place. Holyrood, bereft of a Royal household, had fallen into disrepair and unlike his joyous entry as a thirteen-year-old King of Scots, he was greeted by a "harangue" from the provost, William Nesbit, clad in "a black gown lined with black velvet". Sir Anthony Weldon, an Englishman in the King's retinue, despaired of the city and its hard-bitten Calvinism.

> For his majesty's entertainment, I must needs ingenuously confess, he was received in the parish of Edinburgh (for a city I cannot call it) with great shouts of joy, but no shews of charge for pageants; they hold them idolatrous things, and not fit to be used in so reformed a place . . . for the religion they have, I confess they hold it above reach, and, God willing, I will never reach for it.
> They christen without the cross, marry without the ring . . . They keep no holy-days, nor acknowledge any saint but St Andrew . . . their sabbath exercise is a preaching in the forenoon, and a persecuting in the afternoon . . . they think it impossible to lose the way to heaven, if they can but leave Rome behind them . . .

To conclude, the men of old did no more wonder that the great
Messias should be born in so poor a town as Bethlem in Judea that I
do wonder that so brave a prince as King James should be born in
so stinking a town as Edinburgh in lousy Scotland.

Such a view showed that however much the Union of the Crowns
might have joined together the two countries, old feelings of
antagonism between Scotland and England were very difficult to
lose.

The removal of the King's court to London also meant that the
Castalian Band had been broken up for ever. Montgomerie was dead
and although Ayton and Alexander accompanied James they quickly
adapted themselves to the English literary tradition. Loss of court
patronage left the poets who remained in a literary vacuum, and as
they had effectively divorced themselves from the folk tradition
their sense of alienation was complete. The forfeiture of the court to
London was a bitter blow.

Ah why should *Isis* only see Thee shine?
Is not thy FORTH as well as *Isis* Thine?
Though *Isis* vaunt shee hath more wealth in store,
Let it suffice Thy FORTH doth love Thee more:
Though Shee for Beautie may compare with *Seine*,
For Swannes and Sea-*Nymphes*, with imperiall *Rhene*,
Yet in the Title may bee claim'd in Thee,
Nor Shee, nor all the World, can match with mee.
Now when (by *Honour* drawne) thou shalt away
To Her alreadie jelous of Thy Stay,
When in Her amourous Armes Shee doth Thee fold,
And dries thy Dewie Haires with Hers of Gold,
Much questioning of Thy Fare, much of Thy Sport,
Much of Thine Absence, Long, how e're so short,
And chides, (perhaps) Thy Comming to the North,
Loathe not to thinke on Thy much-loving FORTH:
O love these Bounds, whereof Thy royall Stemme
More than a hundredth wore a Diademe.

William Drummond of Hawthornden who wrote those lines
from his poem, *Forth Feasting, A Panegyricke to the Kings Most
Excellent Majesty* is one of the few bright lights in Edinburgh's
literary history during the seventeenth century. He was born on 13th

December, 1585, the son of the laird of Hawthornden, which is in the parish of Lasswade, a village lying seven miles to the south of Edinburgh on the River Esk. After graduating from the Tounis College he studied law at Bourges and Paris and in 1610, on the death of his father he returned to Hawthornden to take up a life of poetry and reclusive study. Although he had little taste for public life, and cultivated the image of the poet as a romantic wandering through the woods which lie around his castle on its crag above the river in the glen, Drummond became a kind of poet laureate to the city of Edinburgh, ready to advise the council on literary or cultural affairs. In 1633, Charles I, who had succeeded James, entered the city to be crowned King of Scotland.

> Delight of heaven, sole honour of the earth,
> *Jove* (courting thine ascendant) at thy birth
> Proclaimed thee a King, and made it true,
> That Emperies should to thy worth be due,
> He gave thee what was good, and what was great,
> What did belong to love, and what to state,
> Rare gifts whose ardors turne the hearts of all,
> Like tunder when flint attomes on it fall;

Drummond's *Entertainment of the High and Mighty Monarch, Prince CHARLES, King of great Brittaine, France and Ireland, into his ancient and Royall Citie of Edenbourgh, the 15 of June 1633* was matched by a pageant where the spirit of Edina welcomed the Royal party at the West Bow and the shade of the legendary King Fergus made a regal speech at the Tolbooth.

Beneath those words of welcome and flattery, problems lay ahead for the new king. Four years after his visit Charles introduced to the Church of Scotland a new service book which smacked too much of the Catholic doctrine to be fully acceptable to everyone. Its use in St Giles on 23rd July 1637 led to a riot and to the probably apocryphal story of Jenny Geddes hurling her stool at the hapless David Lindsay, the newly appointed Bishop of Edinburgh.

> The Dean he to the altar went, and, with a solemn look,
> He cast his eyes to heaven, and read the curious-printed book:
> In Jenny's heart the blood upwelled with bitter anguish full;

58

Sudden she started to her legs, and stoutly grasped the stool!
With a row-dow — at them now! firmly grasp the stool!

As when a mountain wild-cat springs on rabbit small,
So Jenny on the Dean springs, with gush of holy gall;
'Wilt thou say mass at my lug, thou Popish-puling fool?'
No, no!' she said, and at his head she flung the three-legged stool.
With a row-dow — at them now! Jenny fling the stool!

A bump, a thump! a smash, a crash! now gentle folks beware!
Stool after stool, like rattling hail, came tirling through the air,
With 'Well done, Jenny! that's the proper tool!
When the Deil will out, and shows his snout, just meet him with a
stool!'
With a row-dow — at them now! there's nothing like a stool!

The Council and the Judges were smitten with strange fear,
The ladies and the Bailies their seats did deftly clear,
The Bishop and the Dean went, in sorrow and in dool,
And all the Popish flummery fled, when Jenny showed the stool!
With a row-dow — at them now! Jenny show the stool!

And thus a mighty deed was done by Jenny's valiant hand,
Black Prelacy and Popery she drave from Scottish land;
King Charles he was a shuffling knave, priest Laud a meddling
fool,
But Jenny was a woman wise, who beat them with a stool!
With a row-dow — yes, I trow! she conquered by the stool!

The rioting in Edinburgh led to renewed threats of intervention
from Charles but with an impotent Privy Council he was unable to
prevent the events that followed. A lengthy document, the National
Covenant, was drawn up, denying in legal terms the King's power
to impose an episcopalian policy in Scotland, and it was signed by
thousands of enthusiastic supporters in Greyfriars Church in
Edinburgh the following year.

In the midst of so much upheaval it was impossible for any Scot of
note to remain neutral and Drummond plumped for law and order
and for adherence to the Crown. This action, passive though it
proved to be, in remote Hawthornden, coupled with his use of
English (which has been interpreted by many as the first cultural

treason after the Union of the Crowns) has placed Drummond somewhat outside the Scottish tradition in many critics' eyes. That is an unfair conclusion, as in Drummond we may see the beginnings of the Scottish writer, who, however much he may have been drawn intellectually to English, still retained an affection, albeit romantic, for Scotland and its past. Drummond was no exception. In his castle at Hawthornden which Scott, suffering from much the same kind of syndrome, described as:

> Who knows not Melville's beechy grove,
> And Roslin's rocky glen,
> Dalkeith, which all the virtues love,
> And classic Hawthornden?

Drummond also researched Scottish records and genealogy and arranged for his work to be splendidly executed by the Edinburgh printer Andro Hart.

His interest in England was probably not so much the result of a dislike of Scots but rather a foreboding that to keep in the literary swim he had to follow the manners of an English court. Certainly he was well-known south of the Border: he was a regular correspondent with his cousin at James's court, William Alexander, Earl of Stirling, who was also a poet (Charles Lamb in later years proclaimed Drummond's name as the most euphonious in English literature) and he was a friend and confidant of Ben Jonson who visited Hawthornden in 1618.

In some respects it is odd that Johnson should have ever attempted the journey. He was forty-six, weighed almost twenty stones and in bad physical condition, but he was anxious to leave London and to see other parts of the country in which James had interested him. He arrived in Edinburgh in September when he was given the freedom of the city and treated to a lavish public banquet. Another English poet, John Taylor, was in the city at the time and he was left in no doubt as to the warmth of the welcome for England's poet laureate.

> Now the day before I came from Edenborough I went to Leeth, where I found my long approved and assured good friend Master Beniamin Iohnson, at one Master Iohn Stuarts House: I thanke him for his great kindnesse towards me; for at my taking leave of him,

he gave me a piece of gold of two and twenty shillings to drink his health in England; and withall willed me to remember his kind commendations to all his friends: so with a kindly farewell, I left him as well, as I hope never to see him in a worse estate: for he is amongst Noblemen and Gentlemen that knowe his true worth, and their owne honours, where, with much respective love, he is worthily entertained.

Jonson left Edinburgh to spend Christmas with Drummond at his castle at Hawthornden, and although the two men were very different in outlook and temperament — Jonson is supposed to have drunk the cellar dry — the notes of their conversations on contemporary political and literary matters still makes fascinating, if scurrilous reading.

The poets' rhyming words of greeting: "Welcome, welcome, royal Ben" — "Thank ee, thank ee, Hawthornden", are no doubt fanciful but Jonson's visit had a profound effect on Drummond. It strengthened his own notion of himself as a poet in the English tradition, it gave him a taste of intellectual debate that had been denied to him and it also provided him with gossip about mighty affairs. Drummond stored all that knowledge, replenishing it in later correspondence, and he used it occasionally in a number of epigrams about imagined court life which circulated, for obvious reasons, in private manuscripts.

> The Queen is to make two knights of
> the Garter
> The one is a greate foole the other a
> greater farter.

Drummond eventually signed the Covenant but in his heart he remained a loyalist and the events of the sixteen forties were a sore trial to him and to his beliefs. The Covenanters had raised an army in 1639 to defend their rights and although Charles had met most of their demands, fighting broke out again in the following year and an English army under Viscount Conway was defeated in the north of England. Charles was left with little option but to sue for peace with the Covenanters in the hope that they would support him in his own struggle with the English Parliament.

The outbreak of Civil War in 1642 led to an extraordinary amount of political manoeuvering by the Covenanters between the Royalist cause and the Parliamentarians, and they changed sides several times. Their motive was a simple one: they wanted to establish presbyterianism in England and they also wanted to be paid for their efforts. Although they handed Charles over to the Parliamentarians they were enraged by his execution (he was, after all, a descendant in a long line of Kings of Scots) and when his son Charles was proclaimed King in Edinburgh Cromwell invaded Scotland and defeated the Covenanting army at Dunbar in September 1650. The Marquis of Montrose, a superb soldier who had been a consistent Royalist, was taken prisoner and condemned "to be carried to Edinburgh Cross, and hanged up on a Gallows Thirty Foot high, for the space of Three Hours, and then to be taken down, and his head to be cutt off upon a Scaffold, and hanged on Edinburgh Toolbooth; his Legs and Arms to be hanged up in other public Towns of the Kingdom, and his body to be buried at the Place where he was executed."

On the way to his execution, Montrose's tumbril is supposed to have passed Moray House in the Canongate where he was jeered at and spat upon by his great enemy the Duke of Argyll. But Montrose is best remembered for the gallantry and dignity of his bearing as he faced an awful death. A poem written before his execution resounds with his composure and his faith.

> Let them bestow on ev'ry Airth a Limb;
> Open all my Veins, that I may swim
> To Thee my Saviour, in that Crimson Lake;
> Then place my pur-boil'd Head upon a Stake;
> Scatter my Ashes, throw them in the Air:
> Lord (since Thou know'st where all these Atoms are)
> I'm hopeful, once Thou'lt recollect my Dust,
> And confident Thou'lt raise me with the Just.

The year before, the execution of Charles had embittered Drummond of Hawthornden and he had died in the same year, 1649, leaving all his books to the growing library in the Tounis College. At the end of his life most of his friends had predeceased him and he rarely left his castle in "classic Hawthornden". Another recluse who was a near contemporary of Drummond's was John Napier, laird of Merchiston, an area to the south of Bruntsfield Links which is now a city suburb. He is best remembered for his invention of logarithms and for his work on scientific inventions which were far in advance of their times: an elementary calculating machine, an armoured tank, a design for a submarine and new form of artillery which would use the power of the sun's rays. In an age where the fear of witchcraft consumed simple folk's minds, Napier was an awesome figure in Edinburgh and he was supposed to have a jet-black cock as his familiar.

The Scots crowned Charles II at Scone in 1651 and marched south to ignominious defeat with the Royalist force at Worcester, leaving Cromwell to establish the Commonwealth which incorporated Scotland into British affairs. During this nine year period Edinburgh lost her status as a capital city but there was law and order and a blessed period of prosperity and peace. Gilbert Blackhal, a priest with the Scots Mission in Paris, on a visit to the city, noted how deeply ingrained was the presbyterian religion in all people's minds.

Twelfe houres chopped as I did enter in Leith, and our Puritans were at that time more as halfe Jewes; for they had forbidden al servile work to be done from Saterday at noone, until the next Monday, under great penaltyes; so that a boate durst not go upon ferries to pass any man over, what pressant affair soever he could have; and, therefore, I could not pass at Leith, or return back again to Edenbrough, specially upon their day of general communion, because theis dayes they send searchers to al the innes to sie who are their absent from their churches; and, if any be found, the hostes are finned for loging them or suffering them to be absent. So I did choose rather to be in the fields then in any town; and, therfor did ridde up the water to Queenes ferry, wher I found that same prohibition in vigour. I offered a shilling for a boate which cost but two pens ordinarily, but, if I would have given tenne pounds, the pouer fellowes durst not sette a boate to sea; wherefor I resolved to ridde to the Bridge of Sterling, four and twenty miles out of my way, rather than stay in any of theis puritanical litle tounes, which are much more zealous than the greatest.

But there was no lack of industry during the week. Edinburgh's first newspaper, *A Diurnall of Passages of Affaires*, was published in

Leith in 1652 and a stage-coach service was inaugurated between the city and London. Cromwell died in 1658, and as so often happens with the death of a strong ruler, the country was left in confusion, leading to the Restoration of the Monarchy in 1660. Charles was proclaimed King at the Mercat Cross on 14th May and the city entered into a brief period of enthusiasm for the Royal family, a trait it has managed to keep ever since for its far distant kings and queens.

It did not last. Although Charles II had signed the Covenant in an effort to gain Scottish support, he made it quite plain at an early stage that he had no intention of honouring his commitment. He nominated his own members of the Scottish Privy Council and ruled Scotland through a series of commissioners who were nothing less than colonial governors for the English Parliament. The Court of High Commission was revived in 1664 with the intention of enforcing episcopalian policies and the Covenanters, who regarded with deep suspicion any religion but their own, were once again forced into the field. Brutal reprisals were put in hand for those Covenanters who attended the open-air coventicles (the Covenanters held their services in remote country areas, usually in the open) or refused to go to Church. Edinburgh again became a centre of butchery as many Covenanters went uncomplainingly to their deaths in a mood of religious exaltation at the hands of the public executioner in the Grassmarket.

> Sing with me! sing with me!
> Weeping brethren, sing with me!
> For now an open Heaven I see,
> And a crown of glory laid for me.
> How my soul this earth despises!
> How my heart and spirit rises!
> Bounding from the flesh I sever:
> World of sin, adieu for ever!

Hogg was one of several nineteenth-century writers who were impressed by the religious certainty of the Covenanters (the lines come from his *Covenanter's Scaffold Song*) and of the injustice of the state's oppression. Unlike Scott who found the sect tiresome in *Old Mortality*, Hogg wrote admiringly and sympathetically of their cause in *The Brownie of Bodsbeck*. His contemporary, John Galt,

64

although not an Edinburgh man, also lived in the city in the age of Scott, and in his novel *Ringan Gilhaize* there is a graphic description of the horrors that the Covenanters had to face in the foetid atmosphere of the Tolbooth.

> On reaching Edinburgh I was placed in the tolbooth, where many other sufferers for the cause of the Gospel were then lying. It was a foul and unwholesome den: many of the guiltless inmates were so wasted that they were rather like frightful effigies of death than living men. Their skins were yellow, and their hands were roped and warpt with veins and sinews in a manner very awful to see. Their eyes were vivid with a strange distemperature, and there was a charnel-house anatomy in the melancholy with which they welcomed a new brother in affliction, that made me feel, when I entered among them, as if I had come into the dark abode of spectres, and manes, and dismal shadows.
>
> The prison was crowded over-much, and though life was to many not worth the care of preservation, they yet esteemed it as the gift of their Maker, and as such considered it their duty to prolong for His sake. It was, therefore, a rule with them to stand in successive bands at the windows, in order that they might taste of the living air from without; and knowing from dismal experience, that those who came in the last suffered at first more than those who were before, it was charitable self-denial among them to allow to such a longer period at the window, their only solace.

Despite the strength of their religious convictions, the Covenanting opposition was crushed in June 1679 at Bothwell Brig by an English army commanded by the Duke of Monmouth. Two years later, James, Duke of York, brother to Charles II was made commissioner to Scotland and he immediately passed an Act which demanded that persons in public office should continue to bear allegiance to the King and his successors — James had his eyes firmly fixed on the throne. Hardly surprisingly the Act did little to appease the country and an extreme form of Covenanters, the Cameronians, took up arms against James, only to be put down by two men who have passed into Covenanting mythology as 'bluidy' repressors — John Graham of Claverhouse and Sir George Mackenzie of Rosehaugh.

Mackenzie was the King's Advocate in Scotland and it fell to him to prosecute the Covenanters and in so doing to uphold the law of the day. His interest in legal studies led him to press for the establishment of a library in Edinburgh and the Advocates' Library was started in a house at the north-east corner of Parliament Close in 1689. Three years later the first catalogue was printed and it included a wide range of books including history, criticism and rhetoric, subjects which Mackenzie called, "the handmaidens of jurisprudence". The Advocates' Library later became the National Library of Scotland (in 1925) and down the years it has played a splendid role in helping Edinburgh to develop as a centre of learning and letters. The university library was also expanding and had become a place of interest to visitors to the city like the Rev. Thomas Morer, an English chaplain in a regiment stationed at the Castle.

> South of the Cow-gate, and on a Rising stands the College, consisting of one small Quadrangle, and some other Lodgings without Uniformity or Order, built at several times, and by divers Benefactors, who thought probably to be better distinguish'd by this variety of Forms and Situations in those Buildings. In the midst hereof is the Library, a large and convenient Room made about 60 Years ago for that purpose. The Roof is covered with Lead, and is neatly kept within; well furnish'd with Books, and those put in very good Order, and Cloister'd with Doors made of Wire which none can open but the Keeper, and which is thought a better way than our multitude of Chains incumbering a Library, and are equally troublesome and chargeable to us. It has (as all other Publick Libraries) many Benefactors, whose Books are distinguished by their several Apartments, and the Donors Names set over 'em in Golden Letters. A Device grateful and honourable enough for the Parties concern'd, incourages others to follow their Examples; such especially who may be charmed to the doing of a Good Work, tho' not always upon a Principle of Goodness. Over the Books are hung the Pictures of divers Princes, and most of the Reformers, as Luther, Melanothon, Quinglius, Calvin etc and near them Buchanan's Scull, very intire, and so thin that we may see the Light through it. And that it is really his appears from hence, because one Mr Adamson, Principal of the College, being a young man of 24 Years of Age when Buchanan was buried, either out of Curiosity or Respect to the Dead, brib'd the Sexton some time after to procur him the Skull, which being brought, he fastened Verses to it, and at his Death left it and them to the College.

DARK AGES

The Buchanan was none other than Mary's cheerless tutor.
Although Mackenzie was styled "the bluidy Mackenzie" by Davie
Deans he should be remembered both for his contribution to
scholarship and for his writing which ranged from fiction to political
philosophy. He was one of the few intellectual giants of his day, and
he is buried in the same Greyfriars Church that saw the signing of the
National Covenant.

The Covenanting movement may have captured the imagination
of the late seventeenth century but its influence has also had the effect
of painting a picture of a grey, humourless Scotland where the
all-powerful clergy reigned supreme, frustrating people's pleasures
and keeping them in a state of bended-knee reverence. That an
opposition existed to the leashed imagination of the reformed
church can be seen in the scurrilous pamphlet, *The Scotch Presbyterian
Eloquence*, which appeared anonymously in 1692 and which led to a
furious war of words between the opposing religious factions. In the
extract that follows the imagined sexual hypocrisy of two
Edinburgh ladies is savagely lampooned.

There was among them a married woman, near Edinburgh,
who had paid several fines for not going to church, yet scrupled
not to commit adultery with one of the Earl of Marr's regiment,
and the fellow himself that was guilty, told, out of detestation to
their damnable hypocrisie, that the vile woman had the confi-
dence, in time of her abomination, to say to him, "O you that are in
Marr's regiment, but you be pretty able men, but yet ye are great
Covenant breakers! Alas, few or none of you are godly."
There are very many instances of this nature, but I shall only add
one more, which was told me by a gentleman of good reputation
and credit, who himself confessed to me, with regret, that in the
heat of his youth he had been guilty of the sin of fornication with a
gentle woman of that holy sect. He says, that being with her in a
garret, and she hearing somebody coming up the stairs, she said to
him, "Ah, here's my aunt. I must devise a trick to divert her."
Upon which, she fell a whining and howling aloud, as these people
use to do at their private devotions. "Oh, to believe, to believe!
Oh, to have experience!" said she. And by that means she diverted
her aunts further approaching, who instantly retired, commending her niece's zeal and devotion. The gentleman conceals the
woman's name, out of regard to her honour and his own; begs

pardon for the sin, and tells it only to discover the abominable nature of their hypocrisie.

Charles had died in 1685 to be succeeded by his notoriously unpopular brother, and his attempts to establish Catholicism and Arbitrary Power were hotly resented by the Edinburgh mob who took to the streets at the merest hint of Popery. There was universal joy in the city when the Glorious Revolution brought William and Mary to the throne of Britain — it seemed at long last that the country's religious problems were finally over although the re-establishment of the Presbyterian church government, it should be remembered, deprived a large number of episcopalian ministers of their charges. There were also, still those, like the romantic Jacobite, Graham of Claverhouse, by then Viscount Dundee, who rode from the city in disgust, only to meet his death at the Battle of Killiecrankie in July 1697.

> To the Lords of Convention 'twas Claver'se who spoke,
> 'Ere the King's crown shall fall there are crowns to be broke;
> So let each Cavalier who loves honour and me,
> Come follow the bonnet of Bonny Dundee.
>
> Come fill up my cup, come fill up my can,
> Come saddle your horses, and call up your men;
> Come open the West Port, and let me gang free,
> And it's room for the bonnets of Bonnie Dundee!
>
> Dundee he is mounted, he rides up the streeet,
> The bells are rung backward, the drums they are beat;
> But the Provost, douce man, said, 'Just e'en let him be,
> The Gude Town is weel quit of that Deil of Dundee!
>
> As he rode down the sanctified bends of the Bow,
> Ilk carline was flyting and shaking her pow;
> But the young plants of grace they looked couthie and slee,
> Thinking, 'Luck to thy bonnet, thou Bonny Dundee!'
>
> With sour-faced Whigs the Grassmarket was crammed
> As if half the West had set tryst to be hanged;
> There was spite in each look, there was fear in each e'e,
> As they watched for the bonnets of Bonny Dundee.

DARK AGES

Scott's view of Dundee is the conventional one of the lordly rebel who captured people's hearts but who failed to conquer their minds. Despite the romance of his adventure, the rest of the country remained solidly presbyterian and pro-government. But for all the country's preference for William, he, himself, had little time for Scotland, paying scant attention to the country apart from keeping down the troublesome Jacobite Highlanders and making sure that taxes were paid. William also has the "distinction" of being the first British monarch never to visit his northern capital. (Edinburgh had to wait until the reign of George IV, but that is another story.)

The Scottish parliament set about reforming the religious affairs of the country but they were powerless to interfere in William's foreign policy of waging what amounted to a personal war with France, Scotland's old partner in the fondly remembered days of the Auld Alliance. Edinburgh citizens, although they bore little love for the Highlanders, were dismayed by the King's connivance in the despicable murder of the Macdonalds in Glencoe, but the event that set the country ablaze with rage was the failure of the ill-starred Darien expedition in 1689. Anxious to break into world markets a Scottish trading colony was established on the isthmus of Darien in Panama — they had taken advice from the Scots-born William Paterson, founder of the Bank of England — but the settlers were under-financed, ill-equipped and harassed by the Indians and by the Spanish. The Company failed, most of the would-be settlers lost their lives and the £400,000 which had been scraped together by a country which was never wealthy, was mostly lost. In their pride and their anger the Scottish people turned their hostility on the English and on William for failing to act on their behalf. It was partly due to the scheme, though, that the idea was born in William's mind (he was to die in 1702) that the only way of solving the problems of ruling Scotland was in the unification of the two countries. So, from the turn of the century until 1707 Edinburgh rang with argument and counter-argument as parliament met under the Commissioners to discuss the proposals.

In the midst of this confusion, someone or other issued from the house, which was at the back of the Canongate, calling out: "A plot, a plot! Treason, treason! Down with the bloody incendiaries at the Black Bull!"

69

The concourse of people that were assembled in Edinburgh at that time was prodigious; and, as they were all actuated by political motives, they wanted only a ready-blown coal to set the mountain on fire. The evening being fine, and the streets thronged, the cry ran from mouth to mouth through the whole city. More than that, the mob that had of late been gathered to the door of the Black Bull had, by degrees, dispersed; but, they being young men, and idle vagrants, they had only spread themselves over the rest of the street to lounge in search of further amusement: consequently a word was sufficient to send them back to their late rendezvous, where they had previously witnessed something they did not much approve of.

The master at the tavern was astonished at seeing the mob again assembling; and that with such hurry and noise. But, his inmates being all of the highest respectability, he judged himself sure of protection, or at least of indemnity. He had two large parties in his house at the time; the largest of which was of the Revolutionist faction. The other consisted of our young tennis-players and their associates, who were all of the Jacobite order; or, at all events, leaned to the Episcopal side. The largest party were in a front room; and the attack of the mob fell first on their windows, though rather with fear and caution. Jingle went one pane; and then with a loud hurrah; and that again was followed by a number of voices, endeavouring to restrain the indignation from venting itself in destroying the windows, and to turn it on the inmates. The Whigs, calling the landlord, inquired what the assault meant: he cunningly answered that he suspected it was some of the youths of the Cavalier, or High-Church party, exciting the mob against them. The party consisted mostly of young gentlemen, by that time in a key to engage any in a row; and, at all events, to suffer nothing from the other party, against whom their passions were mightily inflamed.

Hogg's *Private Memoirs and Confessions of a Justified Sinner* is set in the Edinburgh of the period, and although its concern is with the heresy of the Elect who can do as they will without endangering their hope of salvation, The Editor's Narrative gives a useful picture of the kind of street fighting that took place in pre-union Edinburgh.

Although the new century was to bring with it the "mighty affair" of union with England, it also heralded a new awakening of a culture that had been virtually in a coma since the removal of the Court to London. As a recent critic, Tom Scott, has remarked, "The seventeenth century is a poetic wasteland, few birds being heard to sing, although the jackdaw clacked loudly enough in the pulpit." For Edinburgh it was certainly true. After Drummond there was no poet of any import until Ramsay, but there was much intellectual activity born of reformation zeal. (An exception should be made of Francis Sempill who, although not of Edinburgh, based one of his best poems *Hallow Fair* on memories of the city and its surrounding countryside.) James Gregory built Britain's first reflecting telescope and invented differential calculus, the Royal College of Physicians was founded, helping to make the city a world centre of medical studies, the Royal Botanic Garden was established by Sir Robert Sibbald, the palace of Holyrood was rebuilt by Sir William Bruce and most importantly of all, the legal profession asserted itself to become the future axis of intellectual life within Edinburgh. Mackenzie of Rosehaugh had founded the Advocates' Library, Lord Stair published *The Institutions of Law in Scotland* and Sir Thomas Murray of Glendoich produced an edition of all the acts of parliament, both books becoming standard texts for generations of lawyers to come. Despite the restrictions on the imagination in seventeenth century Edinburgh, there was much hope for the future.

Shortly before the Union an anonymous English traveller visited Edinburgh and left a description of a city that had changed little since earliest times. It was a picture that would be very different within the space of fifty momentous years.

> Now helpe me, Art, to describe this mighty city and university, the metropolis of this ancient kingdom of Scotland, that took me up a full half day to see thoroughly. This town extends itself east and west in length, and consists chiefly of one wide street of tall buildings, with some piazzas on the sides. Its situation is on a steep hill between two larger hills, and so the fronts of the houses towards the streets are not so high as the backward parts are, they being left further down the sides of the hill, according to the precipice of the hill, on which part they stand. And some of these houses are seven and eight storeys high towards the street; and more backward, and in the Parliament Close, it seems they were houses fourteen storeys high before they were burnt down by a late fire; but I suppose it was of the back parts they were so high, for the hill there is very steep.

PRECIPITOUS CITY

This town is very populous, and has abundance of poor people in it, so that the streets are crowded with beggars; but I don't take it to be so large as York or Newcastle, though indeed neither of them have so wide a streets or are of so tall buildings as the great street here. The people here are very proud, and they call the ordinary tradesmen merchants; there is no large river up to this town, but of the north side of it, at some distance is a small one. At the best houses here they dress their victuals after the French method, though perhaps not so cleanly, and a soup is commonly the first dish, and their reckonings are dear enough. The maid servants attended without shoes or stockings . . . .

Chapter Five

The Union and After

There is a story told that when the Act of Union, the political alliance joining together Scotland and England, came into force on 1st May 1707, someone broke into the tower of St Giles and played upon its bells, the old Scottish folk-song, *How can I be sad on my wedding day?* Even if the story has become too much part of the city's legend to have any basis in fact, it deserves to be true because not only has it an eloquent title but it is fitting that the folk tradition should provide the epitaph for Scottish political hopes in the eighteenth century.

The failure of the Darien Scheme in 1689 had soured relationships with London. Many Scots suspected, rightly, that England had done all in her power to prevent the adequate provision of supplies to the Scots settlers in the Darien peninsula (which joins north and south America) and had acted in collusion with Spain in attacks on the colony. The failure of the expedition and the loss of the hard-earned £400,000 had enraged the Scottish nation and anti-English feelings ran high in Edinburgh. They were exacerbated by the seven "lean years" of poverty and by the passing of the Alien Act of 1705 which would have made Scots aliens in England and which prevented the passage of trade between the two countries. Several Scottish politicians in fact wanted union with England and after months of intrigue the Scottish Commissioners agreed with their English counterparts on twenty-five articles which would form the basis of the unification of their two countries. On 3rd October 1706 the Scottish Parliament went into its last session to debate the Articles of Union which received their second and decisive reading on 16th January in the following year, against a background of violence and unrest within the city.

Sent to Edinburgh to report on Scottish attitudes was Daniel Defoe who found himself in a state of alarm about the nightly disturbances in the narrow streets of the capital.

> I had not been Long There but I heard a Great Noise and looking
> Out Saw a Terrible Multitude Come up the High street with a
> Drum at the head of Them shouting and swearing and Cryeing
> Out all scotland would stand together, No Union, No Union,
> English Dogs and the like.

Another visitor, an English barrister, Joseph Taylor, discovered that
the passing of the Act was seen by many as being of great benefit to
both countries, and that in spite of the disturbances there were those
who welcomed it. His view was coloured by the company he kept
for the country was fairly evenly divided between the Unionists and
the opposition who had as their spiritual leader, the remarkable
Andrew Fletcher of Saltoun.

> Now the whole Act being finish'd, the Vote was put whether it
> should be carry'd approven, or no, and 'twas carry'd approven, by
> 34 voices. As soon as this was over, we left the house, and that
> night Collonel Ogilby, the Lord Chancellor's brother, the Lord
> Hardress, and severall Lords and parliament men, came to our
> lodgings, and embrac'd us with all the outward marks of love and
> kindness, and seem'd mightily pleas'd at what was done; and told
> us we should now be no more English and Scotch, but Brittons.
> And thus we merrily spent the night in drinking to the Success of
> the treaty and a happy union.

The Union with England was to change the face of the country
and was also to administer a cultural shock wave which reverberated
down the century. When the citizens of Edinburgh awoke on the
morning of 1st May to the sound of St Giles's bells they found
themselves about to step out into a world that was neither Scots nor
British and that split was to become a source of anguished doubt for
their descendants in years to come.

Writers and poets began to be affected by the increasing need to
write in English, both to gain a wider audience and to make
themselves understood. As trade and political links with London
began to be opened up there was a greater need than ever before to
use English and elocution classes began to spring up in the city as
more and more people began to become nervous of using Scots.
Seven years before the Union, Allan Ramsay had left his Lanarkshire

home to be apprenticed to a wig-maker in Edinburgh. In 1712 he set up shop in the Grassmarket as a master wig-maker and in that same year he helped to found the Easy Club, a society for "mutual improvement in Conversation". Like other Edinburgh clubs, the members used pseudonyms and Ramsay took for himself the name Isaac Bickerstaff, thus reflecting the Club's interest in the London *Spectator* which was read aloud before each meeting began. Ramsay also took an early interest in Scots poetry, and he has left us with a good self-portrait in verse.

> *Imprimis* then, for tallness I
> Am five foot and four inches high:
> A black-a-vic'd snod dapper fallow,
> Nor lean, nor overlaid wi' tallow.
> With phiz of a Morocco cut,
> Resembling a late man of wit,
> Auld-gabbet *Spec*, wha was sae cunning
> To be a dummie ten years running.

His interest in poetry led him not only to change his club name to Gawin Douglas but to explore the roots of Scots poetry and song. Since the Union there had been a revival of interest in the romance of the past and songs had been collected almost as evidence of Scotland's claim to nationhood. In 1706 James Watson, an Edinburgh printer with violently anti-Unionist inclinations, published his *Choice Collection of Comic and Serious Poems both Ancient and Modern*, a collection which helped his contemporaries to reach back to an earlier literary tradition.

Ramsay followed Watson's lead in 1724 when he published the first of his five volumes of *The Tea-Table Miscellany*, a collection of songs to be sung to traditional airs, and *The Evergreen*, a collection of medieval Scots poems from the Bannatyne Manuscript. Before then Ramsay had abandoned wigs in favour of a literary career and had opened a bookseller's shop first in Niddry's Wynd and then in 1726 at the east end of the Luckenbooths under the twin signs of Ben Jonson and Drummond of Hawthornden. That he had chosen the spirits of an English dramatist and a Scots poet for his trade is indicative of the duality of his attitudes towards his art. In 1718 he had published his first collection of poems by "the Author at the

PRECIPITOUS CITY

Mercury opposite to Niddry's Wynd". Almost half of them were in English and the others were in Scots. Of the latter the most popular were those about Edinburgh and they were to make Ramsay an eminent and well-loved man within the city.

His earthy directness and love of the city's low life helped to capture in his poetry the vibrant, noisy, busy, city centre where he carried on his business. In the Canongate he bemoaned the death of Lucky Wood who kept a tavern renowned both for its fare and for the honesty of the owner.

> The Writer lads fow well may mind her,
> Furthy was she, her luck design'd her
> Their common mither, sure nane kinder
>   Ever brake bread;
> She has na left her make behind her,
>   But now she's dead.
>
> To the sma' hours we aft sat still,
> Nick'd round our toasts and snishing mill;
> Good cakes we wanted ne'r at will,
>   The best of bread,
> Which often cost us mony a gill,
>   To Aikenhead.

Further down the street, near the Palace of Holyrood lived Lucky Spence, a famous madame who recruited for her brothel from "young lasses that had a little pertness, strong passions, abundance of laziness, and no fore-thought". In his poem to her, Ramsay lets the bawd give some practical advice to her tiro prostitutes.

> When e'er ye meet a fool that's fow,
> That ye're a maiden gar him trow,
> Seem nice, but stick to him like glew;
>   And whan set down,
> Drive at the jango till he spew,
>   Syne he'll sleep soun.
>
> Whan he's asleep, then dive and catch
> His ready cash, his rings or watch;
> And gin he likes to light his match
>   At your spunk-box,

76

Ne'er stand to let the fumbling wretch
  E'en take the pox.

Cleek a' ye can be hook or crook,
Ryp ilky poutch frae nook to nook;
Be sure to truff his pocket-book,
  Saxty pounds Scots
Is nae deaf nits: in little bouk
  Lie great bank-notes.

The Church did its best to quell the kind of drunken licentiousness celebrated by Ramsay and his later compatriots, Fergusson and Burns, and most presbyteries employed watchmen to report on sexual misbehaviour or excessive inebriation. Culprits had to submit when caught, to public retribution from the minister or, worse still, to the stool of repentance or to a short stay in a house of correction like the infamous one in Leith Wynd (near the present Jeffrey Street). It was little wonder, then, that Ramsay should mourn with such glee the death of one of those snoopers, John Cowper.

Fy upon Death, he was to blame
To whirle poor John to his lang hame:
But though his arse be cauld, yet fame,
  Wi' tout of trumpet,
Shall tell how Cowper's awfou name
  Cou'd flie a strumpet.

He kend the bawds, and louns fou well,
And where they us'd to rant and reel
He paukily on them cou'd steal,
  And spoil their sport;
Aft did they wish the muckle De'il
  Might tak him for't.

For his own pleasure, Ramsay would join his colleagues for a day's golf and drinking at Bruntsfield Links which lie about a mile south from the city centre. Parched from the excercise they would spend a few hours at Maggy Johnston's drinking, "a small sort of ale agreeable to the taste, very white, clear and intoxicating", sometimes with disastrous results.

When in our poutch we fand some clinks,
And took a turn o'er Bruntsfield Links,
Aften in Maggy's at Hy-jinks,
    We guzl'd scuds,
Till we could scarce wi' hale out drinks
    Cast aff our duds.

We drank and drew, and fill'd again,
O wow but we were blyth and fain!
When ony had their count mistain,
    O it was nice
To hear us a' cry, Pike ye'r bain
    And spell ye'r dice.

Fou closs we us'd to drink and rant,
Until we did baith glowre and gaunt,
And pish and spew, and yesk and maunt,
    Right swash I true;
Then of auld stories we did cant
    Whan we were fou.

It was not all pleasure. Bookselling was a demanding profession and in addition to selling books, in 1725 Ramsay opened what is generally held to be the first lending library in Britain, a move that was not calculated to attract himself to the godly. Books were considered, by the more extreme Churchmen, to be objects of profanity and many thought it a mortal sin to lend boods at two pence a time, thus making money out of evil. Despite the threats from religious bigots, both shop and library flourished, and bookselling as a profession came to be an important part of Edinburgh's literary life. It was in the shop below Ramsay's on the Luckenbooths that the young William Creech learned the trade.

Ramsay also fell foul of the Church through his involvement with the theatre which had for long been looked on as the domain of the Devil. Hugo Arnot, who wrote an early history of Edinburgh in 1779, was able to state without blushing that throughout the century, "most popular divines represented the playhouse as the actual temple of the Devil, where he frequently appeared clothed in the corporeal substance and possessed the spectators, whom he held as his worshippers". As a result, drama was the weakest link in the Scottish literary output and the theatre had lain long in a moribund state. There had been a glimmer of light in 1692 with the production of *The Assembley* by Archibald Pitcairne but it was hardly likely to ease the Church's suspicions as the author was a Jacobite and an enthusiastic atheist.

The Assembly pokes outrageous fun at the General Assembly of the Church of Scotland (its governing body) in the period after the accession to the throne of William and Mary, when the Presbyterian church government was restored. Pitcairne disliked the Church so much that he painted all his ministers as craven fools who are determined to spoil other people's pleasures. It is set in Edinburgh where two rakes, Will and Frank set the scene.

> For my own Part, I find no Reason to complain; for I find them as good Whoring and Drinking times as ever: Only with this Difference; whereas, before we were *most Christian Drunkards*, we're now turned *most Catholick;* and the Compliments we took before out of *Cassandra* and *Cleopatra* for our Mistresses, we're now beholden to the *Song of Solomon* for them. The Money we were wont to give to Bawds, we now give to Phanatick Ministers Wives: And whereas before Honest Fellows coin'd new Oaths at a Glass of Wine, we now send our Representative to Parliament to do it for us.

Pitcairne's play enjoyed something of an underground reputation in taverns and clubs at a time when it could never have been performed on the stage in Edinburgh. Not that the city was in any way kept in a grip of steel by the Church. There was a healthy scepticism amongst all classes and Pitcairne took great delight in telling his friends that when, one rainy day, he took unexpected shelter in a church, he was astonished to see the minister weeping during the sermon. "What the devil gars the man greet (cry)?" he asked his neighbour. "Faith," said the man, "ye wad maybe greet yoursel' if ye was up there and had as little to say." This kind of cosy infidelity was a very necessary antidote to the stricter attitudes of the Church.

It was not until the winter of 1724 that Edinburgh enjoyed a season of drama when an actor called Anthony Aston brought his troupe of travelling players from England to perform in the Skinner's Hall. It was a successful venture and his theatre attracted enthusiastic audiences but the city council began to take notice of the company's alleged improprieties and the *Edinburgh Courant* of 13th March 1729 reported that, "the Company of Scotch Comedians as they called themselves, have all of a sudden elop't without counting with their creditors". During his stay Aston had become friendly with Ramsay who had helped the company by writing prologues and by selling tickets from his shop.

Between 1730 and 1737 Allan Ramsay managed the Edinburgh Players and was able to use his considerable influence to bring up productions from London. The Players also toured as far afield as Newcastle and Scarborough and Ramsay worked hard to drum up support for legitimate theatre, free from oppression of either Church or State. He went on to found his own theatre in Carrubber's Close off the High Street in 1736 but the following year the government passed an act which prevented theatre performances taking place outside London. The theatre in Edinburgh had to close and Ramsay, furious about the indignity of the action both to himself and to his city, wrote several satires to the Court of Session on the prohibition.

> Shall London have its houses twa
> And we doomed to have nane ava?
> Is our metropolis, ance the place
> Where langsyne dwelt the royal race
> Of Fergus, this gate dwindled down
> To a level with ilk clachan town,
> While thus she suffers the subversion
> of her maist rational diversion?

Ramsay had also written for the theatre when his verse-play, *The Gentle Shepherd*, was published to great acclaim in June 1725. It is generally considered to be second only to *The Thrie Estaitis* in the Scottish dramatic canon, and the simply constructed drama of Scottish rustic life set in the Pentland Hills above Edinburgh was not only a popular success at the time but was a great influence on later Scots poetry. Its fame spread to London and when the poet John Gay was in Edinburgh in 1732 one of his first calls was to Ramsay's shop that he might understand *The Gentle Shepherd* better and so explain the Scots words to his friend Alexander Pope.

After the closing of the Carrubber's Close theatre Ramsay began to retire from public life and although he continued to keep open a busy shop beneath the signs of Jonson and Drummond at the East end of the Luckenbooths, he published little else from his own pen. He led an agreeably Horatian existence amongst his friends and his books and he added to his happiness in 1743 when he built an octagonal villa on the north side of Castle Hill where the present Ramsay Gardens now stands. The local wits dubbed it Goose Pie House, but it had an unsurpassed view to the mouth of the Firth of Forth to the east, to the Ochil Hills to the west, and across the Nor Loch to the pleasant shore of Fife.

He enjoyed both his success and his family life, three daughters had been born to him and "no ae wally-draggle among them, all fine girls", and his son, Allan, was rapidly making a name for himself as a painter in London, having completed his education in Italy. There were still enjoyable evenings to be spent in Jenny Ha's Change House which stood near to Brown's Close where a beer was sold that was so potent it was said "to glue the drinkers' lips together", but as he reached the end of his long life he began to miss those contemporaries who had died. At one time he had aspired to be a London wit but his fellow writers and friends Pope, Steele, Addison and Arbuthnott were all dead as were the other writers of his generation who had known him in Scotland, Robert Blair, James Thomson and Hamilton of Bangour. He died at the age of seventy four in 1758, six years before the love of his later years, the theatre, became legalised, but he died in the secure knowledge that Allan Ramsay, poet of Edinburgh, was well loved by his fellow citizens and that he himself had answered the question posed in an early poem.

> Whenever fame, with a voice of thunder,
> Sets up a chield a warld's wonder,
> Either for slashing folk to dead,
> Or having wind-mills in his head,
> Or poet, or an airy beau,
> Or ony twa-legged rary-show,
> They wha have never seen't are busy
> To speer what-like a carlie is he.

PRECIPITOUS CITY

One of the great events of Ramsay's lifetime had been the arrival in the city on 15th September 1745 of the Jacobite army under the command of the Young Pretender, Prince Charles Edward Stewart, the grandson of James the Second. They arrived in the village of Corstorphine to the west of the city (now a suburb) and following a half-hearted attempt by the City Guard and two regiments of dragoons to offer token resistance, the Highland army entered the Old Town in the early morning of 17th September having been forbidden on pain of punishment not "to taste spirits and to pay for whatever they got". The army set up camp in the King's Park at Holyrood where Charles maintained a royal residence during his two-month stay.

Although there was a romantic attachment to the Jacobite cause the professional and commercial men of Edinburgh were mainly in favour of the Government and there was no little relief when the Jacobite army decamped on 1st November for their long march south, to retreat at Derby and to eventual defeat the following year at Culloden. Even Allan Ramsay, for all his sympathies to the Young Pretender's cause, found a convenient excuse to be absent from the city during its occupation. It was left to the women of Edinburgh to offer the warmest welcome as a volunteer in the Government army was to write a year later: "And the ladies in general, are in love with the Pretender's Son's Person, and wear white Breast-Knots and Ribbons in his Favour, in all their private Assemblies." And early in the next century, when fond memories of the Jacobite cause were still fresh, Robert Chambers described in great detail the colourful proclamation of Charles as Prince Regent.

The Prince being thus established in his paternal palace, it was the next business of his adherents to proclaim his father at the Cross. The party which entered the city in the morning had taken care to secure the heralds and pursuivants, whose business it was to perform such ceremonies. About one o'clock, therefore, an armed body was drawn up around the Cross; and that venerable pile, which notwithstanding its association with so many romantic events, was soon after removed by the magistrates, had the honour of being covered with carpet for the occasion. The officers were clothed in their fantastic, but rich old dresses, in order to give all the usual *eclat* to this disloyal ceremony. David Beatt, a Jacobite

82

teacher of Edinburgh, then proclaimed King James and read the commision of regency, with the declaration dated at Rome in 1743, and a manifesto in the name of Charles Prince Regent, dated at Paris, May 16 1745. An immense multitude witnessed the solemnity, which they greeted with hearty but partial huzzas. The ladies, who viewed the scene from their lofty lattices in the High Street, strained their voices in acclamation, and waved white handerchiefs in honour of the day. The Highland guard looked round the crowd with faces expressing wild joy and triumph, and, with the licence and extravagence appropriate to the occasion fired off their pieces in the air. The bagpipe was not wanting to greet the name of James with a loyal pibroch; and during the ceremony, Mrs Murray of Broughton, whose enthusiasm was only surpassed by her beauty, sat on her horseback beside the Cross, with a drawn sword in her hand, and her person profusely decorated with white ribbons, which signified devotion to the house of Stuart.

Serving in the Jacobite army was Alexander MacDonald, Alasdair mac Mhaighster Alasdair, a poet and Gaelic nationalist who had been employed as a teacher in a charity school in Ardnamurchan. According to tradition he had been charged with teaching Gaelic to the Prince, and throughout his life he remained a fierce Jacobite, intensely proud of his Highland heritage. In 1741 he had written the first Gaelic dictionary but the works that bring him his greatest admirers are his love poems, songs and nature poems, and his masterpiece, *Birlinn Chlann Raghnaill* (The Galley of Clanranald) which describes a voyage from South Uist to Carrickfergus. Macdonald survived the campaign, but seven years after the rising his work was still considered treasonable enough to be burned by Edinburgh's hangman in the Grassmarket.

Another literary personality closely identified with the Jacobite cause was the printer and editor Thomas Ruddiman who had come to Edinburgh from his native north-east in 1699. Archibald Pitcairne had found him work in the Advocates' Library and in 1706 he joined the printer Robert Freebairn before setting up in business by himself and printing some of Allan Ramsay's work. Apart from his interest in Scottish vernacular poetry he printed aids to classical scholarship such as his *Rudiments of the Latin Tongue* and Gavin Douglas's translation of the *Aeneid* into Scots. In 1729 he bought the best known newspaper of the day, the *Caledonian Mercury* and in the following year he was appointed Keeper of the Advocates' Library, a post he held for twenty-two years. His successor as Keeper was to be David Hume.

Ruddiman was one of the founders of the Rankinian Club which counted amongst its members the young Lord Kames and the poet William Hamilton of Bangour.

> The father of the Club was the very learned old Mr Thomas Rudiman, a Printer and keeper of the Advocates' library. A nonjuror Clergyman was next in iminence, and they two were contrivers of this meeting. Being keen Jacobites both they thought it was a good opportunity of Assembling, first, Young Gentlemen, whose parents were well inclined to the old cause; 2dly, Gradually to bring in young Prysbiterian Clergymen, Students of Davinity, Law and Physic, to hear the disputations, which often tended to keep alive the Spirit of Jacobitism, or rather the interest of the family of Stewart.

Hamilton was born in 1704 into an influential Whig family and like others of his day was educated at the High School and at the University where he started writing poetry. Although he is best remembered for his much anthologised poem *The Braes of Yarrow* he wrote occasional verse about Edinburgh life, particularly about the dancing Assemblies which had become so popular in the city. The Assembly opened for dancing at four o'clock and "was rigorously closed at eleven" and it was there that young Edinburgh society met, and though Hamilton was a firm favourite, according to Kames, he often let his feelings get the better of him.

> She (Jeanie Stewart) complained to Mr Home, that she was teased with Mr Hamilton's dangling attentions, which she was convinced had no serious aim, and hinted an earnest wish to get rid of him. "you are his friend," said she: "tell him he exposes both himself and me to the ridicule of our acquaintance." — "No, Madam," said Mr Home, "you shall accomplish his cure yourself: and by the simplest method. — Dance with him at to-night's assembly, and shew him every mark of your kindness, as if you believed his passion sincere, and had resolved to favour his suit. Take my word

Allan Ramsay   Robert Fergusson

William Drummond of Hawthornden

The historic meeting between Robert Burns and the young Walter Scott in
Sciennes Hill House, the home of Adam Ferguson

The Scott Monument under construction in 1844.
It was completed in 1846. Calotype by
Hill and Adamson

James Hogg, the Ettrick Shepherd, by
William Allan

Archibald Constable, the 'Prince of
Publishers' by Andrew Geddes

William Blackwood, the founder of
Blackwood's Magazine, by William Allan

Henry MacKenzie, 'The Man of Feeling'
by Colvin Smith

Sir Walter Scott, by Sir Henry Raeburn

Lord Cockburn, a silhouette by
Auguste Edouart

Susan Ferrier, a silhouette by
Auguste Edouart

for it, you'll hear no more of him." The lady adopted the counsel, and the success of the experiment was complete.

Throughout this period Hamilton's politics were gradually becoming more nationalistic and he began to espouse the Jacobite cause with relentless vigour after a visit to Rome where the Young Pretender had met him and asked the famous question, "Mr Hamilton, do you like this prospect or the one from North Berwick Law best?" He remembered the question in 1745 and joined the Jacobite army on its entry into Edinburgh. After Culloden he went into hiding and was successfully kept by two sisters in a safe house in the heart of the Old Town before going into exile in Sweden in September 1746. He died in 1754, shortly after influential friends, including Kames, had secured his pardon, allowing him to retrieve his estates in Linlithgow and Haddington.

During his time in Edinburgh, after leaving University, the young Hamilton had been assisted in finding a publisher by Allan Ramsay, who, as we have seen, chose to be absent from the city during the Jacobite occupation. In some respects Ramsay's prudence was a further demonstration of the opposing nature of his belief: on the one hand his heart told him that Jacobite nationalism was a devout and worthy cause, but on the other his head ruled otherwise. He had fled south to the house of his friend Sir John Clerk whose palladian mansion at Penicuik was considered one of the marvels of the day.

If Clerk has been called one of the most endearing characters of eighteenth-century Scotland, he was certainly also one of the most rounded and influential. Amongst his friends he numbered patrons like Lord Burlington and the "Roman Knights" of London's Spalding Club, while at home he gathered around him an *Academia dell' Arcadia* in the Midlothian countryside. Ramsay, with his admiration for the London wits, must have been spellbound by this intriguing character. Like many other Scots he had been educated in Europe and continued to keep close links with Rome and Paris, especially as his interest in architecture began to grow. He befriended Ramsay's son, Allan and was patron to William Adam, the father of Robert and John Adam and in many ways, through his friendship, encouragement and contacts, helped to lay the foundation of the formal elegance of Scottish Georgian architecture.

PRECIPITOUS CITY

Amongst all these of the first Rate
Our learned CLERK blest with the Fate
Of thinking right, can best relate
   These beauties all,
Which bear the marks of ancient Date,
   Be-north the wall.

The learned Sir John celebrated in Ramsay's poem died in 1755 before the birth of the New Town but his protégé Robert Adam went on to create a profound effect on the face of Edinburgh, designing the Old College on South Bridge and much of Charlotte Square. The building of the New Town properly belongs to the next chapter and its construction pushed the city beyond the narrow limits of the medieval town on its high ridge between the Castle and the Palace of Holyrood. After the Union Edinburgh began to entertain more visitors than ever before and there are numerous traveller's tales describing the city and its environs. The most famous, and certainly the most business-like, visitor had been Daniel Defoe, and just as his eagle eye omitted few details about the mood of the nation during the Union debate, so also has he left an intimate picture of the city in the early days of the the century.

When you stand at a small Distance, and take a View of it from the East, you have really but a confus'd Idea of the City, because the Situation being in Length from East to West; and the Breadth but ill proportion'd to its Length, you view under the greatest Disadvantage possible; whereas if you turn a little to the Right Hand towards *Leith*, and so come towards the City, from the North you see a very handsome Prospect of the whole City, and from the South you have yet a better view of one Part, because the City is encreased on that Side with new Streets, which, on the North Side, cannot be.

The particular Situation then of the whole is thus. At the Extremity of the East End of the City stands the Palace or Court, call'd *Haly-Rood House*; and you must fetch a little Sweep to the right Hand to leave the Palace on the left, and come at the Entrance, which is called the *Water Port*, and which you come at thro' a short Suburb, then bearing to the left again, South, you come to the Gate of the Palace which faces the great Street.

From the Palace, West, the street goes on in almost a straight

Line, and for near a Mile and a half in Length, some say full 2
measur'd Miles, thro' the whole City to the Castle, including the
going up the Castle in the Inside; this is, perhaps the largest,
longest, and finest Street for Buildings and number of Inhabitants
not in Bretain only, but in the World.

From the very Palace Door, which stands on a Flat, and level
with the lowest of the plain Country, the Street begins to ascend;
and tho' it ascends very gradually at first, and is nowhere steep, yet
'tis easy to understand that continuing the Ascent for so long a
Way, the further Part must necessarily be very high; and so it is; for
the Castle which stands at the Extremity West, as the Palace does
East, makes on all three Sides, that only excepted, which joins it to
the City, a frightful and impassable precipice.

Together with this continued Ascent, which, I think, 'tis easy to
form an Idea of in the Mind, you are to suppose the Edge or Top of
the Ascent so narrow, that the Street, and the Row of Houses on
each Side of it, take up the whole Breadth; so that which way
soever you turn, either to the Right, or to the Left, you go down
Hill immediately and that so steep, as is very troublesom to those
who walk in these Side Lanes which they call Wynds, especially if
their Lungs are not very good: So that in a Word, the City stands
upon the narrow Ridge of a long ascending Mountain.

Defoe also complained bitterly about the vile habit of throwing all
manner of refuse into the streets and he and other visitors castigated
the citizens because they "delighted in Stench and Nastiness".
Visitors commented, too, on their inability to understand Scots
which is a natural relation to Anglo-Saxon and a language in its own
right, and Scots in positions of power began to be aware of using a
tongue which the English considered to be a vulgar vernacular. But
in spite of the encroaching anglicisation there continued to be a
healthy suspicion of London and its inward-looking metropolitan
way of life. Shortly before the forty-five, Margaret Calderwood, the
daughter of Sir James Stewart of Coltness, a Solicitor-General for
Scotland between 1714 and 1717, visited London on her way to
Europe and found little in the city to her liking.

You will think it very odd, that I was a fortnight in London and
saw none of the royall family, but I got no cloaths made till the day
before I left it, though I gave them to the making the day after I

came. I cannot say my curiosity was great: I found as I approached the Court and the grandees they sunk so miserably in my opinion, that I was loath to lose the grand ideas I had of Kings, Princes, Ministers of State, Senators etc, which I suppose I had gathered from the romance in my youth. We used to laugh at the English for being so soon afraid when there was any danger in state affairs, but now I do excuse them. For we, at a distance, think the wisdom of our governours will prevent all these things; but those who know and see our ministers every day see there is no wisdom in them, and that they are a parcell of old, ignorant, senseless bodies, who mind nothing but eating and drinking, and rolling about in Hyde Park, and know no more of the country or the situation of it, than they never had been in it; or how should they, when London, and twenty miles round it, is the extent ever they saw of it?

Her attitude betrays a deep-rooted suspicion of London and of government from Westminster, a dislike that was to remain with many Scots down to the present day. Very few people benefitted from the Union. Some members of the nobility like Queensberry, who had helped to engineer the joining together of the two countries, were given substantial financial rewards, thus giving rise to the belief, held by many Scots that they had been "bought and sold for English gold". For most people, though, the only change was one of regret that a nation's birthright had been exchanged for a distant parliament and a consequent lack of control over their own affairs. Even in the next century, Walter Scott writing about the period in his novel, *The Heart of Midlothian*, put those still rampant feelings into the mouths of the Edinburgh citizens of 1736, the year of the Porteous Riots.

"I dinna ken muckle about the law," answered Mrs Howden; "but I ken, when we had a king, and a chancellor, and parliament-men o' our ain, we could aye peeble them wi' stanes when they werena gude bairns — But naebody's nails can reach the length o' Lunnon."

"Weary on Lunnon, and a' that e'er came out o't!" said Miss Grizel Damahoy, an ancient seamstress; "they hae taen awa our parliament, and they hae oppressed our trade. Our gentles will hardly allow that a Scots needle can sew ruffles on a sark, or lace on an overlay."

88

THE UNION AND AFTER

It was fairly common for the Edinburgh mob to take to the streets, to throw stones, and the city was only kept in a degree of quiet during this period by the presence of troops in the Castle. In September 1736 there was a potent demonstration to the government of the anti-union feelings of the majority of the capital's citizens. Earlier that year two smugglers, Wilson and Robertson, were sentenced to death for a petty crime and condemned to be hanged on the scaffold in the Grassmarket. Many people thought the sentence too severe and when Wilson helped his young companion to escape while they were attending a service at the Tolbooth Church under heavy guard, the general opinion was that there should be a reprieve. Following the execution the crowd expressed its disgust by stoning the hangman and the captain of the City Guard, John Porteous, who, in the words of a contemporary witness, "had his natural courage increased to rage by any suspicion that he and his Guard could not execute the law, and being likewise heated by wine", ordered his men to fire on the crowd. Eight people died and at the subsequent trial Porteous was found guilty and sentenced to death.

Porteous had friends in London who were able to put pressure on influential members of parliament, and Caroline, the Queen-Regent, ordered his reprieve. The Edinburgh mob, when they heard of this, were incensed as the move was seen as an affront both to the city and to the dignity of Scots Law. More sinisterly, many citizens thought that the action was a result of having to bow to direct rule from London. Enraged, the crowd assembled at the West Port burned down the door of the Tolbooth and dragged the wretched Porteous out into the street to be hanged. Walter Scott takes up the reconstruction of the action in *The Heart of Midlothian*.

> "Away with him — away with him!" was the general cry. "Why do you trifle away time in making a gallows? — that dyester's pole is good enough for the homocide."
> The unhappy man was forced to his fate with remorseless rapidity. Butler, seperated from him by the press, escaped the last horrors. Unnoticed by those who had hitherto detained him as a prisoner, he fled from the fatal spot without caring in what direction his course lay. A loud shout proclaimed the stern delight with which the agents of this deed regarded its completion. Butler,

then, at the opening into the low street called the Cowgate, cast back a terrified glance, and, by the red and dusky light of the torches, he could discern a figure wavering and struggling as it hung suspended above the heads of the multitude, and could even observe men striking at it with their Lochaber-axes and partisans. The sight was of a nature to double his horror and to add wings to his flight.

Although the conspirators were never discovered the action of the mob only served to reinforce the idea in London that the Scots were an unruly disaffected neighbour who had to be kept under careful scrutiny, and in Edinburgh it only heightened suspicions about the uncaring nature of central government.

Allan Ramsay, for all his schizoid attitude towards London, lamented the loss of the Scottish parliament too and, like many other writers who were to follow him, maintained a romantic belief in Scotland's national sovereignty. Although critics have chided him for his slack editorial intentions in *The Tea-Table Miscellany* and for the confusion of his attitudes, Ramsay kept alive the possibility of using Scots as a literary language and certainly Fergusson and Burns owed a good deal to his example.

He has also left us with a complete, if biased, picture of the Edinburgh of his day, and he had sufficient wit to apostrophise the loss of Scotland's parliament with a lament for the tavern owners whose trade had been denuded by the sudden lack of thirsty parliamentarians.

> O Cannigate! Poor elritch hole!
> What loss, what crosses does thou thole!
> London and Death gars thee look drole,
>   And hing thy head;
> Wow, but thou has e'en a cauld coal
>   To blaw indeed.

> Hear me ye hills and every glen,
> Ilk craig, ilk cleugh and hollow den,
> And echo shrill, that a' may ken
>   The waefou thud,
> Be rackless Death, wha come unsenn
>   To Lucky Wood.

THE UNION AND AFTER

The Union was brought in with a folk song, and it is fitting that its requiem should be a poem, by Edinburgh's laureate, rich with the language and cadences of the Scottish folk tradition.

Chapter six

The Eighteenth Century Enlightenment

As well as reporting for the government on Scottish attitudes to the Act of Union, Daniel Defoe was an impartial and entertaining observer of life in Edinburgh. Nineteen years after his visit, he published the third volume of his *Tour Thro' the whole Island of Great Britain, Divided into Circuits of Journies* in which he gives us one of the best contemporary accounts of Edinburgh and its society. There is a disgusted description of the noisome filth of the Old Town and wonder at the height and density of the lands, but what caught his eye was not so much the glory of the past as the possibilities of expansion to the north.

> The City suffers infinite Disadvantages, and lies under such scandalous Inconveniences as are, by its Enemies, made a Subject of Scorn and Reproach; as if the People were not as willing to live sweet and clean as other Nations, but delighted in Stench and Nastiness: whereas, were any other People to live under the same Unhappiness, I mean as well of a rocky and mountainous Situation, throng'd Buildings, from seven to ten or twelve story high, a Scarcity of Water, and that little they have difficult to be had, and to the uppermost Lodgings, far to fetch; we should find a *London*, or a *Bristol* as dirty as *Edinburgh*, and, perhaps, less able to make their Dwelling tolerable, at least in so narrow a Compass; for tho' many Cities have more People in them, yet, I believe, this may be said with Truth, that in no City in the World so many People live in so little Room as at *Edinburgh*.
>
> On the North Side of the City is a spacious, rich, and pleasant Plain, extending from the Lough, which joins the City, to the River of *Leith*, at the mouth of which is the Town of *Leith*, at the distance of a long *Scots* mile from the City. And even here, were not the North side of the Hill, which the City stands on, so exceeding steep, as hardly, (at least to the Westward of their Flesh-market) to be clamber'd up on Foot much less to be made passable for Carriages. But, I say, were it not so steep, and were the

92

Lough fill'd up as it might easily be, the City might have been
extended upon the Plain below, and fine beautiful Streets would,
no Doubt, have been built there; nay, I question much, whether, in
Time, the high Streets would not have been forsaken, and the
City, as we might say, run all out of its Gates to the North. . .

Defoe's prophecy was to come true by the time the century was out
and the move to the North was to have a mighty effect not only on
the shape of the city but also on the vision of those who lived there.

There had already been some modest development in the city by
Ramsay's time. James Court, where David Hume and James
Boswell lived for a time, was a new building of note in the
Lawnmarket and there had been a rash of speculative building to the
south of the Canongate. By mid-century the city council was in
agreement that if Edinburgh was to prosper as a British city and as a
Scottish capital, it had to grow. In 1759 the drainage of the Nor Loch
began and a bridge was built across it to join the Old Town with the
"rich and pleasant plain" to the North. The next step was to
announce a competition for the planning of the new extension to the
city, "plans of a New Town marking out streets of a proper breadth
and by-lanes, and the best situation for a reservoir, or any other
public buildings which may be thought necessary".

On 17th April 1767 it was announced that James Craig, a little
known architect, had submitted the best plan and was entitled not
only to the commission but also to a gold medal and to the freedom
of the city. His prize-winning plan shows a carefully laid out, formal
city with a symmetry and elegance which was perfectly in keeping
with the eighteenth century Smile of Reason. It allowed for a long
canal (never completed), tree-lined walks, landscaped parks, a
formal Register House (designed by Robert Adam) and a Theatre
Royal at the east end of Princes Street where the Post Office now
stands. The New Town was conceived of as being British and as
equalling London and even the street names reflect the ideals of a
united country — George Street, Frederick Street, St. David Street,
St. Andrew Square, Charlotte Square.

At the head of his plans Craig had quoted from a poem *Liberty* by
his uncle James Thomson, to set the seal not only on the symmetry
of his physical plans but also on the universality of his intellectual
vision.

PRECIPITOUS CITY

August, around, what Public Works I see!
Lo! stately Streets, lo! Squares that court the breeze!
See long Canals and deepened Rivers join
Each part with each, and with the circling Main
The whole enlivened Isle.

James Thomson had found it necessary earlier in the century to go
to London in search of a public (he is best known for his long poem
The Seasons), but the marriage of the sciences and the arts that he
describes was to find its happiest home in Edinburgh. For there was
a conscious attempt among the city's intelligentsia — they styled
themselves *literati* — to realise and practise a civilised way of life
based on the best European traditions of the day, to create an
"Athens of the North" or a "heavenly city of philosophers". The
impetus for this movement which has come to be known as the
Scottish Enlightenment came from philosophers like David Hume,
the scientists John Gregory and Joseph Black, the economist Adam
Smith, Lords of Session Kames and Monboddo, Hugh Blair,
Professor of Rhetoric and Belles Lettres, William Robertson,
Principal of the University, and Henry Mackenzie, author of the
sentimental novel which proclaimed the age, *The Man of Feeling*.
    Matthew Bramble, the outwardly misanthropic central character
in *Humphrey Clinker* by Tobias Smollett (another Scottish writer
who had to find his audience in London) declared with awe in one of
his letters home that "Edinburgh is a hot-bed of genius. I have had
the good fortune to be made acquainted with many authors of the
first distinction: such as the two Humes, Robertson, Smith,
Wallace, Blair, Fergusson, Wilkie etc, and I have found them all as
agreeable in conversation as they are instructive and entertaining in
their writings." And the printer William Smellie quoted Mr Amyat,
the King's chemist, as declaring that Edinburgh enjoyed a singular
and noble privilege because, "Here I stand at what is called the *Cross
of Edinburgh* and can, in a few minutes, take fifty men of genius and
learning by the hand."
    Why was it then, at mid-century only forty years after the Union,
that Edinburgh could boast such riches of learning amongst the
literati and such progressive plans for a "heavenly city"? One reason
is financial. The Union with England had brought increased wealth

to the country and as a result the city had to expand. Lawyers found greater employment in the additional legislation due to the Act and trade with Europe and the new colonies was facilitated with the help of London. There may have been a continuing resentment about the connection with England but there were also those who realised that prosperity, law and order were not without their disadvantages. The law, too, was the one sure road to political advancement and, during his period of Secretary of State in the reign of George III, Lord Bute became notorious for the number of public appointments he reserved for Scots.

Lawyers had always kept open their links with Europe and it was common practice, with the spirit of Scots Law being Roman-Dutch, for young men to spend a year at a continental university studying law. The connection with Europe was of long standing and although it had been weakened in the years following the Union of the Crowns, it was reborn during the eighteenth century. This was the second reason for the rise of the *literati* — a desire to assimilate European thought — and it was common to find writers like the economist Adam Smith urging his fellows to better themselves by studying "foreign" (European) literature and philosophy. That they were conscious of their stature is nowhere more proudly stated than in *le bon* David Hume's remark to Gilbert Elliot of Minto in 1757.

> Is it not strange, that, at a time when we have lost our Princes, our Parliaments, our independent Government, even the Presence of our chief Nobility, are unhappy, in our Accent & Pronunciation, speak a very corrupt Dialect of the Tongue which we make use of; is it not strange, I say, that, in these circumstances, we shou'd really be the People most distinguish'd for Literature in Europe?

David Hume was intensely aware of being a Scot, was proud of his country and yet, like many others of the *literati*, he was ashamed of his Scots speech. He even went so far as to submit his work to others so that inadvertant "Scoticisms" could be removed and was eager to embrace English as his written language. In 1787 James Beattie published his *Scoticisms, Arranged in Alphabetical Order, Designed to Correct Improprieties of Speech and Writing*, and its author even sent his son from "North Britain" (he also disowned the country) to learn a purer form of English.

At home, from his Mother and me, he learned to read and write. His pronunciation was not correct, as may well be supposed: but it was deliberate and significant, free from provincial peculiarities, and such as an Englishman would have understood; and afterwards, when he had passed a few summers in England, it became more elegant than what is commonly heard in North Britain. He was early warned against the use of Scotch words and other similar improprieties; and his dislike to them was such, that he soon learned to avoid them; and, after he grew up, could never endure to read what was written in any of the vulgar dialects of Scotland. He looked at Mr Allan Ramsay's poems, but he did not relish them.

Another "improver" was Thomas Sheridan, the father of the dramatist, who held classes on elocution in St Paul's Chapel during the summer of 1761. The desire to learn English was understandable if it led to a greater empathy with European thought but it had the disastrously schizophrenic effect of making writers who thought and felt in Scots write in a language which was foreign to them. As a consequence, the *literati*, however rational they may have been in their philosophy, made several curious literary judgements. The insipid poetry of the blind Thomas Blacklock was compared to that composed by Alexander Pope, the now forgotten Dr Wilkie was praised as the equal of Homer and James Macpherson's *Ossian* was given reverential acclaim as being quintessentially Gaelic, while the unknown poet Duncan Ban MacIntyre was living in the city.

A member of the City Guard who had once been arrested for illegally distilling whisky, MacIntyre lived a life of obscurity and ridicule while he lived in the city. (With their Lochaber axes and comic, tall, cocked hats, the City Guard or "black banditti" were figures of fun in Edinburgh.) He is best known for his long poem, *Praise of Ben Dorain*, but he has also left us with poems which show the gulf that was beginning to grow between the social classes in Edinburgh.

Many noble beaux are there,
urbane and elegant,
having powder on their wigs
right up to the crowns;

96

auburn, plaited tresses
twisted into curls;
and like silk is the bushy top,
when it is smoothed by comb.

Many patrician ladies
go up and down the street,
all wearing gowns of silk
that brush against the ground;
stays are worn by the damsels,
compressing them above,
with beauty spots on pretty faces
to increase their coquettry.

As we have seen the chief glory of the lands in the Old Town was that, however dirty or disease-ridden they might have been, there existed within them a mixter-maxter of the social classes and even if equality was only hinted at, the only distinct division in the tenements was that the quality occupied the upper floors. All that changed with the construction of the New Town as the lawyers and the nobility began to take up residence in George Street, Frederick Street and St Andrew Square. William Creech noted with some regret that the changes only sharpened the divisions, "in 1763 people of quality and fashion lived in houses, which, in 1783 were inhabited by tradesmen or by people in humble or ordinary life. The Lord Justice Tinwald's house was possessed by a French teacher — Lord President Craigie's by a rouping wife or sales-woman of old furniture."

The New Town became the haunt of judge and advocate who were justly regarded as important members of the Edinburgh *literati*. Henry Home, Lord Kames, was regarded as the ideal Man of Reason. Schooled in the law and versed in letters, he was also an agrarian improver and an historian who wrote elegantly on moral philosophy. He also continued to use Scots speech, as did most of the Lords of Session, and was content to describe himself as "I ken very weel that I am the coarsest and most black-a-vised bitch in a' the Court o' Session." The judges were a hard-drinking fraternity and thought nothing of tippling heavily during trials, Lord Cockburn remarking of the age that, "black bottles of strong port were set down beside the Bench with glasses, carafes of water, tumblers and

97

biscuits; and this without the slightest attempt at concealment."

For many of the famous judges, drink was not needed to reinforce their eccentricities. Lord Kames sentenced one of his chess-playing cronies to death with the grim remark, "Checkmate, Matthew", and Lord Braxfield told one of his victims that he would be "nane the waur o' a hangin". Braxfield also sent William Brodie to a gallows of Brodie's own making when the city discovered the notorious double life of their respected member of the city council. A cabinet maker and Dean of Wrights, Brodie was also a burglar by night who kept the citizens in a state of alarm with his exploits. (As the man who had fitted most of the city's locks he was in more than a privileged position!) In 1788 he was betrayed by an accomplice, arrested and hanged, but he achieved a grim immortality by becoming the idea for R. L. Stevenson's story *Dr Jekyll and Mr Hyde*, and the dual personality was to tease the Scots for years to come. The Union had something to do with it; so also did the desire to give up Scots in favour of English and to assimilate the manners of the country to the south. Exacerbated by drink it was a powerful recipe for men to lead quiet lives of respectability by day and raucous, drunken, licentious riot by night.

Drink was an important part of Edinburgh society and every visitor to the city marvelled at the huge amounts of alcohol consumed by all classes with equal vigour. Most people started the day with the "morning", a glass of ale, claret was served at breakfast and half-past eleven saw the "meredian" when it was considered time to go to the tavern for the first real drink of the day. As dinner was served early in the afternoon, claret, champagne, brandy and whisky-cup made a welcome appearance and were drunk far into the night. Much of the drinking was done in the many taverns that stood in the closes that ran off the High Street: Lucky Middlemasses in the Cowgate, Rob Gibb's by Parliament House, Fortune's in Stamp Office Close, Douglas's in Anchor Close. It was in these taverns that the drinkers were oblivious to social conventions, judges rubbed shoulders with clerks, advocates with carriers, the nobility with the most eccentric begger. They were also the homes of the convivial clubs which met to eat and drink and to discuss grave philosophical or political matters — the Cape Club, the Select Society, the Feast of Tabernacles, the Crochallan Fencibles.

The lawyers took the lead in drinking and it was not surprising that the tavern-keepers were in bad spirit when the courts were not in session.

Nae body takes a morning dribb
O' Holland gin frae Robin Gibb;
And tho' a dram to Rob's mair sib
   Than is his wife,
He maun take time to daut his Rib
   Till siller's rife.

This vacance is a heavy doom
On Indian Peter's coffee-room,
For a' his china pigs are toom;
   Nor do we see
In wine the sucker biskets soom
   As light's a flee.

Those lines were spoken by one of Scotland's most gifted and least recognised poets, Robert Fergusson, who died at the tragically early age of twenty-four. They also go some way to illuminating the split that existed in the Edinburgh of the Enlightenment. While correct English was the norm of the *literati*, a natural, heightened Scots and a delight in song was Fergusson's crowning achievement.

He was born in Cap-and-Feather Close (now disappeared under the North Bridge) on 5th September 1750 and he was educated at Dundee High School and the University of St Andrews. Leaving without taking a degree, Fergusson was soon back in Edinburgh where he became a lowly clerk in the Commissary Office. From his poetry we can see that he delighted in tavern life and he became a member of the Cape Club on 10th October 1772, taking the name "Sir Precenter". Every member of the Club had to use a pseudonym and discussion was more bohemian than at the other clubs, and more inclined to things Scottish, the ballad editor David Herd taking the name "Sir Scrape Graysteil". Over oysters and gin and ale and rizzard haddock (fish dried in the sun) the Club held regular meetings in James Mann's tavern in Craig's Close, and Fergusson became a quick favourite.

But chief, O Cape! we crave thy aid,
To get our cares and poortith laid:
Sincerity, and genius true,
Of Knights have ever been the due:
Mirth, music, porter deepest dy'd,
Are never here to worth deny'd:
And health, o' happiness the queen,
Blinks bonny, wi' her smile serene.

The spirit of Edinburgh shines through Fergusson's poetry and brief quotations cannot hope to do him justice. His Edinburgh poems should be read in full for the picture they paint of the city he knew so well. The world of club and tavern is celebrated in *Caller Oysters*, a poem which summons up the image of a congenial world where drink and good cheer could banish the reality of the squalid streets outside.

When big as burns the gutters rin,
Gin ye hae catcht a droukit skin,
To Luckie Middlemist's loup in,
    And sit fu snug
O'er oysters and a dram o' gin,
    Or haddock lug.

When auld Saunt Giles, at aught o'clock,
Gars merchant lowns their chopies lock,
There we adjourn wi' hearty fock
    To birle our bodles,
And get wharewi' to crack our joke,
    And clear out noddles.

The legal world is given a wry smile in *The Rising of the Session* and in *The Sitting of the Session,* the Tron Kirk bell is sourly addressed and he celebrates two Edinburgh events, the Leith races and All Hallows fair with wit and gusto. In many of his poems drink plays an important role. A drunk is arrested by the City Guard, punters drown their sorrows at the races, for Ferguson was well aware of the city's second religion.

And thou, great god of *Aqua Vitae!*
Wha sways the empire of this city,
When fou we're sometimes capernoity,

Be thou prepar'd
To hedge us frae that black banditti,
The City Guard.

His most ambitious and his most successful poem is *Auld Reekie*, a
loving hymn of praise (plus the occasional rap over the knuckles) for
the city and its people in all their different moods. It also contains one
of the best descriptions of the city's night life.

Now Night, that's cunzied chief for fun,
Is wi' her usual rites begun;
Thro' ilka gate the torches blaze,
And globes send out their blinking rays.
The usefu' cadie plies in street,
To bide the profits o' his feet;
For by thir lads Auld Reikie's fock
Ken but a sample, o' the stock
O' thieves, that nightly wad oppress,
And make baith goods and gear the less.

Their work done, the keepers of the Luckenbooth stalls shut up shop
for the day and prepared for a boisterous evening's entertainment in
the taverns around the Old Tolbooth. Fergusson painted a vivid
picture of the narrow street ablaze with colour, people jostling about
and the caddies, messenger boys whom Edward Burt had described
as "a very useful Black-Guard, who attend the Coffee-Houses and
public places to go of Errands" speeding up the business of the night.
    Fergusson was not afraid to remember the city's shortcomings
and there were those for whom the night could only bring further
shame and degredation.

Near some lamp-post wi dowy face,
Wi heavy een, and sour grimace,
Stands she that beauty lang had kend,
Whoredom her trade, and vice her end.
But see wharenow she wuns her bread,
By that which Nature ne'er decreed;
And sings sad music to the lugs,
'Mang burachs o' damn'd whores and rogues.

Meanwhile in another tavern drink has taken its toll early in the evening and the threat of violence hung heavily in the air.

> Frae joyous tavern, reeling drunk,
> Wi' fiery phizz, and ein half sunk,
> Behald the bruiser, fae to a'
> That in the reek o' gardies fa':

But when the ten o'clock drum rang the curfew, summoning good citizens to their beds and bidding taverns close their doors, it was time for the Club and the Society to come into their own.

> Now some to porter, some to punch,
> Some to their wife, and some their wench,
> Retire, while noisy ten-hours drum
> Gars a' your trades gae dandring home.
> Now mony a club, jocose and free,
> Gie a' to merriment and glee;
> Wi' sang and glass, they fley the pow'r
> O' care that wad harrass the hour:
> For wine and Bacchus still bear down
> Our thrawart fortunes wildest frown:
> It makes you stark, and bauld, and brave,
> Ev'n whan descending to the grave.

When morning came around again and "kisses the air-cock o' St Giles" the stench of the previous night is added to with the emptying of numberless chamber pots into the streets below. Rosey-hued morn quickly takes on the aura of the midden much to Fergusson's amusement.

> On stair wi' tub, or pat in hand,
> The barefoot housemaids looe to stand,
> That antrin fock may ken how snell
> Auld Reikie will at morning smell:
> Then, with an inundation big as
> The burn that 'neath the Nore Loch Brig is,
> They kindly shower Edina's roses,
> To quicken and regale our noses.

In spite of all that he saw and disapproved of in the city, Fergusson remains in many people's minds, Edinburgh's poet, a man who could never be parted for long from Auld Reikie, a poet who celebrated her with loving grace.

> Reikie, fareweel! I ne'er cou'd part
> Wi' thee but wi' a dowy heart;
> Aft frae the Fifan coast I've seen
> Thee tow'ring on thy summit green;
> So glowr the saints when first is given,
> A fav'rite keek o' glore and heaven;
> On earth nae mair they bend their ein,
> But quick assume angelic mein;
> So I on Fife wad glowr no more,
> But gallop'd to Edina's shore.

Fergusson's poetic career only lasted for three years and in December 1773 Walter Ruddiman's *Weekly Magazine*, which had published all his poetry, printed one of his last poems *Codicile to Rob Fergusson's Last Will* and he became a continual absentee from the Cape Club. His illness lasted several months but because he was unable to work he quickly became destitute and to add to his misfortune he fell into a deep depression and refused the company of others. In the summer of 1774 he injured himself falling down a flight of stairs, and suffering from delirium, he was incarcerated in the Edinburgh Bedlam where he died on 17th October in conditions of extreme horror and neglect.

Despite his early death, Fergusson has continued to exert a powerful influence on poets who have written in Scots, and by his natural and potent use of the language, was able to show that it was not always necessary to turn to an artificial use of English. Robert Burns read his poetry in 1782 to the accompaniment of an excitement that "strung anew my wildly sounding, rustic lyre with emulating vigour". Burns was not an Edinburgh man, but he came to play an important part in the city's history.

The intellectual life of the *literati* and of the poetic underworld was not confined to writing and drinking in taverns. Balls or Assemblies were popular entertainments and Oliver Goldsmith who visited the city in 1753 remarked on the gaiety of the dancing and of the beauty of the Scots girls. The theatre, too, was popular even if it was still officially banned. The Canongate Theatre had been refurbished and re-equipped at the time of Goldsmith's visit and a professional manager, West Digges, had been employed to mount a regular season of new plays. Digges came from an aristocratic background and had a mercurial temper — there were times when he refused to pay his actors and Edinburgh was shocked by the contemptuous treatment meted out to his many mistresses.

Today, he is best remembered for his first production in 1756 at the Canongate Theatre of *A New Tragedy called DOUGLAS, written by an ingenious gentleman of this country* . . . . . The play had in fact been written by John Home, a well-connected minister of the Church of Scotland at Athelstaneford in East Lothian, and its production was to give rise to the oft-quoted shout from the audience on the first night, "Whaurs your Wullie Shakespeare noo?". When the play opened on the 14th December it did in fact cause an uproar with the city being divided in its opinion of the play's merits. There were those who where astonished and delighted that a Scot should have written such a powerful piece of drama, while others saw it as the thin end of the wedge to supplant godly religion. Alexander "Jupiter" Carlyle, who was minister at Inveresk near Musselburgh, remembered the furore in his *Autobiography* which is one of the best chronicles of the Enlightenment.

> The play had unbounded success for a great many nights in Edinburgh, and was attended by all of the literati and most of the judges, who, except one or two, had not been in use to attend the theatre. The town in general was in an uproar of exultation that a Scotchman had written a tragedy of the first rate, and that its merit was first submitted to their judgment. There were a few opposers, however, among those who pretended to taste and literature, who endeavoured to cry down the performance in libellous pamphlets and ballads (for they durst not attempt to oppose it in the theatre itself), and were openly countenanced by Robert Dundas of Arniston, at that time Lord Advocate, and all his minions and expectants.

In the aftermath of the play's success (the theatre was packed for each night of its Edinburgh run and it was subsequently performed in London), Home was forced to resign his post and Carlyle, along with several other Edinburgh ministers, faced prosecution by the local presbyteries. As a result of the fierce fight put up by many ministers, the Church eventually relented and in 1767 the Theatre

THE EIGHTEENTH CENTURY ENLIGHTENMENT

Royal in Shakespeare Square was licensed. By the turn of the century it had moved to a new building at the top of Leith Walk.

That the Church may well have had good reason to fear the theatre as a potential seducer of its congregations is well illustrated in the story of the playwright, John Logan, whose *Runnemede* was produced on 5th May 1784 in Edinburgh. Logan was a minister in South Leith, but after his stage success he turned to excessive drink, womanising and adultery, misbehaving himself so badly in public, even by the standards of the day, that he was forced to leave Edinburgh to seek anonymity in London. As an interesting sequel to the story of theatre in the city and the Church's opposition to it, Alexander Carlyle was able to note that in the same year as Logan's success, the sitting of the General Assembly of the Church of Scotland had to be timed to allow delegates to see Mrs Siddons who was then appearing in the city. The poet Thomas Campbell also remembered her appearance, but for different reasons.

The grave attention of my Scottish countrymen and their canny reservation of praise till they were sure she deserved it, had well-nigh worn out her patience. She had been used to speak to animated clay; but now she felt as she has been speaking to stones. Successive flashes of her elocution, that had always been sure to electrify the south, fell in vain on these northern flints . . . she coiled up all her powers to the most emphatic possible utterance of one passage, having previously vowed in her heart that if *this* could not touch the Scotch, she would never again cross the Tweed. When it was finished, she paused, and looked to the audience. The deep silence was broken only by one voice exclaiming, *"That's no' bad!"* This ludicrous parsimony of praise convulsed the Edinburgh audience with laughter. But the laugh was followed by such thunders of applause that, amidst her stunned and nervous agitation, she was not without fear of the galleries coming down.

Mrs Siddons returned to Edinburgh for two other engagements but patronage of the theatre in Edinburgh was poor and despite the encouragement of the Duke of Hamilton and Henry Dundas there was a general decline in standards until early the following century.

By the 1780s the first part of the Enlightenment, the Golden Age, was over. David Hume had died, a sceptic still, in 1776, James Boswell expressing his surprise that a man could face impending

105

death with such equanimity; Kames, whose life had spanned two centuries, died at the age of eighty-six in 1782 and Monboddo, Adam Smith and William Robertson were all approaching the end of their lives. But their writings had greatly increased the number of booksellers in the High Street — Peter Hill, Elphinstone Balfour, Bell and Bradfute, William Creech and William Laing. It was in those shops that the impetus was to come for the great publishing explosion of the next century.

The number of printing works increased and by 1790 the first *Statistical Account of Scotland* noted that there were sixteen printers in Edinburgh. In spite of the duty levied on them, newspapers like the *Edinburgh Evening Courant* prospered with the help of increased advertising and the townspeople began to show a greater interest in what was happening in other further-flung parts of the world. By 1783 fifteen coaches a week went to London and although the times of the journey had been cut and the coaches were more comfortable, the eighty-year-old Lord Monboddo still preferred to make the journey by horse. Edinburgh also became a popular place to visit and amongst those who lived briefly in city were writers like John Gay, author of *The Beggar's Opera*, who lived in Queensberry House in the Canongate, and the novelist Tobias Smollett who in 1776 lodged with his sister in the now demolished St John Street.

Many of those early travellers have left a graphic picture of the city and amongst the best are those by Thomas Pennant who in 1771 was moved to exclaim that Edinburgh "possesses a boldness and grandeur of situation beyond any that I have ever seen"; Edward Topham, whose *Letters from Edinburgh*, written three years later recorded with gratitude the friendly hospitality he received from the citizens "who are infinitely more civil, humanized and hospitable than any I have ever met"; the Methodist John Wesley offered a sour note when he described Edinburgh as "one of the dirtiest cities I have ever seen", which is hardly surprising when we read Edward Burt's description in 1754 of the Edinburgh habit of hurling all household refuse into the streets below.

> We supped very plentifully, and drank good *French* Claret, and were very merry till the Clock struck Ten, the Hour when every-body is at Liberty, by beat of the City Drum, to throw their Filth out at the Windows. Then the Company began to light Pieces

of Paper, and throw them upon the Table to smoke the Room, and, as I thought, to mix one bad Smell with another.

Being in my Retreat to pass through a long narrow *Wynde* or alley, to my new Lodgings, a Guide was assigned to me, who went before me to prevent my disgrace, crying all the Way, with a loud voice, *Hud your Haunde*. The opening up of a Sash, or otherwise opening a Window, made me tremble, while behind and before me, at some little Distance, fell the terrible Shower.

Well, I escaped all the Danger, and arrived, not only safe and sound, but sweet and clean, at my new Quarters; but when I was in Bed I was forced to hide my Head between the Sheets; for the Smell of the Filth, thrown out by the Neighbours on Back-side of the House, came pouring into the room to such a Degree, I was almost poisoned with the Stench.

This practise, referred to contemptuously as "The Flowers of Edinburgh" continued until the end of the century and it made the clean, open spaces of the New Town a more desirable prospect than ever before.

Amongst the printers who had set up in Edinburgh was William Smellie whose office was in Anchor Close. In the same lane, under an arch bearing the legend BE MERCIFULL TO ME, stood Dawney Douglas's tavern which became the home of the drinking club founded by Smellie, The Crochallan Fencibles. Douglas was in the habit of singing Gaelic songs to his customers and one, *Crodh Challein* (Colin's Cattle), because it had a euphonious title, became the name of one of Edinburgh's most famous drinking clubs.

Educated in the little village of Duddingston to the east of the city (now a suburb) and at the High School, Smellie came from a modest background and yet by dint of hard work and voracious reading he became one of the essential components of the Enlightenment. In 1771 he was involved as editor and principal writer of the *Encyclopaedia Britannica* which had been produced "by a Society of Gentlemen in Scotland, printed in Edinburgh for A. Bell and C. Macfarquhar and sold by Colin Macfarquhar at his printing office in Nicholson Street". Smellie was reputed to have written most of the encyclopaedia without having to check his references and although the publication of his work passed to Constable after his death and then to Cambridge University Press before becoming an international publication, the original dictionary of arts and sciences as envisaged by "the Society of Gentlemen in Scotland" was for many years a standard work.

Although he was a sober, upright man of substance by day, Smellie lived two lives. The nights at the Crochallan Fencibles were given over to deep drinking and the singing of bawdy songs. It was little wonder that when Robert Burns came to Edinburgh, Smellie should first have shown the good business sense to publish the "Edinburgh edition" and then to have introduced him to another side of the city far removed from the drawing rooms of those who fawned on the ploughman poet. That Burns enjoyed the latter and was grateful for the introduction is evident from this boisterous rhyme.

> Shrewd Willie Smellie to Crochallan came;
> The old cock'd hat, the grey surtout, the same;
> His bristling beard just rising in its might,
> 'Twas four long nights and days to shaving night;
> His uncomb'd grizzly locks, wild staring, thatch'd;
> A head for thought profound and clear, unmatch'd;
> Yet tho' his caustic wit was biting-rude,
> His heart was warm, benevolent and good.

Another literary go-between associated with Burns was the bookseller William Creech whose breakfast room in Craig's Close became the meeting place for literary discussion and which came to be known as Creech's Levee. Creech was a hard-headed businessman who bought copyrights from the *literati* for pittances. A solid, respectable citizen he became Lord Provost in 1811 and included amongst his closest friends intellectuals like Dugald Stewart, Hugh Blair and Adam Fergusson and the novelist Henry Mackenzie who had written the novel whose title had become his own nickname — *The Man of Feeling*.

Mackenzie is one of the most interesting writers of this time as his life spanned the two great periods of the Enlightenment, the first being the age of Hume, and the second, in the next century, that of Sir Walter Scott. Born in 1745, Mackenzie was educated at the High School where, by the time he was twelve, he could read most of the

THE EIGHTEENTH CENTURY ENLIGHTENMENT

Latin classics. He was an official of the Exchequer, an occupation which gave him a measured, orderly life, and he quickly became known as a literary dabbler who, in his old age, befriended many young writers and offered them help and advice. There is a splendid portrait of him during that later period in *Peter's Letters to his Kinsfolk*, a book which we shall meet again in the next chapter.

> I found him in his library, surrounded with a very large collection of books — few of them apparently new ones — seated in a high-backed easy chair — the wood-work carved very richly in the ancient French taste, and covered with black haircloth. On his head he wore a low cap of black velvet, like those which we see in almost all the pictures of Pope. But there needed none of these accessories to carry back the imagination. It is impossible that I should paint to you the full image of that face. The only one I ever saw which bore any resemblence to its character, was that of Warren Hastings — you well remember the effect *it* produced, when he appeared among all that magnificent assemblage to take his degree at the installation of Lord Grenville. In the countenance of Mackenzie, there is the same clear transparency of skin, the same freshness of complexion, in the midst of all the extenuation of old age. The wrinkles, too, are set close to each other, line upon line; not deep and bold, and rugged like those of most old men, but equal and undivided over the whole surface, as if no touch but that of time had been there, and as if even He had traced the vestiges of his dominion with a sure indeed, but with a delicate and reverential finger. The lineaments have all the appearance of having been beautifully shaped, but the want of his teeth has thrown them out of their natural relation to each other. The eyes alone have bid defiance to the approach of the adversary. Beneath bleached and hoary brows, and surrounded with innumerable wrinkles, they are still as tenderly, as brightly blue, as full of all the various eloquence and fire of passion, as they could have been in the most vivacious of his days, when they were lighted up with that purest and loftiest of all earthly flames, the first secret triumph of conscious and conceiving genius.

Mackenzie was, in fact, a hard-headed businessman who during his lifetime edited two literary periodicals, *The Mirror* and *The Lounger*, which attempted to imitate the style and manners of literary London, earning for him his other epithet, "our Scottish Addison".

Both publications were complete failures and the awkward, ponderous English written by his contributors lacked the delicate precision of the Augustan prose employed with such ease by Addison and Steele. As a critic, Mackenzie denied the worth of work written in Scots and consequently praised inferior poets whose verse has disappeared into time's wastepaper basket. Fergusson, who never had to pander to southern tastes, cared little for Mackenzie's polite sensibility which he lampooned in a poem, *The Sow of Feeling*, and when Mackenzie came to review Robert Burns's Kilmarnock poems in the December 1786 issue of *The Lounger*, it is salutory to find that the poems he singled out for most praise were written in English.

Burns's first collection, *Poems Chiefly in the Scottish Dialect* was published in Kilmarnock on 31st July 1786. The book contained some of his best work (even if it did leave out poems like *Holy Willie's Prayer* which may have given offence) and he was canny enough in the Preface to stress his lack of formal education and his untutored skills, "unacquainted with the necessary requisites for commencing Poet by rule, he sings the sentiments and manners, he felt and saw in himself and his rustic compeers around him, in his and their native language." The Edinburgh *literati* fell for this white lie and early reviews referred to the bard of humble origin who had been given, god-like, the gift of poetry, but it was Henry Mackenzie's review which crowned Burns's success. Hailed as "the heaven-taught ploughman" he set off for Edinburgh on 27th November 1786 to arrange further publication of his poetry, and also to prove himself among the society which had lavished so much praise upon him.

Burns was born on 25th January 1759 in Alloway in Ayrshire, the son of a tenant farmer. Despite the family's financial hardships Burns received a sound education from his father, learning both from the Bible and anthologies of English literature and from the great oral folk tradition of the Scottish Lowlands. As a young man he led an agreeable life and by 1784 he was tenant of Mossgiel farm near Mauchline in Ayrshire. He had already started writing songs and verse, and also religious satires, and verse letters to his many friends. Reading Fergusson's poems had inspired him to believe that he could aspire to the same standards and he readily acknowledged the debt he owed.

THE EIGHTEENTH CENTURY ENLIGHTENMENT

O thou my elder brother in Misfortune,
By far my elder brother in the muse,
With tears I pity thy unhappy fate!
Why is the Bard unfitted for the world,
Yet has so keen a relish of its pleasures?

It was entirely in keeping with Burns's generosity that one of his first acts in Edinburgh was to raise a stone on Fergusson's pauper grave in the Canongate cemetry.

Burns arrived in the city as winter was beginning to get its grip on the land and he lodged in Baxter's Close, off the Lawnmarket with a friend, John Richmond, who rented the rooms from a Mrs Carfrae. Although he was ostensibly on business, Burns was quickly taken up by the *literati*, and as he wrote to his landlord Gavin Hamilton, their adulation was both a surprise and something of a comical delight.

For my own affairs, I am in a fair way of becoming as eminent as Thomas a Kempis or John Bunyan; and you may expect henceforth to see my birthday inserted among the wonderful events, in the Poor Robin's and Aberdeen Almanacks, along with the black Monday & the battle of Bothwel bridge — My Lord Glencairn & the Dean of Faculty Mr H. Erskine, have taken me under their wing; and by all probability I shall soon be the tenth Worthy, and the eighth Wise Man of the world.

His principal patron became the Earl of Glencairn who arranged for "the gentlemen of the Caledonian Hunt" to subscribe money for his second collection of poems, and when the influential Duchess of Gordon gave him an entrée to Edinburgh society, everbody was anxious to meet the rustic genius. Although society was charmed by his easy manners and conviviality, Burns was well aware that in dealing with the upper classes he was not only walking a social tightrope but was also in danger of becoming, in his own words, "the learned pig in the Grassmarket".

He had been a Mason before living in Edinburgh and on 1st February he was admitted to membership of the Canongate Kilwinning Lodge, in the month after he had been a guest at the

111

Grand Lodge of Scotland, when the toast had been, "Caledonia and Caledonia's Bard, Brother Burns". He also made frequent forays to the Old Town taverns and to the Crochallan Fencibles, evenings which must have given him blessed relief from the studied, stultifying manners of the New Town drawingrooms. In his earlier poems Burns had attacked false modesty and the restrictions of gentility which stood in the way of high-spirited fun, and it is not difficult to believe that the *literati's* loss was the tavern's gain when Burns launched out in one of the ribald songs from *The Merry Muses of Caledonia*. One can imagine the shocked silence and recourse to smelling salts of the Edinburgh lady who overheard a verse from *Ellibanks*!

> There's no a lass in a' the land,
>   Can fuck sae weel as I can;
> Louse down your breeks, lug out your wand,
>   Hae ye nae mind to try man:
> For ye're the lad that wears the breeks,
>   And I'm the lass that loes ye;
> Deil rive my cunt to candle-wicks,
>   Gif ever I refuse ye!

Burns, like many other men of his day, had an easy, uncomplicated attitude towards fornication which was generally held as one of the few pleasures freely enjoyed by rich and poor. Although the Church ranted and roared against sexual relationships, it could do little to prevent them, especially when unwanted pregnancies did not always end in marriage, and all that was required of the offending couple was the tight-lipped humiliation of appearing in disgrace before the Church Session. (For the woman it was different — she had to bring up the child, often with the help of her parents.) Several illegitimate children were born to Burns during his lifetime and the long-suffering Jean Armour had to wait many years before he married her and gave his name to their children. In Edinburgh it was very different. Burns was paraded like a prize bull, dangerous, but kept firmly under control, and when his affairs with servant girls were brought to light, they only added to the delighted sexual frisson of the gentry's wives and daughters.

On his second visit in December 1787, Burns met Mrs Agnes

M'Lehose a niece of Lord Craig, a judge of the Court of Session. Deserted by her philandering husband she entered into an intense relationship with Burns by exchange of letters. In their correspondence he was Sylvander and she Clarinda and from her house in Potter Row she kept up a stylised courtly relationship which was never to be consummated and which today acts as a metaphor for the way in which Burns was regarded by the upper classes — as a poet he might have been invited to the safety of the drawing room, but he would never have been admitted as a lover to the privacy of the boudoir. Naturally enough, Clarinda soon tired of her Sylvander when she discovered that his feelings needed a more physical outlet, but the affair has left us with one of Burns's finest songs, *Ae Fond Kiss*.

> Fare-thee-weel, thou first and fairest!
> Fare-thee-weel, thou best and dearest!
> Thine be ilka joy and treasure,
> Peace, Enjoyment, Love and Pleasure!

> Ae fond kiss, and then we sever!
> Ae fareweel, Alas for ever!
> Deep in heart-wrung tears I'll pledge thee,
> Warring sighs and groans I'll wage thee.

In a sense Burns was unfortunate in coming to Edinburgh after the great intellects of the first period of the Enlightenment had died. He missed intellectual argument and discussion and frequently fulminated against the petty social niceties of everyday life in the city while he was considered something of a social lion. Maria Riddell, writing of him long after his death, remarked that Burns was a sparkling conversationalist, full of wit and learning which too often fell on deaf ears. Henry Mackenzie tried to influence Burns to imitate an Augustan verse which was alien to him, advice which Burns was safe to ignore. He paid due obeisance to the city and its intellectuals in his *Address to Edinburgh* but the best poem written during this period is the earthy *Address to a Haggis* written in Scots.

Burns's wish to see a second collection printed was granted on 17th April 1787 in Henry Mackenzie's house in Brown Square. With the support of the Earl of Glencairn and his hunting friends, William Creech agreed to publish the poems and Burns accepted one hundred guineas for the sale of the copyright plus any money from the subscription. It was a niggardly arrangement which subsequently allowed Creech to print further editions without having to pay royalties but Burns was delighted to see the book printed by Smellie and published on 21st April that same year. The publication established Burns as one of the outstanding poets of the day. It was published in London by Cadell and Davies and pirated editions were printed as far afield as the United States and Ireland. But however successful he might have been and however much he might have been idolised, his future was still far from secure. Part of the reason for coming to Edinburgh had been to find patronage and he had set his heart on a career in the Excise, but the longer he stayed in the city, the less secure his prospects became. The novelty value of the heaven-taught ploughman was wearing thin and there were those who would have helped but who felt that a commonplace job would spoil his muse.

Eventually, in 1788, Burns accepted the offer of a farm at Ellisland near Dumfries on the Dalwinton estate which was owned by Patrick Miller, an Edinburgh banker. Farming was a skill which had always eluded him and three years later he became an Excise-man at long last, in Dumfries, where he lived for five years before his death in 1796.

Today, Burns is regarded as Scotland's national poet and even those readers with a minimal interest in Scotland's literature will know some of his poems or songs and may even have attended one of the annual suppers held in his memory each January. However, few take the trouble to understand the deep-rooted emotions he held for individual liberty and political freedom, feelings which were decidedly at odds with those held by the Edinburgh *literati*. For Burns was not the end product of the Enlightenment, rather, like Fergusson, he was a poet who embodied the survival of a native culture and language which was not parochial but was at one with much of what was happening in Europe in the late eighteenth century.

No account, though, of the Edinburgh of the Enlightenment could end without reference to James Boswell. The son of Lord Auchinleck, one of the last Scottish judges to use Scots in everyday speech and in his legal dealings, Boswell is best remembered as the friend and chronicler of Samuel Johnson whose remarks on the Scotland he visited in 1773 defy repetition. Boswell went on to publish the life of his friend in one of the best literary biographies of all time and to acquire for himself a lasting reputation. Yet during his lifetime he spent more years outside Scotland than he did within it.

For his ambivalent feelings towards his native country he blamed his father's heavy-handed attitudes and emphasis on all things Scottish, and so much did he lack reverence for the place that the passages in his *Journal* dealing with Edinburgh are almost solely concerned with excessive drink and fornication. "I was very drunk, roved the streets, and went and stayed above an hour with two whores at their lodging in a narrow dirty stair in the Bow".

Not unnaturally Boswell was regarded with some suspicion in Edinburgh and when he introduced Dr Johnson in Parliament Hall to Henry Erskine, the patrician Lord Advocate, a shilling was pressed in his hand with the remark that Erskine thought that the normal amount to be paid to the keeper of a performing bear. That anecdote summons up the singular pride of an intellectual movement whose members regarded themselves as being the equals, if not the superiors, of any other nation in Europe.

Chapter Seven

The Edinburgh of Sir Walter Scott

If I were to choose a spot from which the rising or setting sun could be seen to the greatest possible advantage, it would be that wild path winding around the foot of the high belt of semicircular rocks, called Salisbury Crags, and marking the verge of the steep descent which slopes down into the glen on the south-eastern side of Edinburgh. The prospect, in its general outline, commands a close-built, high-piled city, stretching itself out beneath in a form, which, to a romantic imagination, may be supposed to represent that of a dragon; now, a noble arm of the sea, with its rocks, isles, distant shores, and boundary of mountains; and now, a fair and fertile champaign country, varied with hill, dale, and rock, and skirted by the picturesque ridge of the Pentland mountains. But as the path gently circles around the base of the cliffs, the prospect, composed as it is of these enchanting and sublime objects, changes at every step, and presents them blended with, or divided from, each other, in every possible variety which can gratify the eye and the imagination. When a piece of scenery, so beautiful yet so varied — so exciting by its intricacy, and yet so sublime — is lighted up by the tints of morning or of evening, and displays all that variety of shadowy depth, exchanged with partial brilliancy, which gives character even to the tamest of landscapes, the effect approaches near to enchantment.

Walter Scott published that stunning description of the Salisbury Crags in the Park of Holyrood in 1818 in *The Heart of Midlothian*, a novel set almost a century before in 1736, the year of the Porteous Riots; but even today, the evocation of that splendid view remains as bright as it did all those years ago. It was a scene that would have been familiar to Scott from an early age, for until Fame claimed him as her own, his youthful years were spent on the South Side of the city near the University and on the verges of the old town.

Walter Scott was born on 15th August 1771 in a house at the top of College Wynd, an unhealthy stinking warren of tall houses so

116

closely packed together that neighbours in the top flats could shake hands across the narrow street which led down to the Cowgate. It has long since disappeared, but the modern dog-legged Guthrie Street gives some clue to its whereabouts in the year of Scott's birth. (In his book, *Sir Walter Scott: The Formative Years*, Edinburgh 1969, Dr Arthur Melville Clark offers some convincing evidence that Scott was, in fact, born a year earlier, but the opportunity of re-opening that dispute will not come round again until the ter-centenary of the birth next century.) His father, Walter Scott, was a solicitor and a Writer to the Signet, but he came from a Border background where his family had farmed the land at Sandyknowe near the ancient Smailholm Tower. His mother was Anne Rutherford, the eldest daughter of John Rutherford who had held the Chair of Medicine at the University between 1726 and 1765.

When he was but eighteen months old Scott was stricken by poliomyelitis, an illness which left him with a permanent limp in his right leg. Partly as a result of this illness, and because his mother had lost six children in infancy, the family moved to George Square, one of the new fashionable residences lying to the southern side of the Old College. It was a healthy, spacious town house, still standing today in the possession of the Dominicans and a fine example of pre-Adam Georgian architecture. There, the Scott's neighbours at number 25 included some of the brightest names in Edinburgh society: the Duchess of Gordon, who could hold her own in Scots with any Newhaven fishwife, the Lord Advocate Lord Melville, and the "hanging judge" Lord Braxfield, who was to become the model for R.L. Stevenson's *Weir of Hermiston*. Despite the move to a purer part of town, Scott's lameness did not improve and on medical advice he spent much of his childhood away from Edinburgh with his grandparents at Sandyknowe. He also spent a year taking the waters at Bath and although his leg was never cured, by the time he entered the High School in 1779 he was a vigorously strong boy, capable of looking after himself in any scrape as he was later to remember in a letter to a friend, Mrs Hughes.

> I can climb like a cat and in my boyhood was one of the boldest craigs-men in the High School, as the Cats-neck on Salisbury Crags & the Kittle Nine Steps on the Castle rock could tell if they would speak.

The building which housed the High School was not Thomas Hamilton's classical building at the foot of the Calton Hill in Regent Road but a new building at the eastern end of the Cowgate near the present-day High School Yards. There he was schooled early in Latin and although it was a language he never completely mastered he quickly learned to read it and to soak up the history of Rome from its poets and historians. He also read voraciously: Ossian, Spencer, Tasso, Virgil and, significantly, Bishop Percy's *Reliques of Ancient Poetry*.

By the time he left school at the age of twelve, he confessed that he had "a great quantity of general information, ill arranged indeed, and collected without system, yet deeply impressed upon my mind; readily assorted by my power of connexion and memory, and gilded, if I may be permitted to say so, by a vivid and active imagination." From school Scott went up to the town's university where he was to spend two years studying Latin and Moral Philosophy for a general arts degree. But his studies were interrupted by a severe intestinal haemorrhage and he was again forced into convalescence with his grandparents at Sandyknowe. On his return to Edinburgh in 1786 he was indentured as an apprentice in his father's law firm. Such a move was not considered to be inimical to a man of letters and learning and during the latter part of the Enlightenment many of Edinburgh's *literati* were also trained in the law, as Edward Topham reminds us in one of his letters.

> The Gentlemen who are styled Advocates in this country, are almost innumerable; for every man who has nothing to do, and no better name to give himself, is called Advocate. Of those, however, who practise and get business, the number is extremely few; but amongst these few, are some men whose abilities are not only an honour to the country itself: Men who make the bar a school of eloquence, and not, as I am sorry to say with us, a jargon of barbarous, and almost unintelligible words, and who preserve, in their debates, the manners and sentiments of a gentleman.

It was during this period, when he was fifteen, that Scott came into contact with Robert Burns in the company of the great men of his age at Sciennes Hill House, the residence of the philosopher

118

Adam Ferguson. Part of the house still remains in Braid Place and the meeting left a great enough impression on the young Scott for it to be vividly remembered in Lockhart's *Life*.

As for Burns, I may truly say, *Virgilium vidi tantum*. I was a lad of fifteen in 1786-7, when he came first to Edinburgh, but had sense and feeling enough to be much interested in his poetry, and would have given the world to know him; but I had very little acquaintance with any literary people, and still less with the gentry of the west country, the two sets that he most frequented. Mr Thomas Grierson was at that time a clerk of my fathers. He knew Burns, and promised to ask him to his lodgings to dinner, but had no opportunity to keep his word, otherwise I might have seen more of this distinguished man. As it was, I saw him one day at the late venerable Professor Ferguson's, where there were several gentlemen of literary reputation, among whom I remember the celebrated Mr Dugald Stewart. Of course we youngsters sate silent, looked and listened. The only thing I remember which was remarkable in Burns' manner, was the effect produced upon him by a print of Bunbury's, representing a soldier lying dead on the snow, his dog sitting in misery on the one side, on the other his widow, with a child in her arms. These lines were written beneath:

"Cold on Canadian hills, or Mindens plain,
Perhaps that parent wept her soldier slain;
Bent o'er her babe, her eye dissolved in dew,
The big drops, mingling with the milk he drew,
Gave the sad passage of his future years,
The child of misery baptized in tears."

Burns seemed much affected by the print, or rather the ideas which it suggested to his mind. He actually shed tears. He asked whose the lines were, and it chanced that nobody but myself remembered that they occur in a half-forgotten poem of Langhorne's called by the unpromising title of 'The Justice of the Peace'. I whispered my information to a friend present, who mentioned it to Burns, who rewarded me with a look and a word, which, though of mere civility, I then received, and still recollect, with very great pleasure.
His person was strong and robust; his manners rustic, not clownish; a sort of dignified plainness and simplicity, which

119

received part of its effect perhaps from one's knowledge of his extraordinary talents. His features are represented in Mr Naysmith's picture, but to me it conveys the idea that they are diminished as if seen in perspective. I think his countenance was more passive than it looks in any of the portraits. I would have taken the poet, had I not known what he was, for a very sagacious farmer of the old Scottish school — i.e., none of your modern agriculturalists who keep labourers for their own drudgery, but the douce gudeman who held his own plough. There was a strong expression of sense and shrewdness in all his lineaments; the eye alone, I think, indicated the poetical character and temperament. It was large and of a dark cast, and glowed (I say literally glowed) when he spoke with feeling or interest. I never saw such an eye in a human head, though I have seen the most distinguished men of my time. His conversation expressed perfect self-confidence, without the slightest presumption. Among the men who were the most learned of their time and country, he expressed himself with perfect firmness, but without the least intrusive forwardness; and when he differed in opinion he did not hesitate to express it firmly, yet at the same time with modesty. I do not remember any of his conversation distinctly enough to be quoted, nor did I ever see him again, except in the street, where he did not recognize me, as I could not expect he should.

The Edinburgh that Scott knew as a boy was little different from the town that Burns had conquered, and if by then it was not possible to take fifty men of genius by the hand at the Cross of Edinburgh, the city was still a formidable centre of wit and learning. The Napoleonic Wars had denied access to the continent and consequently Edinburgh had become a safe haven for visitors from all points south of the Border. But the city's shape was beginning to show the signs of change that had begun with the construction of Craig's new town.

The most detailed and by far the most human account of this period is contained in Lord Cockburn's *Memorials of His Time*, and nowhere is there a better example of the revolving wheel of time than in his account of the arrival in the city of new customs for dining from London.

The prevailing dinner hour was about three o'clock. Two o'clock was quite common, if there was no company. Hence it was no

120

great deviation from their usual custom for a family to dine on Sundays '*between sermons*' — that is between one and two. The hour, in time, but not without groans and predilictions, became four, at which it stuck for several years. Then it got to five, which, however, was thought positively revolutionary; and four was long and gallantly adhered to by the haters of change as 'the good old hour'. At last even they were obliged to give in. But they only yielded inch by inch, and made a desperate stand at half-past four. Even five, however, triumphed, and continued the average polite hour from (I think) about 1806 or 1807 till about 1820. Six has at last prevailed, and half an hour later is not unusual. As yet this is the farthest stretch of London imitation, except in country houses devoted to grouse or deer, where the species called sportsmen, disdaining all mankind except themselves, glory in not dining till sensible people have gone to bed. Thus, within my memory, the hour has ranged from two to half past six o'oclock; and a stand has been regularly made at the end of every half hour against each encroachment; and always on the same grounds — dislike of change and jealousy of finery.

Cockburn was born eight years after Scott, in 1779, and shared with him a similar background — he was the son of a lawyer and had been educated at the High School and at the University. Where they differed was in their politics, Cockburn being a Whig with an interest in judicial and political reform and an author of several pamphlets urging the extension of parliamentary and municipal franchise. But Cockburn is perhaps best, and most popularly, remembered today as the vivid and readable chronicler of his times, who, in his old age, looked back with a sense of fond regret at the changing face of a city which was starting to push its boundaries further into the countryside he held so dear. He had never held the town council in much esteem, describing them as, "Silent, powerful, submissive, mysterious, and irresponsible, they might have been sitting in Venice." When they bought the grounds of General Scott's elegant house at Bellevue behind Drummond Place, Cockburn feared the worst and with some justification.

But in 1802 Bellevue was sold. The magistrates, I believe, bought it; and the whole trees were instantly cut down. They could not all have been permanently spared; but many of them might, to the comfort and adornment of the future buildings. But the mere beauty of the town was no more thought of at that time than electric telegraphs and railways. Trees never find favour in the sight of any Scotch mason. I remember people shuddering when they heard the axes busy in the woods of Bellevue, and furious when they saw the bare ground. But the axes, as usual, triumphed; and all that art and nature had done to prepare the place for foliaged compartments of town architecture, if being built upon should prove inevitable, was carefully obliterated; so that at last the whole spot was made as bare and as dull as if the designer of the New Town himself had presided over the operation.

Cockburn, in a sense, lived two lives. One was that of the polite Charlotte Square lawyer with an honourable position in the city's society, and the other was that of "Cocky", the country gentleman with a house at Bonaly in Colinton and an interest in natural things and above all, of plodding the Pentland Hills. He regretted the past and yet he was motivated by social change, he was liberal in his attitudes and yet he had a sneaking regard for boisterous evenings spent over food and drink — Ramsay of Ochtertyre called the Edinburgh literati, the "eaterati" — and like others of his age he was Scottish, but half-anglicised, orphaned (to use Karl Miller's phrase) both from his Scottish past and his English future.

This sort of paradox was not uncommon in early nineteenth century Edinburgh. There was a certain penchant for leading double lives and this was continued with the dawning of the new century: the Burke and Hare scandal erupted in 1828 with Cockburn acting for the defence, Hogg wrote his *Confessions of a Justified Sinner*, and there was a growing interest in German-Gothic literature which dealt with dual personalities. All around the world was rapidly changing, and fearful for its future, many writers took refuge in an exaggerated love for the past and for Scotland's heritage and her language. Walter Scott took full advantage of this interest in his later writing but it was from the Borders that he was to draw his first inspiration.

While he was studying for the law, like many other advocates of his day, Scott refused to let the daily drudgery of office routine dim his "vivid and active imagination". Edinburgh could not hold him and he turned to his grandparents in Sandyknowe from whom he had heard the ballads and stories of the Borders history, traditions

122

which were to enrich his writing and to give him his first literary success. He also befriended Robert Shortreed, Sheriff-Substitute of Liddesdale, whom he accompanied on his forays into the wild and barren country of the West Marches of the debatable lands of the Scottish border. It was still a place far removed from civilisation without roads or inns but it was hospitable to the young Scott who quickly got to know the ballads and stories of the taciturn shepherds, the descendants of the stormy, freebooting moss troopers. "He was makin' himself a' the time, but I didna ken maybe what he was about till years had passed. At first he thought of little, I dare say, but the queerness and the fun." Scott was, in fact, putting these "raids", as he called them, to good literary use by collecting what he heard, but Robert Shortreed was under no doubts about the fun they shared.

> Sic an endless fund o' humour and drollery as he then had wi' him! Never ten yards but we were either laughing or roaring or singing. Whenever we stopped, how brawlie he suited himself to everybody! He aye did as the lave did; never made himsel' the great man or took on any airs in the company. I've seen him in a' moods in these jaunts, grave and gay, daft and serious, sober and drunk, but drunk or sober, he was aye the gentleman. He looked unco heavy and stupid when he was fou, but he was never out o' gude humour.

It was during this period, too, that Scott's political and patriotic cast of mind was firmly moulded. He looked on the French Revolution as a threat to civilisation and when Britain went to war with France in 1793, Scott saw his duty as lying clearly with the forces of law and order. The following year, in April 1794 he took part in a pitched battle in the Edinburgh Theatre with Irish medical students who had booed the national anthem and had called for revolutionary songs. Two months later he was again on duty, this time as a special constable on the occasion of the King's birthday, but the only danger he had to face was the smashing of the Lord Justice-Clerk's windows by a handful of boys.

His lameness prevented him from enlisting in the volunteers, but there was the cavalry. In 1797, after the rise of Napoleon, there was a real danger of invasion after the mutiny of the Channel Fleet at Spithead. Scott and his friends acted quickly. On February 14th they met in the Royal Exchange Coffee House and formed two troops of the Royal Edinburgh Volunteer Light Dragoons with Scott being elected quarter-master. In full dress uniform (which cost £22), of scarlet coat with blue collar and cuffs and silver epaulettes trimmed with silver lace, white breeches, black leather boots and spurs and a helmet crested with leopard skin and a red-and-white hackle Scott threw himself into his duties. At the Botanic Gardens in Leith Walk or more commonly on Portobello beach he would ride his charger, sabre drawn, at poles with turnips on them — to represent French soldiers — and would swipe at them, shouting, "Cut them down the villains, cut them down." Even when the threat of invasion had died down Scott continued to glory in his military training to the amusement of his friends, and Charles Kirkpatrick Sharpe, a neighbour in George Square who was later to become a life-long friend from his secluded house at 28 Drummond Place, remembered with amusement the dishevelled figure in the fine uniform returning home after a day on the sands.

But he had made many friends; the romantic John Irving, Adam Ferguson, son of the Professor of Philosophy, and above all Will Clerk son of Sir John Clerk of Pennycuik who lived in the splendid mansion to the south of Edinburgh, now sadly fallen into disrepair. He was a member of the Speculative Society and became a confidant of Henry Mackenzie, who regaled him with tales of a bygone literary Edinburgh. When the court was in session, Scott was a member of a convivial group, "The Club", which met in Carrubers Close where oysters were eaten in a dark basement lit by tallow candles, and claret, brandy and rum punch was downed in great quantities. On one occasion he drank so much that the nickname of "Colonel Grogg" was given to him and he was persuaded that he had spent the entire night in song, despite the fact that he remained tone-deaf throughout his life. Afterwards there would be dancing with girls who appeared wearing masks after dark, and then, on the way home, long after the rest of the city was asleep, fights with walking sticks in Liberton's Wynd.

Scott tended to fall asleep rather than become belligerent when he was in his cups, but excess in drink was still taken for granted in the city of his young manhood. Lord Newton, a Lord of the Court of Session, started the day with six bottles of claret and most judges tried cases with a bottle or two of claret or port to steady their hangovers. For the late-night revellers, getting out of the closes of the old town was a perilous business, for at ten o'clock, as in previous times, the cry of "gardyloo" would go up "like a shriek of the water-kelpie" and the days slops would be hurled from countless windows into the street below. It was with good reason that Dr Johnson had said to his companion Boswell, "I can smell you in the dark."

Cockburn had remarked that, "to get drunk in a tavern seemed to be considered as a natural, if not an intended consequence of going to one", but there came a time in Scott's life when he felt it proper to settle down and to foreswear his wild junkettings in tavern and club. On Christmas Eve, 1797 he married Charlotte Charpentier, the daughter of an emigré French family, and the couple set up house at 39 North Castle Street which was to remain their Edinburgh home. They also took a cottage at Lasswade, a village on the River Esk to the south of Edinburgh, before moving to Ashestiel on the River Tweed near Selkirk when Scott was appointed Sheriff-Depute of Selkirkshire. With the help of a remarkable, self-educated Borderer, John Leyden, who was studying for the ministry in Edinburgh, Scott set about the collection and eventual publication of his three volumes of Border ballads.

In 1802 Walter Scott published the first volume of his collected Border ballads and stories, the *Minstrelsy of the Scottish Border*, and so his literary career was launched in earnest. He also started work on a long poem, *The Lay of the Last Minstrel*, at the suggestion of Lady Dalkeith, the daughter-in-law of the Duke of Buccleuch. That same year, in October, a new magazine, the *Edinburgh Review*, was founded by an Anglican chaplain, Sydney Smith and three advocates, Henry Brougham, Francis Horner and Francis Jeffrey. Its publisher was Archibald Constable who had been described by Scott as the "prince of booksellers" and a man of whom Lord Cockburn had said, "the literature of Scotland has been more indebted than to any other of his vocation".

One of those founders, Sydney Smith, had said that "it requires a surgical operation to get a joke well into a Scotch understanding", but there was nothing funny about the *Edinburgh Review*. Its first issue of 750 copies quickly sold out and it soon created an almost insatiable demand. By 1807 the circulation was 7,000 and it reached its peak eleven years later with monthly sales of well over 14,000 copies. Francis Jeffrey became the permanent editor a year after its first appearance and working from his house in 18 Buccleuch Place he vested the role of editor with a previously unheard of dignity and professionalism. He was paid a salary of £300 by Constable who also arranged for substantial sums of money to be paid to the magazine's contributors, another welcome innovation. Jeffrey was a fluent, quick-witted man who managed to combine an active legal and political career with his work on the *Review*. He went on to become a Member of Parliament and Lord Advocate, with a house in 24 Moray Place and a country house at Craigcrook on Corstorphine Hill, but it was the editor who encouraged young writers like Thomas Carlyle, who enjoyed the greatest renown in Edinburgh.

> I got ready admission into Jeffrey's "study", or rather "office", for it had mostly that air; a roomy not overneat apartment on the ground floor, with a big baize-covered table, loaded with book rows and paper bundles; on one or perhaps two of the walls were bookshelves, likewise well filled, but with books in tattery ill-bound or unbound condition, — "bad new Literature, these will be," thought I; "the table ones are probably on law!" Fire, pair of candles were cheerfully burning, in the light of which sat my famous little gentleman; laid aside his work, cheerfully invited me to sit, and began talking in a perfectly human manner. Our dialogue was altogether human and successful; lasted for perhaps twenty minutes (for I could not consume a great man's time), turned upon the usual topics, what I was doing, what I had published, — *German Romance* Translations, my last thing; to which I remember he said kindly, "We must give you a lift!" an offer which, in some complimentary way, I managed, to his satisfaction, to decline. My feeling with him was that of unembarrassment; a reasonable veracious little man, I could perceive, with whom any truth one felt good to utter would have a fair chance. Whether much was said of German Literature, whether anything at all on my writing of it for him, I don't recollect: but certainly I took my leave in a gratified successful kind of mood; and both those topics the latter in practical form, did soon abundantly spring up between us; with a formal return call by him (which gave a new speed to intimacy), agreement for a little paper on *Jean Paul* and whatever could follow out of an acquaintanceship well begun.

THE EDINBURGH OF SIR WALTER SCOTT

The *Edinburgh Review* was Whig in its politics but it gained its reputation from its lofty and frequently savage literary judgements; indeed, today, Jeffrey is best remembered for telling Wordsworth that *The Excursion* would never do. Although he made amends somewhat by praising Keats and Byron, Jeffrey could never bring himself to be enthusiastic about the Lake School of poetry and like many another Scot, before and after him, he distrusted poetry which laid bare in public its maker's starkest emotions.

> Indeed in Scotland generally the display of personal character the indulging of your whims and humours in the presence of a friend, is not much encouraged; everyone there is looked upon in the light of a machine or a collection of topics. They turn you round like a cylinder to see what use they can make of you, and drag you into a dispute with as little ceremony as they would drag out an article from an Encyclopaedia. They criticise everything, analyse everything, argue upon everything, dogmatise upon everything; and the bundle of your habits, feelings, humours, follies and pursuits is regarded by them no more than a bundle of old clothes.

The fact that William Hazlitt, writing from London about the Scot, Jeffrey and his magazine, is testimony enough to the national interest taken in the *Edinburgh Review*.

Walter Scott, although a Tory, was a frequent contributor to the *Review* until his patience with the editor's criticism and his politics ran out in April 1808 when Jeffrey published a sharply critical thirty-five page review of *Marmion*, attacking its author for continuing to write long narrative poems in the Border ballad tradition.

> To write a modern romance of chivalry, seems to be such a phantasy as to build a modern abbey or an English pagoda. For once, however, it may be excused as a pretty caprice of genius; but a second production of the same sort is entitled to less indulgence, and imposes a sort of duty to drive the author from so idle a task, by a fair exposition of the faults which are, in a manner, inseperable from its execution.

Scott turned his attention thereafter to writing for the newly-founded London-based magazine, the Tory *Quarterly Review* but it was no match for the fiery critical journalism of the *Edinburgh Review*. It was published less frequently than its rival, it lacked flair and its main virtues were respectability and financial stability. Something more nimble and lively was required to challenge Jeffrey's dominance and the answer came in a magazine which was to be published in the Georgian New Town far away from the traditional publishing and bookselling centre of the High Street and the Bridges.

The idea for the magazine came from William Blackwood, a man who came from a very different kind of background than those enjoyed by the patrician Whigs of Edinburgh's legal caste. Unlike Jeffrey, Blackwood had kept his Scots speech and unlike Jeffrey he had acquired from an early age an intimate knowledge of the book trade. In 1816, William Blackwood, against all the advice of his fellow booksellers, decided to move his business from 64 South Bridge to the newly-built Princes Street in the Georgian New Town. It was a move without precedent as bookselling and publishing had traditionally been kept firmly within the preserve of the High Street. Blackwood had entered the bookselling trade in 1790 when he had joined the old established firm of Bell and Bradfute, whose shop was in Parliament Square close by the College and the Law Courts. After a six-year apprenticeship and following experience in Glasgow and London, he set himself up as bookseller and publisher in partnership with Robert Ross. He was not slow to prosper, selling his books, according to custom, "at seven o'clock p.m. for several consecutive nights with a free dinner before-hand for all *bona fide* customers".

By the time of his move to the New Town, Blackwood was by any standards a wealthy and successful man. He was the Scottish agent of Byron's publisher, John Murray; his own great Catalogue of 1812 listing more than fifteen thousand rare books in his possession had lifted him into the front rank of connoisseurs of antiquarian books; and he was a confidant of many of the leading literary figures of the day. To crown his success, in 1816 prior to his move, he published Walter Scott's *Tales of my Landlord*, selling 6,000 copies in a week, and daring to suggest to Scott alterations to the text, criticisms which brought an angry rebuke from the great man:

> I have received Blackwood's impudent letter. God damn his soul!
> Tell him and his coadjutor that I belong to the Black Hussars of
> Literature, who neither give nor receive criticism. I'll be cursed but
> this is the most impudent proposal that was ever made.

Blackwood was forced to apologise to Scott, but the incident only
served to cement a growing friendship between the two men, a
friendship that was to stand the firm of William Blackwood in good
stead in the years to come.

The building to which Blackwood moved his business, number
17 Princes Street, was bright and spacious and quickly became a
centre of literary activity in Edinburgh, attracting the curious from
the street for witty discussion and debate about the literary affairs of
the period. Today, it is a branch bookshop of the John Menzies
organisation and is scarcely recognisable as a Georgian building, but
contemporary references remark on its elegance and charm. There is
a particularly concise and loving description of the saloon in J.G.
Lockhart's *Peter's Letters to his Kinsfolk*:

> The only great lounging book-shop in the New Town of
> Edinburgh is Mr Blackwood's. The prejudice in favour of sticking
> by the Old Town was so strong among the gentlemen of the trade,
> that when the bookseller intimated a few years ago his purpose of
> removing to the New, his ruin was immediately prophesied by not
> a few of his sagacious brethren. He persisted however in his
> intentions and speedily took possession of a large and airy suite of
> rooms in Princes Street, which had formerly been occupied by a
> notable confectioner, and whose thresh-hold was therefore
> familiar enough to all the frequenters of that superb promenade.
> There it was that this enterprizing bibliopole hoisted his standard,
> and prepared at once for action. Stimulated, I suppose, by the
> example and success of John Murray, whose agent he is, he
> determined to make, if possible, Princes Street to the High Street,
> what the other has made Albemarle to the Row.

John Gibson Lockhart became one of its first editors when
Blackwood established his famous magazine the following year and
he was to remain a discerning and critical observer of the literary
scene in Edinburgh, writing about its foibles with ease and
vividness. The *Letters* which he published in 1819 achieved an instant

succès de scandale, moving easily and ceaselessly between satire and serious comment. The satirical portraits, especially those of prominent Whigs, attracted a good deal of wrath and exaggerated his reputation as "the scorpion which delighteth to sting the faces of men", but his serious comments such as the following about William Blackwood remain amongst the best evocations of literary life of the day.

> The length of vista presented to one on entering the shop, has a very imposing effect; for it is carried back, room after room, through various gradations of light and shadow till the eye cannot trace distinctly the outline of any object in the furthest distance. First, there is as usual a spacious place set apart for retail business and a numerous detachment of young clerks and apprentices, to whose management that important department of the concern is intrusted. Then you have an elegant oval saloon, lighted from the roof, where various groups of loungers and literary dilettanti are engaged in looking at, or criticising among themselves, the publications just arrived by that day's coach from town. In such critical colloquies, the voice of the bookseller himself may ever and anon be heard mingling the broad and unadulterated notes of its Auld Reekie music; for unless occupied in the recesses of the premises with some other business, it is here that he has his usual station. He is a nimble active looking man of middle age, and moves about from one corner to another with great alacrity and apparently under the influence of high animal spirits. His complexion is very sanguineous, but nothing can be more intelligent, keen and sagacious than the expression of the whole physiognomy; above all, the gray eyes and eye-brows as full of locomotion as those of Catalini. The remarks he makes are, in general, extremely acute — much more so indeed, than those of any member of the trade I ever heard speak on such topics. The shrewdness and decision of the man can, however, stand in no need of testimony beyond that which his own conduct has aforded — above all, in the establishment of his Magazine . . .

It was from this office that William Blackwood resolved to publish a magazine which would challenge the Whig domination of Jeffrey's *Edinburgh Review*. Two editors were engaged to run the new publication, James Cleghorn, who had been a farmer and Thomas Pringle, a minor poet, and the first issue appeared on 1st

April 1817. It was no competition for the intellectual vigour of its rival and for six monthly issues it limped on, printing births, marriages and deaths, recording odd scientific facts and publishing other nonsenses masquerading as literature. Blackwood realised that the venture was in danger of proving a costly and shameful failure and he acted quickly. Cleghorn and Pringle were sent packing and their places were given to two entirely different men. Lockhart and John Wilson, who took for himself the pseudonym of "Christopher North".

Wilson was thirty-two when he was engaged by Blackwood. The son of a wealthy Paisley gauze manufacturer, he was a prodigious athlete and in his youth he had tramped the width and breadth of Britain and Ireland often in the guise of a tinker. Like Lockhart he was an advocate and had come to live in Edinburgh in 1814 after spending seven years in the Lake District where he had been a friend and neighbour of Wordsworth and De Quincey. That he was a well-known figure in Edinburgh is amply testified to by the young Thomas Carlyle.

> A very tall strong-built and impetuous looking young man, age perhaps about 28, with a profusion of blond hair, with flashing countenance of the statuesque sort, flashing pair of blue eyes, which were fixed as if on something far off, was impetuously striding along, regarding nobody to right or left, but gently yet rapidly cleaving the press, and with large strides stepping along, as if too late for some appointment far ahead. His clothing was rough (I think some loose, whitish jacket of kersey stuff), hat of broadish brim, on the big massive head, flanked with such overplus of strong unclipt flaxen hair, seemed to have known many showers in its time; but what struck one most was the glance of those big blue eyes, stern yet loving, pointing so authentically to something far away.

Lockhart had aristocratic connections and, like many Scots before, had finished his education at Oxford where he had developed a satirical vein which he was to use to good effect in his new career. A tall, elegant, darkly handsome, man Lockhart's haughty demeanour won him few friends. Even James Hogg who collaborated with the two editors in that first issue was more than a little afraid of him.

> He was a mischievous Oxford puppy, for whom I was terrified,

dancing after the young ladies, and drawing caricatures of every one who came in contact with him . . . I dreaded his eye terribly; and it was not without reason, for he was very fond of playing tricks on me, but always in such a way, that it was impossible to lose temper with him.

Much of the planning for the new magazine had to be done in secret, partly because Blackwood was unsure how Cleghorn and Pringle would react, and partly because he had in his possession a piece of literary dynamite — the Chaldee Manuscript. Although there is some doubt as to who wrote the final version of that scurrilous piece of work there is good reason to believe that Hogg wrote the first draft and sent it to Blackwood who in turn passed it on to Lockhart and Wilson. The two men were known as great topers and there is a story that they sat up all night over numberless bottles of port in 53 Queen Street, re-drafting Hogg's original. Whatever the truth of the story, the appearance of the Chaldee Manuscript in the October 1817 issue of *Blackwood's* changed the magazine overnight from its vapid torpor to a controversial, vibrant magazine of Olympian standards.

The introduction to the Manuscript shamelessly states its mock intentions: "We have been favoured with the following translation of a Chaldee M.S. which is preserved in the great library of Paris (Salle 2d no.53 B.A.M.M.) . . . ". What followed in the Manuscript was a satire, couched in the language of the Old Testament, of the leading literary and political personalities of the day, the Whigs and their allies being damned out of hand and the Tories of the Blackwood group being praised for their sagacity and foresight. It was a tour-de-force and, for a few brief days, Edinburgh and *Blackwood's Magazine* stood at the centre of the British literary stage, Half the city roared with laughter at its now obscure and half-forgotten references (Scott appears as "the great magician who dwelleth in the old fastness hard by the River Jordan which is by the Border") and the other half bellowed with indignation and ill-concealed rage. Even readers in distant London were delighted or pained, according to their literary and political tastes.

The first edition quickly sold out and Blackwood, aware that his magazine had become an overnight *literary sensation*, promptly removed the Chaldee Manuscript from the next edition. This move

Robert Burns by Alexander Naysmith

Baxter's Close in the mid nineteenth century, the site
of Robert Burns' first lodging in Edinburgh. Water
colour by Henry Duguid

Edinburgh from Calton Hill by J M W Turner

Robert Louis Stevenson

Sydney Goodsir Smith, Hugh MacDiarmid and
Norman MacCaig at a Burns' Supper at the
Peacock Hotel, Newhaven

Sydney Goodsir Smith in the Abbotsford Bar

only created a black market for the Manuscript but it did not lessen the magazine's popularity. For Lockhart and Wilson had not been content to rest their laurels on the one article. In the same edition there were slashing attacks on Keats and the "Cockney School of Poetry", on Coleridge's *Biographia Literaria* and a derisive article on Leigh Hunt, written by 'Z', who by his familiarity with the subject, was none other than Lockhart himself.

The outrage caused by the appearance of the magazine brought in its tow a number of lawsuits against Blackwood — one from Leigh Hunt demanding the name of 'Z', another from a prominent Whig, John Graham Dalyell who had been savagely lampooned. The writ stated his objections in no uncertain terms: " . . . William Blackwood did insert and publish a wicked, false and scandalous libel, grossly calumnating the person of the said John Graham Dalyell in an indecent, irreverent and blasphemous application of scriptural language." While Blackwood was trying to pour oil on these troubled waters, a further howl of rage went up from Dalyell — Lockhart had written an anonymous letter to Leigh Hunt claiming that Dalyell had penned the article by 'Z'. Looking at events today it does seem that Blackwood had lost control of events at 17 Princess Street and was being forced to face the inevitable consequences. He was threatened with excommunication, given a horse-whipping and sent to Coventry by the book trade in the city. Adam Black, who was later to become a fine publisher, remembered the bitterness that existed between Blackwood and his rival, Constable.

> As might have been expected, this petty warfare, in which no quarter was given, had a baneful influence upon Edinburgh society, and especially on the book trade. I recollect a booksellers sale, at which a number of the trade were assembled when Constable came in late. Seeing Blackwood he pointed to him, and said, "I cannot associate with that man," and immediately left the room followed by several others. I remained, though friendly to Constable, not choosing to act as an adherent of either party. But it was not easy to maintain a position of neutrality between two proud and hot-tempered men.

And Mrs Grant of Laggan, a Highland lady resident in Edinburgh, wrote in her memoirs about the city being " in an uproar about *Blackwood's Magazine* which contains in a very irreverent and unjustifiable form, a good deal of wit and cunning satire." James Hogg, rightly cautious about the *literati's* attitude to him returned to his farm in Ettrick where he wrote to Scott, pleading with him, "For the love of God, open not your mouth about the Chaldee M.S." Even Lockhart and Wilson, while continuing to exhort Blackwood to "keep your mind in good fighting condition" were forced by circumstance to flee the city for refuge in Windermere.

By and by the storm died down and although the magazine continued to publish its hoaxes, rib-poking and learned tomfoolery, much of the abusive criticism was published for its own sake, and within a few years *Blackwood's* had lost its literary crown. Wilson stayed on as editor and with James Hogg created for *Blackwood's* the *Noctes Ambrosianae*, imaginery accounts of boozy evenings spent in hi-jinks at Ambrose's Tavern in Gabriels Road, where the main protagonists were Christopher North, Timothy Tickler and the Ettrick Shepherd. Astonishingly, Wilson, without an ounce of learning on the subject in his head, was also appointed to the Chair of Moral Philosophy in the University as the Tory's nominee. He arranged for a friend, Alexander Blair in Birmingham, to write his lectures, but when the mail-coach failed to arrive, as happened on numerous occasions, Wilson, nothing daunted, would rant and rave, and roar at his students in a violent pretence of rhetoric and learning. So popular did these lectures become that townsfolk would come off the street to gaze in wonder at the huge red-headed man in full flight, brow-beating his class with highflown words and phrases.

It was an image of himself that Wilson liked to recreate in the *Noctes*, but he also grew to be a pest, lashing out at Hogg and then trembling in fear that his anonymous articles be detected. Another Blackwood writer, John Galt was to feel the brunt of Wilson's high Tory politics when he carefully edited references to machine-breaking from that fine novel by Galt, *The Annals of the Parish*. But Wilson's particular scorn was reserved for his "friend" and "collaborator", Hogg.

> Pray, who wishes to know anything about his (Hogg's) life? Who indeed cares a single farthing whether he be at this blessed moment dead or alive? Only picture yourself a stout country lout with a

THE EDINBURGH OF SIR WALTER SCOTT

bushel of hair on his shoulders that had not been raked for months,
enveloped in a coarse plaid impregnated with tobacco, with a
prodigious mouthful of immeasurable tusks, and a dialect that sets
all conjecture at defiance, lumbering suddenly in upon the elegant
retirement of Mr Miller's backshop . . . what would he (Hogg)
himself have thought, if a large surly brown bear, or a huge
baboon had burst open his door when he was at breakfast?

If that description from the *Noctes* was supposed to have been
written by a friend, then how much more hurtful must have been the
many other backbiting remarks from his enemies that Hogg had to
endure during his years in Edinburgh? Born and brought up a
shepherd in Yarrow in the Border country, Hogg had been
encouraged in his writing by his master, Wiiliam Laidlaw of
Blackhouse, who was friendly with Scott. Indeed, Scott met Hogg
during his Border raids for ballads and even though Hogg's mother
did not relish the committing of the oral tradition to print the two
men were to remain life-long friends. Hogg had published some
verse in the *Scots Magazine* and in 1801 had published a small volume
of poems, *Scottish Pastorals*, but the ensuing years were dogged by
several unsuccessful attempts to set himself up as a farmer, first in
Harris and then in Dumfries-shire.

In 1810 he moved to Edinburgh where he published a collection of
songs and became the editor and main contributor of *The Spy*, a
weekly literary magazine which ran for a year. As it turned out,
farming's loss was to be literature's gain.

Having appeared as a poet, and a speculative farmer besides, no
one would now employ me as a shepherd. I even applied to some
of my old masters, but they refused me, and for a whole winter I
found myself without employment, and without money, in my
native country; therefore, in February 1810, in utter desperation, I
took my plaid about my shoulders, and marched away to
Edinburgh, determined, since no better could be, to push my
fortune as a literary man. It is true, I had estimated my poetical
talent high enough, but I had resolved to use it only as a staff, never
as a crutch; and would have kept that resolve, had I not been driven
to the reverse. On going to Edinburgh, I found that my poetical
talents were rated nearly as low as my shepherd qualities were in
Ettrick. It was in vain that I applied to newsmongers, booksellers,

135

editors of magazines, &c. for employment. Any of these were willing enough to accept any of my lucubrations, and give them publicity but then there was no money going — not a farthing; and this suited me very ill.

That is not an uncommon experience for any fledgling writer but Hogg was determined that it should only be a temporary one. His involvement with *The Spy* brought him into contact with Edinburgh's literary society and he joined a debating society, The Forum, which met in the church in Carruber's Close, so that he could improve both his elocution and his self-confidence. By the time his long poem, *The Queens Wake*, was published in 1813 his fortunes had changed and he was able to admit to himself, not without pride that, "though I sometimes incurred pointed disapprobation, I was in general a prodigious favourite." He was, as we have seen, also drawn into the Blackwood group, becoming a frequent contributor to the magazine, and taking for himself the immortal soubriquet, The Ettrick Shepherd.

But Hogg was an anachronism in nineteenth-century Edinburgh. His country directness and honesty initially delighted his patrons but as time wore on it began to embarrass them, and though some of his friends kept up a pretence of friendship they were in fact exploiting him behind his back. Hogg's world of the tavern and of the common country people had to be kept strictly apart from the world of the drawing room, and what were originally seen as his virtues were used in print to crucify him. From all accounts Hogg was an open, honest man, touched by vanity perhaps, but nevertheless so in love with the image of himself as an urban celebrity, that it is easy to see, even when he tells the story against himself, how he became the butt of sophisticated young men at the numerous dining clubs that existed in the city.

I observe that in the extended MS I had detailed all the proceedings of a club, the most ridiculous that was ever established in any city, and, owing to some particular circumstances, I cannot refrain from mentioning them here (his *Memoirs*). The club was established one night, in a frolic, at a jovial dinner party, in the house of a young lawyer, now of some celebrity at the bar, and was christened *The Right and Wrong Club*. The chief principle of the club was, that whatever any of its members should assert, the whole were bound to support the same, whether *right or wrong*. We were so delighted with the novelty of the idea, that we agreed to meet the next day at Oman's Hotel, and celebrate its anniversary. We were dull and heavy when we met, but did not part so. We dined at five, and separated at two in the morning, before which time the club had greatly risen in our estimation; so we agreed to meet next day, and every successive day for five or six weeks and during all that time our hours of sitting continued the same. No constitutions on earth could stand this . . . the result was, that several of the members got quite deranged, and I drank myself into an inflammatory fever.

Hogg spent five years in Edinburgh before being granted a farm at Altrive Lake in Ettrick by the Duke of Buccleuch, but he was to remain a kenspeckle figure on the Edinburgh scene, choosing always to live in one of the areas off the New Town, in Teviot Row, Stockbridge or at Ambrose's in Gabriels Road. His first novel, *The Brownie of Bodsbeck*, was published in 1818 and this was followed by *The Three Perils of Man* in 1822 and by *The Confessions of a Justified Sinner*, thought by many critics to be the finest novel of the age, in 1824. Although he was not of Edinburgh, and throughout his residence kept his heart firmly in the Borders, Hogg knew the city and, like his predecessor Burns, was equally at home in the Grassmarket tavern as he was in the salons of Heriot Row. And like his fellow Borderer Scott he has left us with a complete and loving description of the city as he saw it while bathing in the River Forth off Portobello.

Isna Embro a glorious city? Sae clear the air, yonner you see a man and a woman stannin on the tap o' Arthur's Seat! I had nae notion there were sae mony steeples, and spires, and columns, and pillars, and obelisks, and doms in Embro! And at this distance the ee canna distinguish atween them that belangs to kirks, and them that belangs to naval monuments, and them that belangs to ile-gas companies, and them that's only chimley-heids in the auld toon, and the taps o' groves, or single trees, sic as poplars; and aboon a' and ahint a', craigs and saft-broo'd hills sprinkled wi' sheep, lichts and shadows, and the blue vapoury glimmer o' a Midsummer day — het, het, het, wi' the barometer at ninety; but here, to us twa, bob-bobbin amang the fresh, cool, murmurin, and faemy wee waves, temperate as the air within the mermaids palace.

Portobello is now an eastern suburb of Edinburgh lying on the river, but in Hogg's day it was a lively seaside resort with salt-water baths. It enjoyed considerable popularity and for a few months John Gibson Lockhart and his wife lived at 37 Belfield Street. Once a wilderness, it had prospered in the eighteenth century with the construction of a coaching inn by a retired sailor who had fought with Admiral Vernon's fleet at the Battle of Puerto Bello. It was in Portobello, too, that Walter Scott, still acting as a reserve officer, found the time to work on his second long poem, *Marmion*. A fellow officer, James Skene, remembered him exercising his powerful black steed on the sands. "Now and again you would see him plunge in his spurs, and go off at the charge, with the spray dashing about him." Little wonder that the stanzas on which Scott was working were the dramatic scenes describing the Battle of Flodden.

Marmion was published by Constable in 1808 and within two months had sold out its first edition of two thousand copies in spite of a hefty selling price of one-and-a-half guineas. It consolidated the reputation that Scott had gained with the *Minstrelsy of the Scottish Border* and *The Lay of the Last Minstrel*. Although *Marmion* is perhaps most popularly known for its two songs, *Where shall the lover rest?* and *Lochinvar*, it also contains Scott's famous evocation of the Edinburgh that he adored.

> Such dusky grandeur clothed the height
> Where the huge castle holds its state
>   And all the steep slope down,
> Whose ridgy back heaves to the sky,
> Piled deep and massy, close and high,
>   Mine own romantic town!

Scott continued to spend parts of the year in the Borders executing his legal duties in Selkirk-shire, but more and more of his time came to be spent in his Edinburgh home and as well as becoming a well-known personality in the city, he had also become a partner in the printing firm owned by his old school friend, James Ballantyne. The printing works were in Pauls Work on the north side of the Canongate below Calton Hill. Scott wanted Ballantyne to set himself up as a publisher to rival Constable but the publication of a series of dreary unsellable antiquarian books put the firm in financial danger, leaving Ballantyne with a huge debt to Scott. It was then that Constable intervened and so began an intricate business relationship where credit was backed by bills and not by real money. The arrangement was later to have dire results for Scott and his family.

The theatre, too, claimed Scott's attention and although the city lacked a strong dramatic tradition, it did have an intimate theatre in Corri's Rooms in Leith Walk and a dramatist in Joanna Baillie whom many thought could help bring about a theatrical revival in Scotland. Scott became a trustee of the theatre along with Henry Mackenzie and the Lord Provost who, by chance, was a stocking weaver by profession and a devotee of the stage (although Scott hinted slyly that his interest "was owing to a large order for hose, pantaloons and plaids"). In January 1810 Joanna Baillie's play, *The Family Legend*, was staged by Henry Siddons, son of the renowned Sarah Siddons, and its first night was a glorious success with "thunderous cheers of enthusiasm, and hats and handkerchiefs tossed into the air". Scott's hand in the production brought him new friends in the theatre, including the great Shakespearean actor of the day, John Philip Kemble.

Although Scott continued to have an interest in the theatre, he was not enthusiastic about the attempts to dramatise his own work (although later in life he grew to love the actor Charles Mackay's portrayal of Baillie Nicol Jarvie). *The Lady of the Lake* was turned into a melodrama, and was played in London, Dublin and Edinburgh, where Scott found Mrs Siddons' portrayal of Ellen "too Columbinish" for a Highland heroine. His interests in the dramatic, already displayed in his long poems, had turned him to the novel and as early as 1805 he had started work on *Waverley* which was to be a prose piece about the 1745 Jacobite uprising. When he had shown it to Ballantyne and to his close friend William Erskine, Lord Kinedder, both had disliked it so much that, like many another disappointed author, Scott had condemned it to his bottom drawer. It was only after he moved house to Abbotsford by the River Tweed near Galashiels that he finished the manuscript and gave it to Constable who published it in 1814. By the end of the year it had sold five thousand copies, had made its author £2,000 and had received universal critical praise. But its author had chosen not to put his name on the title page.

There are several reasons for this. Scott himself claimed that it would have been unbecoming for a Clerk to the Court of Session, which he then was, to have been known as a novelist. It may have had something to do with not wanting to show the world how many lives he was leading, but the best reason for the anonymity has been put forward by Professor David Daiches who points to a motto adopted by Scott — *Clausus tutus ero* ("I shall be safe when closed up"). As the novels were to become so much of his life and his main financial prop, Scott may have chosen to keep that part of his mind and art private, or like many other Scottish writers (Hugh MacDiarmid, Lewis Grassic Gibbon, for instance) he may have shied away from putting his name to writing which was so intimate that it made him vulnerable. The puzzle of "The Great Unknown" teased the people of Edinburgh until 1827 when the identity of the author had become such an open secret that Scott announced it to a crescendo of applause at a dinner held in the Assembly Rooms in George Street on February 23rd.

By then, "the author of *Waverley*" had published twenty-three novels, including such masterpieces as *Guy Mannering* (1815), *Rob Roy* (1817), *Heart of Midlothian* (1818), *Ivanhoe* (1819), *Kenilworth* (1821), *Quentin Durward* (1823) and *The Fortunes of Nigel* (1822). His writing brought him great anonymous fame and a considerable fortune but, as he explained to his son-in-law Lockhart, he also found time in the midst of a frantic social life for his own work and to offer the occasional helping hand to others.

> Ay, it was enough to tear me to pieces, but there was a wonderful exhilaration about it all: my blood was kept at fever pitch — I felt as if I could have grappled with anything and everything; then there was hardly one of my schemes that did not afford me to the means of serving some poor devil of a brother author. There were always huge piles of material to be arranged, sifted and indexed — volumes of extracts to be transcribed — journeys to be made hither and thither, for ascertaining little facts and dates — in short I could commonly keep half-a-dozen of the ragged regiment of Parnassus in tolerable ease.

Edwin Muir has said of Scott's novels that when a nation loses its identity it creates a legend to take its place, and other commentators have criticised Scott for dealing with historical subjects in his novels,

140

and yet in most of them there is a working out of several contemporary themes especially those of the conflicting allegiances of the old Scotland to the new Britain, of the Scots speech to the new middle-class English usages, of the sobriety of law and order to the romance of fiction. Certainly Scott's age was one of rapid change: of war and social unrest, of a move towards parliamentary reform, and in Scotland of a move away from things Scottish. In that turbulent world, his novels must have offered crumbs of comfort to those who wanted to return to the romantic Edinburgh Scott described in *The Abbot.*

> "This, then is Edinburgh?" said the youth, as the fellow-travellers arrived at one of the heights to the southward, which commanded a view of the great northern capital — "this is that Edinburgh of which we have heard so much?"
>
> "Even so," said the falconer; "yonder stands Auld Reekie; you may see the smoke hover over her at twenty miles' distance, as the goss-hawk hangs over a plump of young wild ducks; ay, yonder is the heart of Scotland, and each throb that she gives is felt from the edge of Solway to Duncansby Head. See, yonder is the old Castle; and to the right, on rising ground, that is the Castle of Craigmillar, which I have known a merry place in my time."
>
> "Was it not there," said the page in a low voice, "that the Queen held her court?"
>
> "Ay, ay," replied the falconer — "Queen she was then, though you must not call her so now."

As fascinated as he was with the past, Scott kept up a lively interest in everything and everyone around him. His portrait was executed twice by Sir Henry Raeburn, the doyen of British portrait painters who kept his studio at 32 York Place. Born in 1756 the son of a Stockbridge mill-owner, Raeburn enjoyed a fame similar to Scott's and he painted many of the leading personalities of the day. The first Scott painting was completed in 1808, commissioned by Constable after the success of *Marmion*, and the second, a senatorial sitting a year before Raeburn's death, in 1822, when Scott was at the height of his powers.

Scott's opportunity to blend past with present and to portray the grandeur of his country's history came in August 1822 when George IV visited the city. According to Lockhart, the Town Council relied

heavily on Scott to help them out with their preparations and he
responded with gusto, hitting on the notion of presenting Highland
Scotland with a review of troops and the presence in the city of the
main clan chiefs whom he asked to dress "in the masquerade of the
Celtic Society". Later many were to criticise him for the
over-preponderance of kilts, tartans and bagpipes, but the visit itself
was a triumph. There was a ceremonial welcome at Leith, where the
stones on the landing stage had been inscribed *O felicem diem!*, a
banquet in Parliament Hall, a Royal Command performance of *Rob
Roy*, many assemblies and dinners and a review of the troops in
glorious weather on Portobello beach.

At the end of the visit Scott was exhausted with a painful body
rash and a return of the intestinal complaint he called "a gravellous
tendency — a sort of Macadamization of those parts which would be
best in their original structure and much exasperated by a disposition
to bile". The return of these attacks which had begun as early as 1817
made Ballantyne believe that his valuable author was on death's
doorstep and put the honest Hogg in a genuine state of alarm.

> Dear Scott
> I never knew that you were so dear to me till last night when I saw
> your seat taken by another — that circumstance engendered ideas
> that were unbrookable. I fear that you were very ill last night that it
> was found necessary to let blood . . . . .

In fact disaster of another kind was fast approaching Scott and his
publishers. The financial arrangements they had made had been built
on sand and the tempest was about to break. Spurred on by
speculative fever in London, Constable's English agents, Hurst,
Robinson and Co. had invested unwisely in a ruinous hop harvest.
In turn Constable and Ballantyne were drawn in by the domino
effect of having bills of exchange and credit which were quite
worthless, and Scott with his vast business interests in their affairs
was drawn into the debacle. Because he had been living on credit he
was unaware of the extent of his debts which were an astonishing
£116,838.11.3. Ruin stared him in the face and an incredulous Scott
family were forced to acknowledge that they had become paupers
overnight. Edinburgh was astonished and offers of help poured in
from all sides, but Scott was adamant that he would clear his debts

142

"with my right hand", and confided his hopes and fears to his Journal.

> What a life mine has been! — half educated, almost wholly neglected or left to myself, stuffing my head with most nonsensical trash, and undervalued in society for a time by most of my companions — getting forward and held a bold and clever fellow contrary to the opinion of all who thought me a mere dreamer — Broken hearted for two years — my heart handsomely pierced again — but the crack will remain to my dying day. Rich and poor four or five times, once at the verge of ruin, yet opened new sources of wealth almost overflowing — now taken in my pitch of pride, and nearly winged (unless the good news hold), because London chuses to be in an uproar, and in a tumult of bulls and bears, and a poor inoffensive lion like myself is pushd to the wall. And what is to be the end of it? God knows.

Shortly before Christmas 1825 Scott was forced to admit defeat and to set in motion the legal machinery to manage his debts. On 20th January 1826 Scott's creditors met in the Waterloo Hotel to establish a private trust deed into which he could pay sums of money to settle his major debts. Abbotsford, his fantasy house by the Tweed, had been saved but 39 North Castle Street was sold together with most of its furniture, much to Scott's great shame. He admitted that he was "subject to attachment even to chairs and tables", and he heard a passer-by comment that he would not mind giving a pound for a chair that had been the Great Unknown's.

Worse was to follow. After a short illness his wife Charlotte died in the summer of 1826 and there followed a series of dreary lodgings in Edinburgh, first in the vile apartments of Mrs Brown at 6 North St. David Street when a good friend, Captain Basil Hall, was shocked by its lowly squalor. "At the top of the stairs we saw a small tray with a single plate and glasses for a solitary person's dinner." Later that year he moved to more comfortable lodgings at 3 Walker Street and from there to his last lodgings at 6 Shandwick Place between 1828 and 1830. Occasionally he would stay with the publisher, Robert Cadell, at 16 Atholl Crescent.

There were still some happy days to be had at Abbotsford with congenial visitors and a solicitous family; *Woodstock* a novel set in sixteenth-century England made £6,000 and his life of Napoleon brought in 10,500 guineas; the government even put the fifty-gun frigate H.M.S. *Barham* at his disposal in 1831 for a winter tour of the Mediterranean. At the beginning of 1832, while in Naples, he received the splendid news that the debt had finally been cleared by his literary efforts. But his health was failing daily. The lameness which had afflicted him as a child returned, and as well as continuing stomach complaints he suffered from chilblains and rheumatism and most seriously of all he began to have blackouts and fainting fits. In May 1832, desperate to see Scotland again, he returned home from Rome by a tortuous overland route. On the way he suffered from several cerebral haemorrhages and the journey itself was long and wearisome. It was July before he reached Edinburgh where he put up at the Douglas Hotel in St. Andrew Square before setting off on the 7th for Abbotsford.

Scott survived the splendid summer, almost revived by being at home on his native heath, but on the 21st September at the age of sixty-one he died peacefully in his sleep, Lockhart noting in his *Life* that it was a perfect early autumn Scottish day, so warm that all the windows were open to hear the gentle ripple of the waters of the River Tweed. A great age in Scottish letters had drawn to an end.

Chapter Eight

The Victorian Age

The news of Sir Walter Scott's death reverberated around the world. It was first reported in a brief obituary in the *Scotsman* the following day, then London took up the news in the *Times* of 25th September, their leading article claiming that Scott had become the President of European Literature. Later the news seeped through to Europe and then to North America where he enjoyed the kind of popularity normally reserved for today's film stars, thus justifying the *Scotsman's* early obituary claim.

> He dies too soon for the wishes of his countrymen — but in the fulness of his glory, with an imperishable name, honoured and lamented by the admirers of genius to the extremities of the earth.

He was buried in Dryburgh Abbey, and as the funeral cortège made its way along the road from Melrose to the ruined twelfth-century abbey, the horses stopped at his favourite view of the Eildon Hills, just as they had always done during their master's lifetime.

Scott's death left a vacuum in Edinburgh: in many ways he had been the centre of the city's literary life, helping and encouraging, adding his voice to literary opinion and standing firm for values which were fast losing their significance in a changing world. Hogg, who had increasingly spent less time in Edinburgh as the years rolled by, died three years later and was buried in Ettrick Churchyard, Blackwood died in September 1834 with Wilson and Lockhart by his side, John Galt, who had come to live in Edinburgh for a brief period in 1821 and who had become a fine novelist, died in 1839 after a time in Canada. Their deaths too impoverished the city.

Control of *Blackwood's Magazine* fell to William's sons, Robert and Alexander, and Christopher North remained a loyal, if somewhat subdued, supporter, attracting to the publishers a new

145

generation of writers. Lockhart had left Edinburgh to live in London where he edited Murray's *Quarterly Review* from 1825 until his death. He had been persuaded to move by his father-in-law's stern belief that a man with family commitments should no longer indulge in literary horseplay, and also by the eloquence of a young London businessman who was later to become Prime Minister of Britain — Benjamin Disraeli. On his return to London after successfully engaging Lockhart for Murray, Disraeli found himself in the stagecoach in the company of another Edinburgh publisher.

> It struck me that I had never met such an ostentatious man or one whose conversation was so braggart. One would think that he had written the Waverley Novels himself, and certainly that Abbotsford belonged to him. He informed me that he intended to build a new wing to Abbotsford next year . . . Something had gone wrong on the journey, the guard or coachman had displeased. He went into an ecstasy of pompous passion. "Do you know who I am man? I am Archibald Constable, etc!"

A week later, Constable was a ruined man.

On Scott's death, Lockhart had written to Blackwood from London: "If the Edinburgh people did well, they would put a statue where Castle Street cuts Princes Street, with the Castle Rock for a background; and they would make a huge Homeric Cairn on Arthur's Seat — a land and sea mark." In fact the people of Edinburgh went one better: they caused a Gothic pile to be built in Princes Street Gardens where from the top the visitor may see lying all around the symmetry of an Edinburgh that the shape of Scott might still recognise. The committee which took the decision to build the monument met two weeks after Scott's death, but they had difficulty raising the funds which soon lagged behind the monument's construction. The design was executed by George Meikle Kemp, a self-taught draughtsman — a fact which may excuse some of the excesses in the monument — who was unfortunately drowned in the Union Canal in 1844, two years before the monument was completed.

After the passing of the Reform Bill, many of Blackwood's authors had begun to drift away, unable to find a niche in the magazine's increasingly High Tory outlook. William Maginn, an

Irishman who styled himself the Ensign O'Doherty and who had brought a sense of outrageous fun to polite Edinburgh, deserted *Blackwood's* for the new, imitative periodicals in London; Thomas De Quincey, the "Opium Eater", who had once taken shelter from his creditors beneath the table in Blackwood's saloon, drifted away; and Dr D.M. Moir, "Delta", who lived in nearby Musselburgh, began to have an increasingly important say in the firm's publishing affairs. Despite his good intentions, he was a menace as an editor, cutting out work that he judged might offend the sensibilities of the magazine's new and genteel readership.

On the other side of the city, the *Edinburgh Review* remained in print throughout the nineteenth century, although its influence was on the wane after Jeffrey retired from the editorship in 1829. Three years later he had become member of parliament for Edinburgh in the first reformed parliament and in the following year he was made a Lord of Session. He died in 1850 and his biography was written two years later by his old friend, Lord Cockburn, but for a picture of this astute editor in his home at Craigcrook Castle we must return to *Peter's Letters to his Kinsfolk*.

> . . . and I drove to Craigcrook, Mr Jeffrey's villa, *molto gustomente* — the expectation of the manifold luxuries I hoped to enjoy there — the prospective delights both of palate and intellect — being heightened and improved by the preliminary gratification I tasted, while the shandrydan rolled along between the refreshed green of the meadows and cornfields. His house is an old turreted mansion, much patched in the whole mass of its structure, and, I believe, much increased in its accommodations since he entered upon possession of it. The situation is extremely beautiful. There are very few trees immediately about the house; but the windows open upon the side of a charming hill, which, in all its extent, as far as the eye can reach, is wooded most luxuriantly to the very summit. There cannot be a more delicious rest for the eyes, than such an Arcadian height in this bright and budding time of the year; but, indeed, where, or at what time, can a fine wood be looked upon without delight? Between the wood and the house, there is a good garden, and some fields, in the cultivation of which Mr Jeffrey seems to take much pleasure; for I had no sooner arrived, than he insisted upon carrying me over his ditches and hedges to shew me his method of farming; and, indeed, talked of

Swedish turnip, and Fiorin grass, and red-blossomed potatoes, in a style that would have done no dishonour to your friend Curwin himself. I had come, thanks to my rustic ignorance, exactly at the hour appointed for dinner (five o'clock), so that I had three parts of an hour of the great man entirely to myself — during the whole of which space he continued to talk about rural affairs, and to trot me up one field and down another, till I was weary, without (*credite posteri!*) making one single allusion to law, politics or literature.

Literary taste was changing. There was a new reading public and they had a voracious appetite; writers now had to compete in the open market-place for their survival and inevitably, some, like Scott, did better than others. Constable had been the first to recognise that money was to be made in the book trade, but to meet the new demands, other publishers set themselves up in the city, amongst them being William and Robert Chambers, who had started as booksellers in Leith Walk and had then moved to Hanover Street before setting up as publishers in Thistle Street where they remain to this day. (By a quirk of fate the firm of William Blackwood moved to Thistle Street in 1972 after a long stay at 45 George Street.) The firm published *Chamber's Journal* and an Encyclopaedia and although the magazine is long since defunct, Chambers still remains at the forefront of British reference book publishing. Both the brothers, who were born in Peebles, made substantial contributions to their adopted city. William was Lord Provost in 1865 and in 1868 and was a great benefactor of the Church of St. Giles, while his brother's work as a writer includes that formidable mine of information, *The Traditions of Edinburgh*, which was written in 1823 at a time when the author wanted to capture some of the grandeur of a passing age.

In 1827 at 57 South Bridge, Adam Black had purchased the copyright of the *Encyclopaedia Britannica*, and like others of his day, slowly changed from a bookseller to a publisher. He built up a list that specialised in philosophy, science and theology and, as the firm expanded, he brought in his nephew Charles as a partner in 1834. By then he had moved his office to 27 North Bridge, a building that had once housed the General Post Office. It was to be his penultimate Edinburgh address (there was a brief stay at 6 North Bridge) before the firm up and moved to London in 1889. Despite their loss to the city, the firm of A & C Black remains one of the great Edinburgh publishers, endowing the James Tait Black Prize which is given annually to the best novel and best biography, on the recommendation of the Regius Professor of English at the University of Edinburgh. It was first awarded in 1919 and is one of Britain's great literary prizes.

The city was growing, pushing further south beyond the Meadows and Bruntsfield Links and making encroachments in the west, onto Corstorphine Hill — the Victorian suburbs were on the march. John Ruskin gave an early warning to the citizens in a lecture given at the Philosophical Institution on 1st November 1853 that constant vigilance was needed to maintain the architectural standards of the city. Sadly, it is a warning that has all too often gone unheeded in recent years.

> Of all the cities in the British Islands, Edinburgh is the one which presents most advantages for the display of a noble building; and which, on the other hand, sustains most injury in the erection of a commonplace or unworthy one. You are all proud of your city; surely you must feel it a duty in some sort to justify your pride; that is to say, to give yourselves a right to be proud of it. That you were born under the shadow of its two fantastic mountains — that you live where from your room windows you can trace the shores of its glittering Firth, are no rightful subjects of pride. You did not raise the mountains, nor shape the shores; and the historical buildings of the Canongate, and the broad battlements of your castle, reflect honour upon you only through your ancestors. Before you boast of your city, before you venture to call it yours, ought you not scrupulously to weigh the exact share you have had in adding to it or adorning it, to calculate seriously the influence upon its aspect which the work of your own hands has exercised?

Nevertheless Edinburgh was still a place to be visited and many writers made the pilgrimage and were captivated by what they found. Harriet Beecher Stowe arrived in the city in 1854 en route for the Highlands.

> Edinburgh has had an effect on the literary history of the world for the last fifty years, that cannot be forgotten by anyone approaching her. The air seemed to be full of spirits of those who, no longer living, have woven a part of the thread of our existence. I do not

know that the shortness of human life ever so oppressed me as it did on coming near to the city . . .

After reading his *Christmas Carol* to a packed audience in the Music Hall, Charles Dickens was presented with a silver quaich by a grateful Lord Provost. The year was 1858, and Dickens was a famous man, but he did not forget that it was Edinburgh, of all the British cities, who had honoured him first when he was made a freeman in 1841.

> I never have forgotten, and I can never forget, that I have the honour to be a burgess and guild-brother of the Corporation of Edinburgh. As long as sixteen or seventeen years ago, the first great public recognition and encouragement I ever received was bestowed on me in this generous and magnificent city — in this city so distinguished in literature and so distinguished in the arts. You will readily believe that I have carried into the various countries I have since traversed and through all my subsequent career, the proud and affectionate remembrance of that eventful epoch in my life; and that coming back to Edinburgh is to me like coming home.

Dickens had first visited Edinburgh as early as 1834 when, as a young journalist on the London *Morning Chronicle*, he had been sent north to cover the granting of the freedom of the city to Earl Grey, the hero of the Reform Bill. As there was no building large enough to accommodate all the guests (all two thousand of them) who were entertained to dinner by the city council, a huge marquee was hurriedly built in the grounds of the Royal High School on Calton Hill. It was a splendid occasion, brilliantly lit by a huge gas chandelier borrowed from the Theatre Royal, but it was Dickens the future novelist who noticed, and reported on, the more human aspects of the day.

> A gentleman who, we presume, had entered with one of the first sections, having sat with exemplary patience for some time in the immediate vicinity of cold fowls, roast beef, lobsters and other tempting delicacies (for the dinner was a cold one) appeared to think that the best thing he could possibly do, would be to eat his dinner, while there was anything to eat. He accordingly laid about him with right good will; the example was contagious and the

clatter of knives and forks became general. Hereupon, several gentlemen who were not hungry cried out "Shame!" and looked very indignant: and several gentlemen who were hungry cried "Shame!" too, eating nevertheless all the while, as fast as they possibly could. In this dilemma one of the stewards mounted a bench and feelingly represented to the delinquents the enormity of their conduct, imploring them for decency's sake, to defer the process of mastication until the arrival of Earl Grey. This address was loudly cheered but totally unheeded: and this is, perhaps, one of the few instances on record of a dinner having been virtually concluded before it began.

Another literary visitor to Edinburgh was Charlotte Brontë in 1850 and she was no less ecstatic about the environment than other earlier travellers had been.

My dear Sir, do not think I blaspheme when I tell you that your great London, as compared to Dun-Edin, 'mine own romantic town', is as prose compared to poetry, or as a great rumbling, rambling, heavy epic compared to a lyric, brief, bright, clear, and vital as a flash of lightening. You have nothing like Scott's Monument, or if you had that, and all the glories of architecture assembled together, you have nothing like Arthur's Seat, and above all you have not the Scotch national character; and it is that grand character after all which gives the land its true charm, its true greatness.

As a child, Charlotte and her sisters and brother, Patrick Branwell, had been fascinated by the Edinburgh of *Blackwood's Magazine*, especially by the characters who peopled the *Noctes Ambrosianae*. Branwell was so consumed with admiration for the magazine that in December 1835 he had written to the editor offering his services on whatever terms the Blackwoods might suggest. "Now, sir, do not act like a commonplace person, but like a man willing to examine for himself. Do not turn from the native truth of my letters but prove me; and if I do not stand the proof I will not further press myself upon you. If I do stand it, why, you have lost an able writer in James Hogg, and God grant you may get one in Patrick Branwell Brontë (age 15)." The letters went unanswered and are still to be seen in a sad little group in the huge Blackwood collection held by the National Library.

The Brontë sisters, despite the grim drudgery of much of their lives, at least had the satisfaction of enjoying some success during their lifetimes. It might not have been so had they lived in Scotland where a lady was not expected to write fiction — indeed, many people doubted whether authorship was any kind of profession at all. Such was the case of Susan Ferrier, the youngest daughter of James Ferrier who was a close colleague of Walter Scott's in the Court of Session. When she sent Blackwood her first novel, *Marriage*, she concealed her identity and returned the proofs through a close friend. She went on to write two other novels, *Inheritance* and *Destiny*, but in the close-knit society of Edinburgh it was impossible to keep up the ruse and pressure was put upon her to lay aside her pen. Which is a pity, for in *Marriage* she has captured something of the dissimilation that was beginning to creep into Edinburgh life.

The day, though cold, was clear and sunny, and the lovely spectacle before them shone forth in all its gay magnificence. The blue waters lay calm and motionless. The opposite shores glowed in a thousand varied tints of wood and plain, rock and mountain, cultured field, and purple moor. Beneath, the Old Town reared its dark brow, and the New one stretched its golden lines, white, all around, the varied charms of nature lay scattered in that profusion, which nature's hand alone can bestow.

"Oh! this is exquisite!" exclaimed Mary, after a long pause, in which she had been rivetted in admiration of the scene before her. "And you are right, my dear uncle. The ideas which are inspired by the contemplation of such a spectacle as this are far — oh, how far! — superior to those excited by the mere works of art. There I can, at best, think but of the inferior àgents of Providence. Here the soul rises from Nature up to Nature's God."

"Upon my soul, you will be taken for a Methodist, Mary, if you talk in this manner," said Mr Douglas, with some marks of disquiet, as he turned round at the salutation of a fat elderly gentleman, whom he presently recognised as Bailie Broadfoot.

The first salutations over Mr Douglas's fears of Mary having been overheard recurred, and he felt anxious to remove any unfavourable impression with regard to his own principles, at least, from the mind of the enlightened magistrate.

"Your fine views here have set my niece absolutely raving," said he with a smile; "but I tell her it is only in romantic minds that fine scenery inspires romantic ideas. I dare say many of the worthy

152

inhabitants of Edinburgh walk here with no other idea than that of
sharpening their appetites for dinner."
   "Nae doot," said the Bailie, "it's a most capital place for that.
Were it no for that, I ken nae muckle use it would be of . . ."

Twenty years later, another woman novelist found that, whatever
society might think, writing was the only way she knew to make an
honest living. Born in April, 1828, in Wallyford near Musselburgh,
Margaret Oliphant married an impoverished artist and soon found
that hack writing was a reasonable means of financial independence.
From her house in Fettes Row articles, biographies, novels and
reviews flowed from her pen, mostly for the formidable John
Blackwood, who had taken over control of the family firm and who
had added George Eliot to his lists. Today most of Mrs Oliphant's
work is forgotten. She wrote too much too quickly and with too
little intellectual equipment to do her work justice; but she did
succeed in keeping her family's head above water and she has the
distinction of being Edinburgh's first full-time woman of letters. In
1897, the year of her death in London, she completed volume two of
her *Annals of a Publishing House*, the story of the Blackwoods, which
remains one of the best mines of literary anecdote of the period.
   Although, as the century progressed, the writing of fiction
slumped into that tartan-clad slough of Balmorality, the Kailyard,
there were still giants in the land who had links with the great days of
the past. Thomas Carlyle had left his Edinburgh home at 21 Comely
Bank in 1828 for Dumfries and then Chelsea, disappointed by the
failure of his application for the Chair of English Literature. He had
enjoyed a close association with the city while a student, and it was in
1822 that he had experienced the sudden flash of insight in Leith
Walk that changed his philosophy to the Everlasting NO. In 1866 he
returned to Edinburgh to become Lord Rector of the University.
Saddened, however, by his wife's death his return to the city
brought recognition, but little happiness.
   Charles Kirkpatrick Sharpe was still a familiar figure in Princes
Street, "an old gentleman, very peculiarly attired in a faded surtout
of utterly antique fashion, with a large and bulging cravat round his
throat, the lower curls of a light-brown wig visible between his hat
and his smooth and still ruddy cheeks, pumps on his thread-
stockinged feet instead of shoes or boots, and in his hand a green silk

umbrella." An historian and antiquarian by inclination he also possessed a notoriously sarcastic wit, and in Edinburgh was known by his visiting card which stated his name C. Sharpe in musical notation. Another writer who had given way to melancholia was Hugh Miller, a stonemason by trade, whose brilliant imagination shines through his two greatest works, *The Old Red Sandstone* and *My Schools and Schoolmasters*. On the 2nd December 1856, in a fit of acute depression, he shot himself in his house in Portobello High Street.

Of the figures in the gallery of Edinburgh writers whom we have met already, D.M. Moir perhaps enjoyed the most widespread popularity during the period. His writing helps to form the beginnings of the sentimental novel which was to have such a baleful effect on Scottish letters, and the book which made his name was the pawky *Mansie Wauch* which is partly set in Edinburgh.

> To those, nevertheless, that take the world as they find it, there are pleasures in all situations; nor was mine, bad though I allow it to be, entirely destitute of them; for our workroom being at the top of the stairs, and the light of heaven coming down through skylights, three in number, we could, by putting out our heads, have a vizzy of the grand ancient building of George Heriot's Hospital, with crowds of young laddies playing through the grass parks, with their bit brown coatees, and shining leather caps, like a wheen puddocks, and all the sweet country out by Barrowmuirhead, and thereaway; together with the Corstorphine Hills — and the Braid Hills — and the Pentland Hills — and all the rest of the hills covered here and there with tufts of blooming whins, as yellow as the beaten gold — spotted round about their bottoms with green trees and growing corn, but with tops as bare as a gaberlunzie's coat — kepping the rowling clouds on their awful shoulders on cold and misty days; and freckled over with the flowers of the purple heather, on which the shy moorfowl take a delight to fatten and fill their crops, through the cosey months of the blythe summertime.

Moir was, of course, a Blackwoodian and amongst his colleagues was another writer of the polite school of letters, William Edmonstoune Aytoun, whose wife was the youngest daughter of Christopher North. Aytoun contributed many humorous articles to *Blackwood's* and he wrote the patriotic *Lays of the Scottish Cavaliers* which, with their imitation of the best of Scott, enjoyed a great popularity in their day. John Blackwood was amongst his closest friends, and it was not an uncommon sight to see the two men pacing Great Stuart Street, Aytoun's address, in the deepest of conversations.

By mid-century Edinburgh had become a polite, bourgeois city, and as the suburbs grew, so did the New Town become a quieter place. Some authors and publishers still lived there, but for the time being, Edinburgh was not the great literary centre that it had been in Scott's day. The presses still thundered on, the city enjoyed its reputation of being a printing centre, but the material was becoming less creative, more concerned with books of an educational nature. In 1843, the firm of Thomas Nelson moved from their Grassmarket offices to Hope Park near the Meadows to set up their revolutionary rotary printing press. They pioneered the production of cheap classics for the mass market, and when fire destroyed their works, undeterred, they moved to larger premises in Dalkeith Road, beneath the Salisbury Crags.

The other great Victorian publisher was the long established house of Oliver and Boyd which had been founded in 1778 by Thomas Oliver as a printing press in the High Street near the Nether Bow. He had been joined by George Boyd in 1807 and in 1820 they had moved to their picturesque and warren-like offices in Tweed-dale Court to push themselves to the forefront of Scottish educational publishing. On a momentous day in 1836 a young bookseller's apprentice called James Thin, employed by James Macintosh of 5 North College Street, called at Oliver and Boyd and was mightily impressed with what he saw, " . . . they had gradually developed into publishers, printers, and bookbinders, and were the only firm who at that time carried on these departments". James Thin founded his own bookselling business opposite the University on South Bridge in 1841, and eventually became the largest bookseller in the city, but that early visit was remembered sixty years later when his two sons, James Hay and George Traquair, became controlling directors of Oliver and Boyd, together with John Grant, the other large bookseller in the city.

Oliver and Boyd had built up close links with the University which was expanding and re-inforcing its importance as a medical centre. Sir J.Y. Simpson discovered chloroform as an anaesthetic, Dr William Pulteney Alison pioneered medical assistance for the poor, Sir R.W. Philp detected the infectious nature of tuberculosis and Sir Henry Littlejohn became the city's first medical officer of health.

They all had good cause to work in Edinburgh. Up in the Old Town which had changed little since it had been abandoned to the poor at the end of the eighteenth century, the remaining tenements were a living nightmare. In 1851 half of the city's population, or 30,000 people, lived in crowded, insanitary hovels in the closes off the High Street and in the slums of the Cowgate — picturesque they may be in their restored state today, but one hundred years ago they were filthy sties — and it is astounding to note that many still kept farm animals in their houses and that the streets were still infected with the "Flowers of Edinburgh". Hardly surprisingly, in December 1861, the seven-storey tenement at 101 High Street tumbled to the ground taking with it over a hundred lives. One boy lived to tell the tale to the rescuers — "Heave awa chaps, I'm no dead yet!" he cried from the rubble — and he is commemorated by the carving of a boy's head set in the stonework above the present-day Paisley Close.

The city had also experienced the benefits of the industrial revolution. The railway had arrived in the 1840s, helping to draw Scotland and England even closer together, and the wheel of empire took away the country's brightest and best, to become soldiers on the North-West Frontier, doctors in southern India, engineers in East Africa and missionaries in the Far East. For the next hundred years it would be difficult for any talented youngster to stay and make a reputation in his or her native country — and that included writers too.

It was into this world, at once modern, and yet strapped to its past, that Robert Lewis Balfour Stevenson was born on 13th September, 1850 at 8 Howard Place in Stockbridge. (By a coincidence, that decade, Kenneth Grahame, the future author of *The Wind in the Willows* was born at 30 North Castle Street, but he left the city in infancy and was brought up in England.) Stevenson came from a long line of marine engineers. His father Thomas and his grandfather Robert were consultants to the Commissioners of Northern Lights and had spun a chain of lighthouses around

Scotland's rugged coasts from the Bell Rock off the Fife shore to
Skerryvore in the Outer Hebrides. His mother, Margaret Isabella
Balfour was the daughter of a minister in the village of Colinton and
a member of a well-established and respectable middle-class family.
As a child Louis, as he came to be styled, suffered from respiratory
illnesses which were not helped by his family's removal to a damp,
exposed house at 1 Inverleith Terrace in 1853. While he was there, he
was a prey to colds and croup but it was not until he was six years old
that the family doctor finally persuaded Thomas to move to a
warmer house for the sake of the child's health. They moved in 1856
to a terraced house which faced south towards the sun, number 17
Heriot Row, with its gas lamp outside the front door.

> My tea is nearly ready and the sun has left the sky;
> It's time to take the window to see Leerie going by;
> For every night at teatime and before you take your seat,
> With lantern and with ladder he comes posting up the street . . . .

> For we are very lucky, with a lamp before the door,
> And Leerie stops to light it as he lights so many more;
> And O! before you hurry by with ladder and with light,
> O Leerie, see a little child and nod to him tonight!

Continuous illness kept him apart from other youngsters during
his childhood — the reader need not look any further than to the
Child's Garden of Verses to find ample evidence of "the child alone"
— and it bred in him a life-long detestation of Edinburgh's fiercely
cold and damp weather.

> To none but those who have themselves suffered the thing in the
> body, can the gloom and depression of our Edinburgh winters be
> brought home. For some constitutions there is something almost
> physically disgusting in the bleak ugliness of easterly weather; the
> wind wearies, the sickly sky depresses them; and they turn back
> from their walk to avoid the aspect of the unrefulgent sun going
> down among perturbed and pallid mists. The days are so short that
> a man does much of his business, and certainly all his pleasure, by
> the haggard glare of gas lamps. The roads are as heavy as a fallow.
> People go by, so drenched and draggle-tailed that I have often
> wondered how they found the heart to undress. And meantime the
> wind whistles through the town as if it were an open meadow; and

if you lie awake all night, you hear it shrieking and raving overhead with a noise of shipwrecks and falling houses. In a word, life is so unsightly that there are times when the heart turns sick in a man's inside; and the look of a tavern, or the thought of the warm, fire-lit study, is like the touch of land to one who has been long struggling with the seas.

Stevenson was saved from becoming a neurotic and skinny, unprepossessing little boy by having as his companion a splendid nurse, Alison Cunningham, the "Cummy" to whom he dedicated *A Child's Garden of Verses*. As well as friendship, she offered him a solid grounding in the bible of the Old Testament and a consequent admiration for the Covenanters, a ripe knowledge of Scots and enough country superstitions to keep him awake at nights. It was all grist to the future writer's mill.

Summers were spent with his cousins at Colinton, then far enough from the city centre to be a rural retreat (some of the flavour of that life can be found in the walk through the woods along the Water of Leith, past the ruined mills to the churchyard in the old village) and North Berwick became a favourite family holiday haunt. At the age of ten he was sent to the Edinburgh Academy where the gangly boy earned a reputation for being bright but slightly aloof and unwilling to join in the organised ritual of a Victorian public school. As his education progressed it was tacitly assumed that Stevenson would follow the careers of his forbears and become an engineer, but the young boy was clearly laying the foundations of his future life as a writer. His father encouraged him to write the history of the Pentland Rising, the story of the defeat of the Covenanters at Rullion Green, and then had the pamphlet printed at his own expense. Writing as a career, though, was out of the question in his parent's eyes — why, even Sir Walter Scott was first and foremost an advocate.

In 1867 Stevenson followed his father's wishes and enrolled in the University of Edinburgh. It gave him the opportunity he had been looking for to break away from the bonds of home and parental authority and to have the day completely to himself. He learned to survive, too, working out in his first year a system to avoid lectures and seminars, and using the time instead to wander all over the city, which he came to know with a fond intimacy. Stevenson's love of

158

Edinburgh and his knowing awareness of the different stratas in its society, together with his knowledge of the steep wynds and narrow staircases of the Old Town has left us with one of the most finely drawn pictures of the city in his *Edinburgh: Picturesque Notes* of 1878.

It is true that the over-population was at least as dense in the epoch of lords and ladies, and that nowadays some customs which made Edinburgh notorious of yore have been fortunately pretermitted. But an aggregation of comfort is not distasteful like an aggregation of the reverse. Nobody cares how many lords and ladies, and divines and lawyers, may have been crowded into these houses in the past — perhaps the more the merrier. The glasses clink around the punch-bowl, some one touches the virginals, there are peacocks' feathers on the chimney, and the tapers burn clear and pale in the red firelight. That is not an ugly picture in itself, nor will it become ugly upon repetition. All the better if the like were going on in every second room; the land would only look the more inviting. Times are changed. In one house, perhaps two-score families herd together; and, perhaps, not one of them is wholly out of reach of want. The great hotel is given over to discomfort from the foundations to the chimney-tops; everywhere a pinching, narrow habit, scant meals, and an air of sluttishness and dirt. In the first room there is a birth, in another a death, in a third a sordid drinking bout, and the detective and the Bible-reader cross upon the stairs. High words are audible from dwelling to dwelling, and children have a strange experience from the first; only a robust soul, you would think, could grow up in such conditions without hurt. And even if God tempers His dispensations to the young, and all the ill does not arise that our apprehensions may forecast, the sight of such a way of living is disquieting to people who are more happily circumstanced. Social inequality is nowhere more ostentatious than at Edinburgh. I have mentioned already how, to the stroller along Princes Street, the High Street callously exhibits its back garrets. It is true, there is a garden between. And although nothing could be more glaring by way of contrast, sometimes the opposition is more immediate; sometimes the thing lies in a nutshell, and there is not so much as a blade of grass between the rich and the poor. To look over the South Bridge and see the Cowgate below full of crying hawkers, is to view one rank of society from another in the twinkling of an eye.

All Edinburgh became his playground and he became a lover, too, of the city's pubs, especially of Rutherford's in Drummond Street. The drouthy atmosphere of earlier days had gone for ever but men still sat down to dinner at five o'clock and were expected to drink through to midnight or later, and still do a full day's work the following bleary-eyed day. Amongst the cruelly oppressed working classes drunkenness was universal, indeed for many it was the only opiate in otherwise poverty-stricken lives, and to cater for their customer's needs pubs in Edinburgh opened at six o'clock in the morning and did not close their doors until eleven at night. Drink was cheap too with whisky twopence a nip or half-a-crown the bottle. It was with good reason that Stevenson noted sardonically, "A Scot of poetic temperament, and without religious exaltation, drops as if by nature into the public house. The picture may not be pleasing; but what else is a man to do in this dog's weather?"

Like Scott before him, Stevenson was made a member of the Speculative Society and though he did not shine conspicuously there it soon became a vital part of his Edinburgh life. His social life, too, was important: friends like James Ferrier and Charles Baxter dined at Heriot Row; he took part in theatricals in the home of Fleeming Jenkin, professor of engineering at the University; and skating on the frozen Duddingston Loch provided an ideal setting for early romantic adventures.

> Now fancy paints that bygone day
> When you were here, my fair —
> The whole lake rang with rapid skates
> In the windless, wintry air.
>
> You leaned to me, I leaned to you,
> Our course was smooth as flight —
> We steered — a heel-touch to the left,
> A heel-touch to the right.
>
> We swung our way through flying men,
> Your hand lay fast in mine,
> We saw the shifting crowd dispart,
> The level ice-reach shine.
>
> I swear by yon swan-travelled lake,
> By yon calm hill above,

I swear had we been drowned that day
We had been drowned in love.

Sexual relations within his own class were well-nigh impossible, and like his contemporaries, Stevenson turned to the brothels and pubs that made up the city's low life in Lothian Road and Leith Walk. Wearing the velvet coat, by which name the prostitutes came to know him, he moved easily and freely within their world, claiming at an early age: "I have been all my days a dead hand at a harridan, I never saw the one yet that could resist me." In the underworld he also came to know a common humanity that was far removed from the starched primness of suburban life.

I walk the streets smoking my pipe
And I love the dallying shop-girl
That leans with rounded stern to look at the fashions;
And I hate the bustling citizen,
The eager and hurrying man of affairs I hate,
Because he wears his intolerance writ on his face
And every movement and word of him tells me how
much he hates me.

I love night in the city,
The lighted streets and the swinging gait of harlots.
I love cool pale morning,
In the empty bye-streets,
With only here and there a female figure,
A slavey with lifted dress and the key in her hand,
A girl or two at play in a corner of waste-land
Tumbling and showing their legs and crying out to me
loosely.

Feelings that are common to many young men, these early experiences left their mark and in later life he was to look back at them with a sense of fondness and regret, especially in the letters to Charles Baxter who became a life-long friend and manager of his financial affairs.

Pray write to me something cheery. A little Edinburgh gossip, in heaven's name. Ah! what would I not give to steal this evening with you through the big, echoing college archway, and away south under the street to dear Brash's, now defunct! But the old time is dead also, never, never to revive. It was a sad time too, but so gay and so hopeful, and we had such sport with all our low spirits and all our distresses, that it looks like a lamplit, vicious fairy land behind me. O for ten Edinburgh minutes, six pence between us, and the ever glorious Lothian Road, or dear, mysterious Leith Walk!

Frequenting the city's underworld also put him firmly in partnership with Edinburgh writers of the past like Fergusson and Burns who delighted in the city's low life and in the hypocrisy of its vision. It gave him the background for a good short story, *The Misadventures of John Nicholson* — a splendid evocation of the Calton Hill and the howffs of Greenside at the top of Leith Walk — and it gave him living proof of Calvin's dynamic aspect of evil which lies at the roots of *Dr Jekyll and Mr Hyde*. It would be wrong, though, to suggest that this side of his life caused problems at home, as it was not until his mercurial cousin Bob Stevenson, a fledgling artist, arrived in Edinburgh that a serious breach took place within the family.

Bob had a dramatic effect on his already impressionable cousin. He was brimming with ideas about *la vie boheme* and had been deeply impressed by the Aesthetes while at Cambridge: in Louis he found an avid pupil. Never the most attentive of students at University, Stevenson embraced the ideals of bohemian life, wore a velveteen jacket, kerchef and wideawake hat, kept late hours and scorned the life of the bourgeoisie.

> O fine religious, decent folk,
> In Virtue's flaunting gold and scarlet,
> I sneer between two puffs of smoke —
> Give me the publican and harlot.

Particularly obnoxious to him were the growing suburbs with their standardised architecture and the Pooter-like existences of their inhabitants. For those he reserved his particular scorn.

> Day by day, one new villa, one new object of offence, is added to another; all around Newington and Morningside, the dismallest structures keep springing up like mushrooms; the pleasant hills are loaded with them, each impudently squatted in its garden, each

roofed and carrying chimneys like a house. And yet a glance of an eye discovers their true character. They are not houses; for they were not designed with a view to human habitation, and the internal arrangements are, as they tell me, fantastically unsuited to the needs of man. They are not buildings; for you can scarcely say a thing is built where every measurement is in clamant disproportion with its neighbour. They belong to no style of art, only to a form of business much to be regretted.

Inevitably, stories about his new-found life trickled back to Heriot Row and in the winter of 1873 the storm broke between father and son. The theories of Herbert Spencer and Charles Darwin had taken a grip on the cousins and their cronies and Thomas Stevenson's discovery of his son's agnosticism plunged the family into a state of war. Much of the blame was placed on Bob and throughout the year the quarrel between father and son lay uneasily below a brittle surface. A wretched winter brought about a respite as Louis's illness flared up again. Tuberculosis was suspected and he was sent off on his first travels to Europe in a life-long search for better health.

It was the beginning of the end of his relationship with the Edinburgh of his childhood. He returned to study law, to complete his studies and to see a brass nameplate, "R.L. Stevenson, Advocate" placed on the door of his parents' house, but writing was taking up more and more of his time. Leslie Stephen, the editor of the *Cornhill*, published him and encouraged him, and in 1875 he became friendly with W.E. Henley, a critic and litterateur who was to be a stormy petrel of a friend for years to come. Henley was then a patient in the old Edinburgh Infirmary, suffering from the ravages of tuberculosis, and he later retained his brief connection with the city by taking up the editorship with Charles Whibley of the *Scots Observer*.

That same year warmer weather was again recommended for Louis and he set off on the longest and most momentous travels of his life: to France, to marriage with Fanny Osbourne, to America, back to Europe and then to Bournemouth, to the beginnings of a dazzling literary career. Thirteen years later, while he was in Bournemouth considering his next move, his father died and he returned to Edinburgh for the last time. By then the breach with his father had been healed and there was little to tie him to the city and to its long damp winters. So the family set off again, with Louis's mother in tow, to the United States and from there to the Pacific where he died of a brain haemhorrage on 3rd December 1894 on the island of Samoa.

He left two unfinished novels, both aglow with his love for the Edinburgh he had known in earlier years — *Weir of Hermiston*, a powerful study of conflict between father and son which has as its protagonist an elderly Scottish judge who is plainly based on Lord Braxfield; and *St Ives*, which is partially set in the village of Swanston, in the lee of the Pentland Hills.

> Once clear of this foolish fellow, I went on again up a gradual hill, descended on the other side through the houses of a country village, and came at last to the bottom of the main ascent leading to the Pentlands and my destination. I was some way up when the fog began to lighten; a little farther, and I stepped by degrees into a clear starry night, and saw in front of me, and quite distinct, the summits of the Pentlands, and behind, the valley of the Forth, and the city of my late captivity buried under a lake of vapour . . . . The east grew luminous and was barred with chilly colours, and the Castle on its rock, and the spires and chimneys of the upper town took gradual shape, and arose like islands, out of the receding cloud. All about me was still and sylvan; the road mounting and winding, with nowhere a sign of any passenger, the birds chirping, I suppose for warmth, the boughs of the trees knocking together, and the red leaves falling in the wind.

Swanston was a favourite childhood haunt and in the distant Pacific islands he was able to remember each detail of this charming, white-washed village that nestles beneath the gaunt ridge of Caerketton. Today, despite the advancing army of bungalows, it remains a place of tranquility — climb the pathway over the golf course up the steep slope of the Pentlands on a misty winter's day when most of south Edinburgh is blotted out with only the Castle and Arthur's Seat and the ridge of the Old Town breaking the skyline to see it at its best. The shade of RLS would have little reason to believe that his view had changed at all.

For Edinburgh from afar became a recurring nostalgic motif in the poetry that he wrote from Samoa and the Pentland Hills were never far away from his mind's eye.

THE VICTORIAN AGE

The tropics vanish, and meseems that I,
From Halkerside, from topmost Allermuir,
Or steep Caerketton, dreaming gaze again.
Far set in fields and woods, the town I see
Spring gallant from the shallows of her smoke,
Cragged, spired, and turreted, her virgin fort
Beflagged. About, on seaward-drooping hills,
New folds of city glitter. Last the Forth
Wheels ample waters set with sacred isles,
And populous Fife smokes with a score of towns.

Stevenson also wrote in Scots — it was still considered proper in his class to have a knowledge of the tongue, even though standard English had become the order of the day in business and social dealings — and in one of his best poems, *Ille Terrarum*, written for Charles Baxter, he viewed Edinburgh in all its different moods.

Frae nirly, nippin', Eas'lan' breeze,
Frae Norlan' snaw, an' haar o' seas,
Weel happit in your gairden trees,
    A bonny bit,
Atween the muckle Pentland's knees,
    Secure ye sit.

Beeches an' aiks entwine their theek,
An' firs, a stench, auld-farrant clique.
A' simmer day, your chimleys reek,
    Couthy and bien;
An' here an' there your windies keek
    Amang the green.

Edinburgh, then, was never far away from his thoughts, and of all the city's writers, Stevenson was most able to view the place in all its complexities, to celebrate it, to chide gently its citizens and to see clearly the two lives that existed within its grey, windy streets. Even at the very end of his life Edinburgh was still pulling at his heart-strings. In the manuscript of *Weir of Hermiston*, Fanny found a dedicatory verse to her which was included as the book's dedication. Its second verse is a moving declaration of love to a woman who had fortified his life and work, but the opening lines are written with the misty eye of nostalgia.

PRECIPITOUS CITY

I saw rain falling and the rainbow drawn
On Lammermuir. Hearkening I heard again
In my precipitous city beaten bells
Winnow the keen sea wind. And here afar
Intent on my own race and place I wrote.

Before his death, Stevenson was much taken up with thoughts of
his homeland and in a letter to Lord Rosebery, to whom he had sent a
copy of *Catriona*, he was at pains to point out that although he had
been "vigorously unhappy" in Scotland, he still wished that he
"could be buried there — among the hills, say, on the head of
Allermuir — with a table tombstone like a Cameronian". The
homesickness he felt had been triggered off by the dedication to him
of a novel, *The Stickit Minister*, by S.R. Crockett.

The publication of that novel in 1893 helped Samuel Rutherford
Crockett, a Free Church minister in the village of Penicuik near
Edinburgh, to give up his calling and turn wholeheartedly to
authorship. From his prolific pen came forty novels, each one of
them being monumentally successful and making him one of the
wealthiest writers of his time. Today they are justly forgotten but in
his day they gave Crockett a lifestyle that was light years away from
the poverty he had known as a student at the University of
Edinburgh. It was not uncommon for undergraduates to be
poverty-stricken — there were no grants and bursaries were fiercely
competed for — and Crockett was always proud of the fact in later
life that he had existed on oatmeal, penny rolls and milk during his
university days. In Crockett's last year as a divinity student, 1878, a
freshman took up residence in Cumberland Street and although he
was lucky enough to have some private means he was especially
observant of his fellow students' plight.

I knew three undergraduates who lodged together in a dreary
house at the top of a dreary street; two of them used to study until
two in the morning, while the third slept. When they shut up their
books they woke number three, who arose, dressed and studied
until breakfast time. Among the many advantages of this
arrangement the chief was that, as they were dreadfully poor, one
bed did for the three. Two of them occupied it at the one time, and
the third at another. Terrible privations? Frightful destitution? Not
a bit of it. The Millenium was in those days. If life was at the top of

166

a hundred steps, if students occasionally died of hunger and hard work combined, if the midnight oil only burned to show a ghastly face 'weary and worn', if lodgings were cheap and dirty, and dinners few and far between, life was still real and earnest; in many cases it did not turn out an empty dream.

The dispassionate observer was James Matthew Barrie, the future creator of Peter Pan who gained a name for himself in his Edinburgh years by writing theatre criticism and book reviews for the *Edinburgh Courant*.

Crockett and Barrie became leading members of the school of writing known as the Kailyard which presented a sloppy picture of a never-never land of rural virtue, normally presided over by the discerning eye of the local minister. Manipulating that rash of sentimentality was Sir William Robertson Nicoll, editor of the *British Weekly*, who was also a patron, from his London office, of the other two main Kailyarders, "Ian Maclaren" (John Watson, a Church of Scotland minister) and Annie S. Swan.

Born near the village of Coldingham in Berwickshire, in 1859, Annie S. Swan spent her early years in Edinburgh, in a house which stood at the top of Easter Road, "then a lovely country lane bordered by fields and hedges, white with May bloom and pink wild roses in summer". Later her father farmed at Gorebridge in Midlothian and he sent his daughter to be educated at Queen Street Ladies College in Edinburgh (later to be Mary Erskine's School). She started writing early, winning a Christmas story competition in the *People's Journal* while at school and achieving overnight success at the age of twenty-four with her second novel, *Aldersyde*. By then she was married to a medical student and living in a flat in Morningside where she kept open house for her husband's student friends. At that time, too, Margaret Oliphant became the first of many critics to attack the bitter-sweet sentimentality of her novels, but Annie S. Swan was unabashed, claiming in her autobiography, "the public had no fault to find with it and asked for more. After all, it is the reading public which passes the final judgment on any book."

Despite that rap over the knuckles Annie S. Swan was an assiduous collector of friends and during her stay in Edinburgh and later in Musselburgh she was the unlikely companion of Patrick Geddes and his wife Anna, pioneers of modern social work and town planning, who were responsible for much restoration work in the Lawnmarket and for the construction of Ramsay Gardens on the site of Ramsay's "Goose-Pie" house. Although she lived latterly in England, Annie S. Swan continued her associations with Scotland through Robertson Nicoll's publications, especially through articles in *The Woman at Home*, a precursor of today's glossy women's magazines. Surprisingly, during her Edinburgh days she never met Dr John Brown — the "Scottish Charles Lamb", as many critics called him — who lived at 23 Rutland Street. His collection of essays, *Rab and his Friends*, is a miniature masterpiece, at its best in his understanding of the human nature of many dogs.

> There, under the large arch of the South Bridge, is a huge mastiff, sauntering down the middle of the causeway, as if with his hands in his pockets: he is old, grey, brindled; as big as a little Highland bull, and he has the Shakespearean dewlaps shaking as he goes.

As the century wore on, Brown's medical practice became of less importance to him and he became a friend of many leading men of the day and a raconteur whose fame spread beyond the bounds of Edinburgh. Thackeray visited him before his death in 1863, and later Brown recorded the memory of that unusual visit.

> We cannot resist here recalling one Sunday evening in December when he (Thackeray) was walking with two friends along the Dean Road, to the west of Edinburgh — one of the noblest outlets to any city. It was a lovely evening — such a sunset as one never forgets; a rich, dark bar of cloud hovered over the sun, going down behind the Highland hills, lying bathed in amethystine bloom; between this cloud and the hills there was a narrow strip of pure ether, of a tender cowslip colour, lucid, and as if it were the very body of heaven in its clearness, every object standing out as if etched upon the sky. The north-west end of Corstorphine Hill, with its trees and rocks, lay in the heart of this pure radiance, and there a wooden crane, used in the quarry below, was so placed as to assume the figure of a cross; there it was, unmistakeable, lifted up against the crystalline sky. All three gazed at it silently. As they gazed, he gave utterance in a tremulous, gentle, and rapid voice, to what all were feeling, in the word "Calvary!"

Although an occasional writer Brown's essays were deservedly popular, and the tradition of writing private literature continued in the city. Alexander Smith's *A Summer in Skye*, an early travel book, has a stunning description of Edinburgh in winter and Edward Bannerman Ramsay, the episcopalian Dean of Edinburgh, wrote the immensely successful *Reminiscences of Scottish Life and Character* which went through twenty editions after its original publication. But for all the busy scribbling in the city at the end of the century there were very few writers of any stature. In November 1889 the *Scotsman* noted gloomily that there were only sixty-two publishers left in the city — many of whom devoted their output to religious and educational books — and that apart from the *Scotsman* which had been founded in 1817, there seemed to be fewer newspapers than in earlier years.

There was, though, a flourishing public library. The Public Library Act of 1850, sponsored by a Scotsman, William Ewart, member for Dumfries, had been adopted in Scotland three years later and the first public library was started in the city in 1886. Later, in 1895, with funds from Andrew Carnegie, the great Scottish benefactor, it opened in its present splendid headquarters on George IV Bridge. Another bright star on the city's cultural horizon was the opening of the Royal Lyceum Theatre in Grindlay Street on 10th September 1883 with a gala performance starring Ellen Terry and Henry Irving. At the other end of the scale were the ridiculous poetry readings given by William MacGonagall, poet and tragedian, who had been born in the city in 1830, the son of a handloom weaver. Although he spent most of his life in Dundee, he was a frequent visitor to Edinburgh and his poem in praise of Scotland's capital would have been considered a doubtful joke had it not come from the hand of MacGonagall.

At the time of the Lyceum's opening, a young medical graduate of the University of Edinburgh sent *Blackwood's* a story, *The Actor's Duel*, which was hurriedly turned down by the editor. Several other attempts were made, with other stories, until the young doctor tired of banging his head against the magazine's stolid management and sent his work instead to the newly-founded *Strand Magazine*. The July 1891 issue of that magazine made Dr Arthur Conan Doyle famous overnight with the publication of *A Scandal in Bohemia*, the first of many Sherlock Holmes stories.

Conan Doyle had been born in Edinburgh on 22nd May 1859, in his parent's house at 11 Picardy Place. His father was a clerk of works at the Office of Works in Holyrood Palace and a devout Catholic who sent Arthur to a rigid education at Stonyhurst. From there he went up to study medicine at Edinburgh in the class of Dr Joseph Bell, a pioneer in forensic medicine, who was to become one of the models for Sherlock Holmes. Like his fellow alumni of the age, Barrie and Stevenson, Conan Doyle disliked Edinburgh for its grim winter and equally bleak university.

> Edinburgh University may call herself, with grim jocoseness, the "alma mater" of her students, but if she is to be mother at all, she is one of a very stoic and Spartan cast, who conceals her maternal affection with remarkable success. The only signs of interest she ever deigns to evince towards her alumni are upon those not infrequent occasions when guineas are to be demanded from them.

He could see no future for himself in Edinburgh and as soon as he had graduated he left his tiny, cluttered flat in Howe Street and set up practice in Southsea, a suburb of Portsmouth.

Apart from the accident of birth, Edinburgh could hardly make any claim on Conan Doyle. The city does not figure as a backdrop in his writing, but his studies under distinguished doctors like Bell, Maclagen and Rutherford and his knowledge of the insanitary horrors of the Old Town gave him fuel for his detective fiction. He returned infrequently on brief visits to lunch with W.E. Henley in Thistle Street, but the thought of living in Edinburgh never crossed his mind. Success lay elsewhere and like many other men of his generation he took the road south, to enormous success as a writer, to a knighthood in 1902 and to a rich and fulfilled life. He died on 7th July 1930 in Sussex, secure in his new-found spiritual belief that he was setting out on the greatest adventure of all.

Chapter Nine

Modern Times

In April 1907 a new magazine, the *Scottish Review*, was launched in Edinburgh from the offices of the publisher Thomas Nelson. It had started life as a religious magazine, but its editor, a young Scottish publisher called John Buchan, who was also busy making his name as an author, was determined that his magazine should eschew the politics and culture of the parish pump. In a letter to Lord Rosebery, he said that its aim would be "to deal fully with all interests, literary, political and social, with something Scottish in the point of view. We want to make it the centre of a Scottish school of letters such as Edinburgh had a hundred years ago."

The magazine remained in existence for two brief years but during Buchan's editorship it published the great literary names of the day and demonstrated a marked distaste for the Kailyard. It folded because it lacked a readership but its publication saw the beginning of a dream in the twentieth century to establish in Edinburgh a literary, intellectual and political magazine that would reflect from a Scottish point of view the growing interest in international affairs. Although they had the capital to underwrite the venture, Nelsons were dismayed by the tepid response and Buchan turned to editing the famous Nelson Sixpenny Classics and becoming a mainstay of the publishing team in London.

Buchan enjoyed a long association with Nelson until his commitments to politics and public life gradually eased him out of full-time publishing, and he came to spend even less time in Edinburgh. His next visits to the city were to be more momentous: in Spring 1933 he was Lord High Commissioner to the General Assembly of the Church of Scotland with his headquarters in the Palace of Holyrood, and four years later he was elected Lord Chancellor of the University of Edinburgh. During his younger years Buchan had not been such an establishment man and had launched several biting attacks on the Kailyarders, calling their work "the land of vapidity and prosiness". A son of the manse himself, he had good cause to reject their virtuous image of kirk-and-manse life and he turned instead to the London of the *Yellow Book*.

But Buchan, although an Edinburgh publisher, was not of Edinburgh. Born in Perth and educated in Glasgow, he spent his early summers in the Borders before his career took him to Oxford and to the glittering prizes of public success. Twenty years later, a fellow Borderer, Christopher Murray Grieve, called Buchan, "Dean of the Faculty of Scottish Letters" in a remarkable series of essays on contemporary Scottish literature which were published in the *Scottish Educational Journal* between 1925 and 1927 from the Moray Place headquarters of the Educational Institute of Scotland.

Grieve had been born on 11th August 1892 in the Border town of Langholm, and after an education at the local academy, where he came under the influence of the composer Frances George Scott, he moved to Edinburgh in September 1908 to take up an appointment as a student-teacher at Broughton Higher Grade School in Macdonald Road. (The Scots had pioneered the monitorial system of education where older pupils assisted in teaching.) By that time Grieve's mind had been enriched by study in Langholm's Telford Library and he was writing poetry. At Broughton the principal teacher of English, George Ogilvie encouraged the young man to write and to edit the school's magazine.

> I remember vividly Grieve's arrival amongst us. I see the little, slimly built figure in hodden grey, the small, sharp-featured face with its piercing eyes, the striking head with its broad brow and the great mass of flaxen curly hair. He hailed from Langholm, and had a Border accent you could have cut with a knife. I am afraid some of the city students smiled at first at the newcomer, but he very speedily won their respect. He certainly very quickly established himself in mine. His first essay (an unseen done in class) is still to my mind the finest bit of work I have got in Broughton.

That promise of that "finest bit of work" had expanded by the time Ogilvie noted it in 1920 and from then, until his death in September 1978 Grieve, under his poetic *nom de guerre*, Hugh

MacDiarmid, was to be the major influence on Scottish writing in the twentieth century. There seemed to be little that was beyond his powers: gem-like lyrical poems in Scots, long philosophical poems of power and passion, a unique understanding of his country's political ills and a determination to bring about a new flowering of Scottish letters. Most of his life, too, was spent away from the physical centre — he lived in the Highlands, London, Whalsay in the Shetlands, the Borders, but he kept in touch with Edinburgh through his myriad publishing enterprises, and if he became a frequent visitor to the city he was also not slow in attacking the place for its faults.

> So the mighty impetus of creative force
> That seeks liberation, that shows even through
> The scum of swinish filth of bourgeois society,
> The healthy creative force will break through
> — Even in Edinburgh — and good, human things grow,
> Protecting and justifying faith
> In regeneration to a free and noble life
> When labour shall be a thing
> Of honour, valour, and heroism
> And "civilisation" no longer like Edinburgh
> On a Sabbath morning,
> Stagnant and foul with the rigid peace
> Of an all-tolerating frigid soul!

MacDiarmid, as might be expected, had no time at all for the Kailyarders, nor indeed for anyone else like the Portobello-born music hall comic, Harry Lauder, who created an image of Scotland as a quaint backwater full of kilts and sporrans, porridge and whisky. In his attacks on these blights on Scottish culture he was joined by another poet, Lewis Spence, who also saw the possibility of regenerating Scots as a living language.

Spence had been born in Broughty Ferry near Dundee but he had links with Edinburgh through his grandfather, a university professor, and he came to live in the city in 1892. While a sub-editor on the *Scotsman*, he founded the Ten Club with the paper's news editor William Robertson. Apart from its social side, the Ten Club spent a good deal of time and energy in print berating Robertson Nicoll and his *British Weekly* and Spence became, with MacDiarmid,

173

a founding figure in the movement — the Scots Literary Renaissance — to find a form of Scots that would "bring Scottish literature into closer touch with current European tendencies in technique and ideation". Spence wrote a classical Scots, reminiscent at its best of the sixteenth-century work of the Scots makars.

> O wad this braw hie-heapit toun
> Sail aff like an enchanted ship,
> Drift owre the warld's seas up and doun
> And kiss wi' Venice lip to lip,
> Or anchor into Naples Bay
> A misty island far astray,
> Or set her rock to Athens' wa',
> Pillar to pillar, stane to stane,
> The cruikit spell o' her backbane,
> Yon shadow-mile o' spire nad vane,
> Wad ding them a'! Wad ding them a'!

From his house at 34 Howard Place Spence was a seminal influence on literary life in Edinburgh, helping to found the Scottish National Party in 1929 and turning to a deep and comprehensive understanding of the world's mythologies, work which gave him an international reputation.

The Edinburgh that both poets knew was in a state of hurried transition. Speculative building had expanded the city, with sprawling suburbs that quickly swallowed up Stevenson's Colinton and extended towards the Pentland Hills and west along the old Glasgow Road. The First World War speeded up the development of the motor car and although Edinburgh developed a marvellous system of electric and cable-car tramways, these were later abandoned, allowing the petrol engine to pollute the atmosphere and foul up the city's streets. The motor car and lorry became problems, still not solved, for a city council which had inherited three different kinds of city, in the Old Town, the New Town and the modern suburbs. Something of that early hustle and bustle of an Edinburgh just before the First World War can be felt in a description penned by G.K. Chesterton who came north on the behalf of the London *Daily News*.

It seems like a city built on precipices: a perilous city. Although the

174

actual ridges and valleys are not (of course) really very high or very deep, they stand up like strong cliffs; they fall like open chasms. There are turns of the steep street that take the breath away like a literal abyss. There are thoroughfares, full, busy, and lined with shops, which yet give the emotions of an Alpine Stair. It is, in the only adequate word for it, a sudden city. Great roads rush down like rivers in spate. Great buildings rush up like rockets. But the sensation produced by this violent variety of levels is one even more complex and bizarre. It is partly owing to the hundred veils of the vaporous atmosphere, which make the earth itself look like the sky, as if the town were hung in heaven, descending like the New Jerusalem.

The First World War, as well as altering the shape of the city, also changed dramatically the lives of its inhabitants who survived. Wilfred Owen and Siegfried Sassoon, two of the finest English poets of the war, spent a period of convalescence in 1917 in the nursing home at Craiglockhart, once a hydropathic hotel and today a teacher's training college, which Sassoon described as "a gloomy, cavernous place even on a July afternoon". In the great powers' upholding of the independence of the Balkan states and "poor little Belgium" MacDiarmid saw the need for self-determination in Scotland; and for others, like the novelist Bruce Marshall, the war expanded horizons beyond the cosiness of home and hearth. Marshall was born on 24th June 1899, educated at two Scottish public schools — Edinburgh Academy and Trinity College, Glenalmond — and during the war he served as a captain with the Royal Irish Fusiliers and lost a leg. Far from finishing him, the injury spurred him on to take a degree at Edinburgh and to start writing seriously.

In 1927 he published his first novel, *Teacup Terrace*, a shrewd satire of middle-class life in the city which scandalised Edinburgh. The city became too small to hold him and he left to work in France where he lives to this day after a fruitful career as a novelist and script-writer. Like other exiles, though, his heart has never been far away from his birthplace and in a recently published novel, *The Black Oxen*, the optimistic post-war years of the nineteen-twenties come alive on the page.

When they arrived at the brightly lit dancing hall in Fountainbridge, three noisy young drunks were being ejected by the chucker-out. Before she reluctantly gave them their tickets the girl at the desk inhaled a sample of Binnie's, Maconochie's and Neil's breaths.

Inside, the orchestra was playing 'Oh, Oh, My Sweet Hortense' and on the dance floor a mixed bag of semi-sober advocates, writers to the signet, solicitors to the supreme court, chartered accountants, students and keelies were revolving with a kaleido-scope of typists, instructresses, brickfaced Murrayfield heiresses and lugubrious tarts.

"Flora Goodwillie, by all that isn't holy." Maconochie drew Binnie's and Neil's attention to an outstandingly pretty red-haired girl sitting unaccountably alone in the dance instructresses' pen. "Bonniest eyes in the whole of Scotland, but an accent you could hang up the washing on. Wonder what made *her* take up the Palais."

"Buffers like yon could stop the Flying Scotsman going full tilt at Longniddry," Binnie said. "Fine I'd like a wee sit out with her. Shouldn't be surprised if she fishes it out for you."

Dismissing Binnie's lewd vignette as so much paranoia, and excited rather than repelled by his description of the girl's relief, Neil left his companions and strode quickly across to the pen.

"May I have this one, please?" he asked.

"Have you got a ticket? Och, what does it matter? After all, this is Hogmanay." What Maconochie had said about the girl's accent was an understatement: you could drive a train across the Firth of Forth on her vowels; but what Maconochie had said about the girl's beauty had been inadequate: her violet eyes must be the loveliest in the whole wide world.

Marshall's description of the Fountainbridge Palais is far removed from Fergusson's Cape Club or Burns' Crochallan Fencibles but it does give some idea of the gulf that continued to exist in the city. The middle classes may have been prepared to drink heavily and go whoring, but their indiscretions were rarely committed with their own class, and it is indicative of a changed social use of language that the young ex-army officers should find Flora's accent so repugnant. *The Black Oxen* follows fifty years of the fortunes of Neil Duncan and his contemporaries, their careers as respectable lawyers and stockbrokers, their sexual hi-jinks and affairs, all set against the background of professional Edinburgh. Much of the action is thinly veiled and one of the novel's comic triumphs is the description of Ma Blinkbonnie's salon which is not a thousand miles away from the Danube Street brothel which was finally closed down in 1976.

Other writers associated with the city at that time also went on to make reputations elsewhere. Sir Hugh Walpole's father was, for a time, Bishop of Edinburgh and Dame Cicely Fairfield who wrote under the name Rebecca West was educated at George Watsons Ladies' College. Although her career as an actress took her to London where she started writing, Hugh MacDiarmid was moved in 1926 to say that her novel, *The Judge*, was "the best Scottish novel of recent years".

Both writers left Edinburgh for domestic reasons and enjoyed success in London — by that time the main publishing centre in Britain. But other writers living in Edinburgh were not so fortunate. The historian George Scott-Moncrieff returned to Edinburgh in 1932, anxious to become part of the new nationalist movement that was sweeping through the country's intellectual circles, only to find that Scottish publishing had been reduced to a "vacuum that would be insufferable in any other country with a five million literate population". In a sense he was right. The larger publishers had become more interested in producing educational books, leaving literary publishing in the hands of enthusiasts like the Porpoise Press who published poetry pamphlets and the work of novelists like Neil Gunn from their offices in 133 George Street, and the Moray Press which was owned by Grants, the Princes Street booksellers. Even MacDiarmid who was fast becoming recognised as a major force in the land found difficulty in being published.

John Buchan had persuaded Blackwood to bring out *Sangschaw* in 1925 and *A Drunk Man Looks at the Thistle* a year later but from then onwards MacDiarmid had to fight hard to find a stable publishing platform. At that time he was editing *The Northern Review*, one of a succession of general cultural magazines which flickered briefly in Edinburgh; Henley's *Scots Observer* was still published in London under the editorship of William Power, and *The Freeman*, a political magazine, was published by Robin Black from India Buildings. The impetus behind this flurry of magazine publishing activity was the emergence of the nationalist movement — the National Party of Scotland had been founded in 1928 in an attempt to bring together the very disparate nationalist groups and in the new party were writers like Lewis Spence, MacDiarmid, R.B. Cunninghame Graham and Compton Mackenzie. Argument and counter-argument was rife and for the first time in many years Edinburgh rang to claims about the legality of the union with England. Even the newly-formed BBC, under the control of David Cleghorn Thomson, entered the debate with a symposium called "Scotland in Search of her Youth", and on 5th November 1929 the novelist Compton Mackenzie, who had returned to Edinburgh in search of his Scottish roots, broadcast his famous address "What's wrong with Scotland?" which ended with the words which gave MacDiarmid the inspiration for one of his best-loved lyrics, *The White Rose of Scotland*.

> We have grafted ourselves upon the rich rose of England. It has flourished on our stock. We have served it well. But the suckers of the wild Scots rose are beginning to show green underneath. Let them grow and blossom, and let the alien graft above, however rich, wither and die. You know our wild Scots rose? it is white, and small, and prickly, and possesses a sharp sweet scent which makes the heart ache.

Another writer who was closely identified with the Nationalist movement was the Orkney novelist Eric Linklater who had spent his years after graduating from the University of Aberdeen in India as an academic and journalist. An infrequent visitor to Edinburgh, his novel *Magnus Merriman* is, nevertheless, an exhilarating glance at the city in the nineteen-thirties, at an Edinburgh whose Old Town was as full of squalid, tumble-down public houses as it had ever been.

> Like a great battlement the north side of the High Street confronted them. From their lower level a long flight of steps led upwards, a narrow passage between black walls whose farther end was invisible, and on whose middle distance a lamp shone dimly. Here and there on the steps, obscurely seen, were vague figures. Under the lamp, with harsh voice and combative gesture, two men were quarreling. Another, oblivious to them and perhaps to all the world, leaned against the wall with drooping head. From the high remote darkness of the passage came the shrill sound of a woman laughing, and from the tavern whose door the lamp

lighted there issued, muffled by the walls, the multifarious sound of talk and argument and rival songs.

Meiklejohn grew more cheerful as they climbed the steps, and he pushed his way impatiently past the men at the door. One of them turned indignantly and asked him where the hell he thought he was going. Meiklejohn paid no attention, and the man followed him into the crowded bar, his temper ruffled, bent on pursuing this new quarrel.

"Hey!" he said, and took Meiklejohn by the shoulder, "did you no hear me? Or are you deaf as well as blind?"

"That's all right," said Meiklejohn.

"Oh, that's all right, is it?" said the man with an offensive parody of Meikljohn's voice.

Magnus spoke soothingly: "He hasn't done you any harm. If he pushed you it was only by accident."

"And what the hell's it got to do with you?" asked the quarrelsome man. "It's him I'm talking to. Can he no answer for himself?" He glared fiercely at Magnus. He was a square-shouldered fellow, very shabbily dressed, but nimble and soldierly, and his face was red and bony and truculent. Then slowly his expression altered. Pugnacity gave place to surprise, to recognition, and finally to beaming pleasure. "Christ!" he said, "it's Merriman, the beggar that stuck his bayonet up the Captain's airse at Festubert!"

For it should not be forgotten that, despite the city's lurch into the twentieth century, the area around the High Street and the Grassmarket was seldom visited by polite society. David Daiches, then a schoolboy at George Watson's College, remembered the area as "a filthy slum with children with ricketts and bare feet running around in obvious poverty and ill-nourished, women with threadbare shawls coming out of the jug and bottle entrance of a pub, trying to drown their sorrows in gin."

After graduating from Edinburgh, David Daiches left the city of his childhood for a dazzling academic career which took him to Oxford, the United States, Cambridge and Sussex before he returned in 1977 to the city he knows so well. Another contemporary, Muriel Spark, in her Edinburgh novel, *The Prime of Miss Jean Brodie*, was also aware of that gulf.

Now they were in a great square, the Grassmarket, with the

Castle, which was in any case everywhere, rearing between a big gap in the houses where the aristocracy used to live. It was Sandy's first experience of a foreign country, which intimates itself by its new smells and shapes and its new poor. A man sat on the icey-cold pavement; he just sat. A crowd of children, some without shoes, were playing some fight game, and some boys shouted after Miss Brodie's violet-clad company, with words that the girls had not heard before, but rightly considered to be obscene.

Born in 1918, Muriel Spark was educated at James Gillespie's School for Girls, which was probably the model for Jean Brodie's Marcia Blaine School. Today, Miss Spark lives in New York and Rome but "Jean Brodie", which has had a stage version and which has been filmed and televised, remains one of the great Edinburgh novels. The central character, Miss Brodie, is a monstrous creation, a wilfully ignorant woman with an unmatched capacity for corrupting her susceptible middle-class girl pupils. Only Sandy, of the girls, has the imagination to see through Jean Brodie's division of the world into the crème-de-la-crème and the rest, and to come to a vivid understanding of her country's pre-occupation with the Calvinistic theory of the Elect.

> Fully to savour her position, Sandy would go and stand outside St. Giles Cathedral or the Tolbooth, and contemplate these emblems of a dark and terrible salvation which made the fires of the damned seem very merry to the imagination by contrast, and much preferable. Nobody in her life, at home or at school, had ever spoken of Calvinism except as a joke that had once been taken seriously. She did not at the time understand that her environment had not been on the surface peculiar to the place, as was the environment of the Edinburgh social classes just above or, even more, just below her own. She had no experience of social class at all. In its outward forms her fifteen years might have been spent in any suburb of any city in the British Isles; her school, with its alien house system, might have been in Ealing. All she was conscious of now was that some quality of life peculiar to Edinburgh and nowhere else had been going on unbeknown to her all the time, and however undesirable it might be she felt deprived of it; however undesirable, she desired to know what it was, and to cease to be protected from it by enlightened people.

Sandy's dilemma, that of the Scot divorced from her or his cultural background, has been at the centre of Scottish culture in the twentieth century. In the novel, she solves it, unsatisfactorily, by becoming a nun — Muriel Spark, herself, was received into the Catholic church in 1954. By then, however, her visits to Edinburgh had become few and far between, one of the last being when her father died.

> I spent most of my time in my room waiting for the hours of visiting my father to come round. I think at such times in one's life one tends to look out of the window oftener and longer than usual. I left my work and my books and spent my time at the window. It was a high, wide window, with an inside ledge, broad and long enough for me to sit in comfortably with my legs stretched out. The days before Easter were suddenly warm and sunny. From where I sat propped in the open window frame, I could look straight onto Arthur's Seat and the Salisbury Crags, its girdle. When I sat the other way round I could see part of the Old City, the east corner of Princes Street Gardens, and the black Castle Rock. In those days I experienced an inpouring of love for the place of my birth, which I am aware was psychologically connected with my love for my father and with the exiled sensation of occupying a hotel room which was really meant for strangers.

It was in the nineteen-thirties that another constitutional exile, Edwin Muir returned to Scotland from London. The son of an Orkney farmer who had moved his family to Glasgow, Muir was a poet of great intellectual stature whose childhood years in the industrial west of Scotland had given him an early leaning towards socialism. Like MacDiarmid he had joined the I.L.P., but while his fellow poet threw himself with typical enthusiasm into the nationalist movement (the Scottish Party and the Nationalist Party had amalgamated in 1934 to form the present Scottish Nationalist Party), Muir was a more detached supporter, keeping himself at arm's length from total involvement. Later he was to quarrel bitterly with MacDiarmid on the literary use of Scots but the two men shared a deep loathing of a capitalist system which allowed a Scottish unemployment rate of 26%. In 1935 Muir wrote *Scottish Journey*, an account of a journey through his Scotland which would be a companion to J.B. Priestley's volume on England.

The book opens in Edinburgh, in a chapter which is full of acute critical insights into the divided nature of the city. Like other writers before him Muir saw clearly the split between the Old and the New Town, between poverty and wealth, and in no passage is this better felt than, almost predictably, in his examination of the city's sexual and drinking mores.

Scottish streets are given an atmosphere of their own simply by the number of drunk people that one encounters in them. Whether the Scottish people drink more than other peoples it would be impossible to say; but they give the impression of doing so, because of the abundant signs of public drunkenness that one finds in such towns as Edinburgh and Glasgow and even in small country towns on a Saturday night. During a fortnight's stay in Edinburgh I did not get through a single evening without seeing at least one example of outrageous or helpless drunkenness, and I had spent two years in London without coming across more than four or five. I think the explanation is that Scottish people drink spasmodically and intensely, for the sake of a momentary but complete release, whereas the English like to bathe and paddle about bucolically in a mild puddle of beer. One might put this down to a difference of national temperament or of national religion or to a hundred other things; there is no doubt, in any case, that the drinking habits of the Scots, like their dances, are far wilder than those of the English. The question is not a very important or interesting one. Much more interesting is the difference which class distinction produces in drunkenness in a Scottish town. There are as many drunk men and women in Princes Street on a Saturday night as in Leith Walk, but there are far fewer signs of them, and this is mainly due to social causes. Even when a man is in other ways incapable, he tries to conform to his particular code of manners, and so drunkenness in Princes Street is quiet and genteel: shown in a trifling unsteadiness of gait or a surprising affability of aspect by which the middle-class Edinburgh man manages to suggest that he is somehow upholding something or other which distinguishes him from the working classes. He is helped in this purpose by certain benevolent circumstances, however, such as that the whisky sold in Princes Street is better than the whisky one buys in Leith Walk, and that it is always easy to get a taxi in Princes Street after ten o'clock. By means of these discreet ambulances the unconscious and semi-conscious are inconspicuously removed. In Leith Walk they lie about the pavement until their friends or the police laboriously lead them away. Thus appearances are kept up, appearances upon which a whole host of the most important things depend.

But it was not only the moral aspect of the city's poverty that distressed Muir: it was a deeper and more spiritual shortcoming within the population, an inadequacy that he saw as treason to Scotland. Just as Sandy pondered St Giles and the Tolbooth, in Muriel Spark's novel, and came to an understanding of being cut off from her heritage, so Muir dissected the city and its people and laid them bare with the cunning precision of the surgeon's scalpel.

> Edinburgh has a style, and that style was at one time, indeed as recently as a century ago, the reflection of a whole style of life. While the city itself remains, this style of life has now been broken down, or rather submerged, by successive waves of change which were first let loose during the Industrial Revolution, an event that has on a large scale swept from the great towns of Europe the innate character which they once possessed. The waves have almost completely submerged London; but Edinburgh, being a high, angular place, is more difficult to drown. So it presents outwardly the face it had a hundred years ago, while within it is worm-eaten with all the ingenuity in tastelessness which modern resources can supply.

Muir had been persuaded to return to Scotland from his work on A.R. Orage's *New Age* by the newly-formed Scottish Centre of International PEN. Formed in 1927 at the instigation of Professor Herbert Grierson, who was Professor of English Literature and Rhetoric at the University of Edinburgh, Scottish PEN had as its first secretary Hugh MacDiarmid and it existed as a meeting place for Scottish writers and on an international level to campaign for freedom of speech for all writers and to deal with problems like translation and international copyright. Its founder was the novelist John Galsworthy. Muir was present at the 1934 International Conference which was hosted by Scottish PEN in Edinburgh. For the organisers, it was little short of a triumph, culminating in a banquet with a Scottish traditional menu devised by Moray MacLaren, a writer with an encyclopaedic knowledge of his country's history; and so demonstrating to the world that Scottish PEN deserved its independence from the London Centre, a victory which Muir and others had helped bring about at the Budapest conference two years earlier.

Another founder and early promoter both of Scottish PEN and of the writers associated with MacDiarmid's Scots Renaissance was the poet Helen Cruickshank, who kept hospitable open house at Dinnieduff in Corstorphine. She was a constant source of encouragement and generosity to her fellow writers: offering MacDiarmid a permanent room in her house — it came to be known as "The Prophet's Chamber" — when he was in Edinburgh; helping Edwin Muir and his wife Willa to move back to Scotland; welcoming James Leslie Mitchell, the novelist, "Lewis Grassic Gibbon", whenever he made the journey north from his exile in Welwyn Garden City. Before her death in 1975 Helen Cruickshank had given unstinting help to successive generations of writers, remaining a much-loved and well-respected figure in the literary life of the city.

In the preparations for the establishment of the SNP, the left-wing of the old National Party was purged and in 1933 MacDiarmid was expelled from the South Edinburgh branch. Later he was to be expelled for his nationalism from the Communist Party which throughout the nineteen-thirties in Scotland depended on an anti-fascist front for its main support. During that period, internationalism and anti-facism were popular in Scotland and the nationalism which the *literati* had helped to create suffered accordingly. It became increasingly difficult for intellectuals with left-wing leanings to come to terms with the nationalist establishment and for many years the SNP remained an amorphous party at the centre of the political spectrum.

Indicative of much of the country's indifference to the cultural and political fate, was the continuing inability of the literary and cultural magazines to survive. *The Modern Scot*, the *Scots Standard*, and the promising *New Alliance*, which George Scott-Moncrieff had helped to found as a joint Scots-Irish publication, all lost the battle to gain a new audience which could articulate the feelings of regeneration within the country. War with Germany in 1939 took away much of the impetus: MacDiarmid spent the war working on Clydeside, Muir was in St. Andrews and Mackenzie in London, but a new generation of writers had found the faith to live and work and write in Scotland, and to express the belief that, despite Hector MacIver's gloomy prognosis that support for the Nationalist cause was "like farting against a hurricane", Scotland was still worth living in.

Hector MacIver had come to Edinburgh in 1934, to teach at the Royal High School, and until his death in 1966 he exercised an extraordinary influence, not only on his own pupils but also on the many writers who swam into his ken. Shortly after his death, Karl Miller, one of his pupils, now a Professor of English in London, edited a moving *festschrift*, in his honour — *Memoirs of a Modern Scotland* — which contains excellent essays not only on the man himself but of his age. A Lewisman by birth, and an aristocrat by inclination, MacIver was in many peoples' eyes, something of an eccentric and stories about him are legion. While dining with Louis MacNeice in Edinburgh's Cafe Royal he sent back his lobster because he doubted its Lewis origins; he knew a waiter in a city hotel who resembled Yeats and christened him William Waiter Yeats; he lodged with a variety of friends including Sir Herbert Grierson. Amongst his friends he numbered Dylan Thomas and Louis MacNeice and after the war he remained a close friend of the Edinburgh poets who had taken up the mantle of the renaissance movement. Principal amongst these was Sydney Goodsir Smith, a poet, who like his eighteenth-century forbears and like Stevenson before him, celebrated the city's low life with wit and humour.

Smith wrote his poetry in a fine, literary Scots which has led Alexander Scott, his friend and fellow makar, to describe him as "our greatest modern Scots poet of love, liquor and disenchantment".

> Efter the glaumert mile frae "Eagle" doun
> Til "Darnley's Wallicoat" was dune
> (And there's anither gane!)
> We werenae juist as sober as we'd been, and —
> I cannae mind the howff, in Rose Street onyweys,
> The "Abbotsford" maybe or "Daddy Milnes" —
> But we were standing at the bar . . .
> When, there she was!
> The door bust open wi a thrang
> O' orra buddies, students and conspiratoories,
> All on the bash to celebrate I dae ken what —
> And there she was, a lassie frae the mune direct,
> That smiled at me.

The son of the Professor of Forensic Medicine at Edinburgh, Smith was born in New Zealand in 1915 and educated in England. During the nineteen-thirties he had experimented with Scots, writing in a cramped artificial style that was to break through in 1948 with the publication of his verse sequence *Under the Eildon Tree*, which is justly regarded as one of the greatest poems of passion in the Scots tradition. Here the poet uses the myth of Thomas the Rhymer as the unifying theme of a work which laments the great lovers of history — Orpheus and Eurydice, Dido and Aeneas, Burns and Highland Mary — and is not above including the "lesser luves" of "the hure of Reekie".

> I got her i' the Black Bull
> (The Black Bull o' Norroway)
> Gin I mynd richt, in Leith Street,
> Doun the stair at the corner forenent
> The Fun Fair and Museum o' Monstrosities,
> The Tyke-faced Loun, the Cunyiar's Den
> And siclike.

A celebration of common humanity is inherent in all of Smith's work and in his poems dealing with Edinburgh there is the underlying raucousness of the pub, good company and late nights, of a world where,

> . . . the bar
> Outby across the road
> By Mary's Bath-tub, aa
> Was cantie, snog and bricht,
> A cheerie howff, and a crousie companie
> O philosophers and tinks — Aa
> "Scholards an' gennemen, beGode!"

Sydney Goodsir Smith worked for a time as Art Critic of the *Scotsman* and painted while pursuing his literary career as poet, dramatist and critic from his house at 50 Craigmillar Park, the great "Schloss Schmidt". He was one of the most remarkable figures of his generation, a man of such good humour and generosity that even five years after his death in 1975, friends like David Daiches "cannot walk into the Abbotsford without still expecting to see him".

There was in the nineteen-forties and fifties a revival of bohemian life in Edinburgh with writers and artists foregathering in pubs like the Abbotsford in Rose Street, the Cafe Royal, and "Daddy" Milnes in Hanover Street. That was the world celebrated by Sydney Goodsir Smith and he himself contributed to the stories and retold them with gusto. Once, on a hungover Saturday morning, unsteadily sure of his surroundings, and in need of refreshment, Sydney went into what looked like a bar and ordered a large drink. There was a bar in the building and a man stood behind it — but Sydney had wandered into a bank (they opened on Saturdays in those days). Other stories abound about that most liked of men, and he added to them with fantastic embellishments. The determined seeker after his wit need not look any further than to his extravaganza *Carotid Cornucopious* — the Caird of the Cannon Gait and Voyeur of the Outlook Touer — a linguistic romp which MacDiarmid described as "doing for Edinburgh no less successfully what Joyce did for Dublin in *Ulysses*". Printed for the Auk Society (Sydney often saw himself as the Auk) it is a work that defies quotation but something of its flavour can be seen in the fantastic names of the Edinburgh pubs visited by Carroty — Sunday Balls in Fairest Redd, the Abbotsfork in Low Street, Doddie Mullun's, Wullie Roose's Coxfork in Bung Strait and the Haw-Haw Hures at Quaenisfanny whaur Divot Fowrballs or Fallfaur was crabnipped.

Throughout his life, Sydney Goodsir Smith, like many of his fellow poets, experienced considerable difficulties in finding a publisher, and his *Collected Poems* did not appear until after his death. Because he wrote in Scots most London-based publishers ignored him and publishing in Edinburgh had declined to such an extent that it was barely kept alive by the remaining Scottish-owned houses and by a handful of enthusiasts who were under-capitalised and who lacked distribution outlets. The Porpoise Press which had done such sterling work had been taken over by Faber, but their role to a certain extent, had been replaced after the war by a group of printers headed by Joseph Mardell of the Stanley Press, who established Serif Books. It staggered on for a few years and published the work of writers like Fred Urquhart, John R. Allan and Maurice Lindsay before it disappeared as suddenly as it had been born.

In 1952 Mardell had printed the first number of *Lines Review*, a literary magazine which was to play a significant role in publishing the work not only of Scottish poets but also of European poets in translation. It was conceived by Alan Riddell, an Australian-born poet who had studied at Edinburgh and its first number was published as a sixtieth-birthday tribute to Hugh MacDiarmid. Later, the printing and publishing of this fine magazine was taken over by Callum Macdonald who had started his printing business with a hand press in the basement of his stationer's shop in Marchmont Road. As well as publishing *Lines* on a regular basis, Macdonald, a Lewis man by birth, became the most influential post-war literary publisher and without him Sydney Goodsir Smith's later poetry would not have seen the light of day. It was with good reason that in 1978 Robert Garioch dedicated his own *Collected Poems* to Callum Macdonald, with the words, "No publisher was ever more considerate."

Robert Garioch — Robert Garioch Sutherland — was a close friend and neighbour of Smith's and like him he writes in Scots. Most of his life has been spent in the city, working as a schoolmaster and, like Robert Fergusson before him, casting a discreet eye over Edinburgh's pomposities and absurdities.

> I saw him comin out the N.B. Grill,
> creashy and winey, wi his famous voice
> crackin some comic bawr to please three choice
> notorious bailies, lauchen fit to kill.
>
> Syne thae fowre crousie cronies clam intill
> a muckle big municipal Rolls-Royce,
> and disappeared, aye lauchan, wi a noise
> that droont the traffic, towards the Calton Hill.
>
> As they rade by, it seemed the sun was shinin
> brichter nor usual roun thae cantie three
> that wi thon weill-kent Heid-yin had been dinin.
>
> Nou that's the kinna thing I like to see;
> tho ye and I look on and canna jyne in,
> it gies our toun some tone, ye'll aa agree.

MODERN TIMES

In his *Sixteen Edinburgh Sonnets* (which like Fergusson's poetry should be read in their entirety as quotation from them cannot hope to do justice), Garioch presents himself as the underdog, the anti-establishment man who prefers the company of the pub to that of the drawing room, but there is a hard edge to his geniality and he is never afraid of holding up a mirror to man's vainglory. In *Did you see me?* the poet, invited to the kind of "great occasioun" that Edinburgh delights in, sees the reception ruined by:

> . . . . the keelies of the toun,
> a toozie lot, gat word of the affair.
>
> We cudnae stop it: they jist gaithert roun
> to mak sarcastic craks and grin and stare.
> I wisht I hadnae worn my M.A. goun.

In other poems like *Cooling Aff*, *And they were richt* and *Heard in the Cougate* Garioch wields a sharply satirical blade at his native city and in one of his best poems, *To Robert Fergusson*, he looks back with fond regret at the Edinburgh of two centuries ago.

> Auld Reekie's bigger, nou, what's mair,
> and folk wha hae the greater share
> of warldlie gear may tak the air
>   in Morningside,
> and needna sclim the turnpike stair
>   whar ye wad byde.
>
> But truth it is, our couthie city
> has cruddit in twa pairts a bittie
> and speaks twa tongues, ane coorse and grittie.
>   heard in the Cougait
> the tither copied, mair's the pitie,
>   frae Wast of Newgate.
>
> Whilk is the crudd and whilk the whey
> I wad be kinna sweirt to say,
> but this I ken, that of the twae
>   the corrupt twang
> of Cougait is the nearer tae
>   the leid ye sang.

And in *Embro to the Ploy* he pokes gentle fun at the newly-founded Festival, imagining a romp where characters from the city's underworld rub shoulders with polite society in the Festival Club which is housed each year in the Assembly Rooms in George Street.

> The auld Assembly-rooms whaur Scott
> foregethert wi his fiers,
> nou see a gey kenspeckle lot
> ablow the chandeliers.
> Til Embro drouths the Festival Club
> a richt godsend appears;
> it's something new to find a pub
> that gaes on sairvin beers
>   eftir hours
> in Embro to the ploy.
>
> Jist pitten-out, the drucken mobs
> frae howffs in Potterraw,
> fleean, to hob-nob wi the Nobs,
> ran to this Music Haa,
> Register Rachel, Cougait Kate,
> Nae-neb Nellie and aa
> stauchert about amang the Great,
> what fun! I never saw
>   the like,
> In Embro to the ploy.

The Festival had opened in 1947 under the direction of Rudolf Byng and it quickly established itself as one of the world's great festivals of music and drama, becoming in the words of the critic Ronald Mavor, "the mostest of the bestest". Much of the impetus and vision had come from Harvey Wood of the British Council in Edinburgh who saw in the Festival an opportunity of healing Europe's wartime wounds, and despite its chronic lack of performance facilities, the Festival and its Fringe continue to be the year's highlights when they take over the city for three late summer weeks.

To give the event a Scottish flavour Lyndsay's *Thrie Estaitis* was produced by Sir Tyrone Guthrie in 1948 in a revised version by the playwright Robert Kemp. In what seemed like poetic justice to many, it was staged in the Assembly Hall of the Church of Scotland on the Mound, and, despite the grim and forbidding statue of John Knox at its main entrance, the hall has gone on to establish itself as a regular Festival venue. Another Scottish play, produced in a later Festival was Sydney Goodsir Smith's *The Wallace*, which generated the kind of enthusiasm Scots usually reserve for football matches, Iain Cuthbertson who played the title role remembering that "when Wallace slew his wife's slayer, the English Sherriff, loud cheering broke out. It was as if Denis Law had scored for the third time."

Although the Festival continued to attract enthusiastic audiences, for the rest of the year drama remained the poor relation of Scottish letters. Although the impresarios, Howard and Wyndham had attempted to establish regular seasons at the Royal Lyceum and during the thirties the Masque Theatre and Millicent Ward's Studio Theatre had brought plays to the city, there was no decent theatre until 1946 when the remarkable Gateway Theatre opened in Elm Row. The former community centre was owned by the Church of Scotland who leased it out through their Home Board to the Edinburgh Film Guild and to a company headed by Campbell White and Robert Kemp who stated its aims as: "by giving an outlet to Scottish material, Scottish actors would be given a chance of being more truly creative".

In 1953 a permanent company was established under the direction of Lennox Milne and the season opened in October with James Bridie's *The Forrigan Reel*. During its short career the Gateway achieved a substantial reputation which the energetic Robert Kemp built up both as its chairman and as a playwright who wrote a vigorous Scots. Eventually financial problems overtook the theatre and it closed its doors in March 1965. It later became a television studio.

Although poets like Sydney Goodsir Smith might have lacked a wide audience on the printed page, they were more fortunate in the new field of radio and television broadcasting. In 1964 Smith celebrated the opening of the Forth Road Bridge in *The Twa Brigs* for the Home Service and in December the following year he wrote *Kynd Kittock's Land* which was produced for television with photographs by Alan Daiches. This poem is perhaps his most sustained work in praise of Edinburgh, the poet's "rortie city" which is such a mixture of historical grandeur and scruffy low life. Smith saw through it all.

> Embro toun is me and me is it — d'ye see?
> The winds will come as winds have been
> But ever and aye there's us
> That sits here bien and snog,
> Members, son, o' an auld companie
> In an auld rortie city —
> Wretched, tae, ye cried us, ach, young man,
> Ye ken nocht aboot it — as ye said yersel.
>
> Times aye cheynge and this auld runt
> Will flouer again (Heh! Heh! Yon's me!)
> And hae nae cheynge ava — we're aye the same,
> The desperate and the deid, the livin raucle yins,
> D'ye ken? Ay, and sae it is,
> Auld Reekie through the keeking glass
> Looks fine, and sae it does.
> And the mornin and the evenin
> Were anither age gane by . . .

There were other agencies, besides the BBC, who had the best interests of Scottish writers at heart. The Saltire Society published booklets of poetry, campaigned for a greater awareness of Scots culture in education and established award schemes to achieve higher standards in architecture. They also published the *Saltire Review*, which was yet another brave attempt to establish a general cultural magazine in the city.

Within the university, Scottish letters received a much-needed boost with the foundation of the School of Scottish Studies which soon became a treasure house of recordings of the Scottish and Gaelic oral traditions. Its founding father was Calum MacLean, a man widely versed in the Gaelic cultures of Ireland and Scotland whose brother Sorley was then teaching in Edinburgh at Borough-muir School. Today, Sorley MacLean, a Skye man, is generally held to be the greatest of living Gaelic poets, and he was a close friend of Sydney Goodsir Smith and of Hugh MacDiarmid whom he had first met in Edinburgh in 1934. Another West Highland poet who still lives in Edinburgh and who has the distinction of writing in Gaelic, Scots and English is George Campbell Hay. In the fifties, Edwin Muir was back in Edinburgh as Warden of Newbattle Abbey College, Scotland's first adult education institute. During his period there he encouraged an interest in contemporary literature and amongst his students were men who went on to make names for themselves as writers: George Mackay Brown, Tom Scott, Archie Hind and Morley Jamieson.

Although Garioch and Goodsir Smith are held to be Edinburgh's finest exponents of Scots in the twentieth century, there were other poets using that language with equal facility, notably Albert Mackie who also enjoyed a succcessful career as dramatist and journalist, and J.K. Annand whose bairn rhymes continue to give delight to successive generations of children. But Scots was not the sole medium of expression for the poets who followed in MacDiarmid's slipstream.

> On the Calton Hill
> the twelve pillars
> of this failed Parthenon
>   made more Greek by the cargo boat
>   sailing between them
>   on the cobwebby waters of the Firth
> should marry nicely with the Observatory
> in the way complements do
>   each observing the heavens
>   in its different way.

That singular voice belongs to Norman MacCaig a poet who writes in English with an Edinburgh accent never far away. He was born in Edinburgh in 1910 and like Robert Garioch was educated at the Royal High School (where he claims he started writing poetry because it invariably took less time to write than prose) and at the University of Edinburgh; his mother was a Gael and over the years it has been his custom to spend the summers in the north-west Highlands. Much of his life was spent as a schoolmaster but in his later years he was his university's first ever Writer in Residence. A friend and lender of encouragement to many — he was, perhaps, MacDiarmid's greatest friend — the young Karl Miller, a pupil of

193

MacIver's at the Royal High School, had good cause to remember his second meeting with this most scholarly and courteous of poets.

> One night shortly afterwards I ran into him again in the vestibule of the General Post Office, where we spent an hour talking about the imagery of Lorca. The GPO was the hub of the Edinburgh I have been describing, with its wild lives, its prim lives, the 'heavenly Hanoverianism' — in Burns's phrase — of its handsome squares and thoroughfares, and the loyal names that were prudently conferred on these by the magistrates who built the New Town: facing me across a street sloe-black in the rain was the Cafe Royal, to my left was Princes Street, and at my back was the Royal Mile. MacCaig did not seem to mind spending an hour talking about Lorca with a schoolboy he hardly knew (only Lorca, we said, could have provided that image of a bisected apple), and the encounter was typical of the town as I knew it then, of its grave interest in literature and of its private courtesy.

There is a division in most of MacCaig's poetry between the romantic and the classical and although the delicacy of his lyrics has become his own critical hallmark, for most readers the greatest joy is the discovery within a vivid and compelling image of the poet's keen, personal insight.

> City of everywhere, broken necklace in the sun,
> you are caves of guilt, you are pinnacles of jubilation.
> Your music is a filigree of drumming.
> You frown into the advent of heavenly hosts.
> Your iron finger shatters sad suns —
> they multiply in scatters, they swarm
> on fizzing roofs. When the sea
> breathes gray over you, you become
> one lurking-place, one shifting of nowheres —
> in it are warpipes and genteel pianos
> and the sawing voices of lawyers. Your buildings
> are broken memories, your streets
> lost hopes — but you shrug off time, you set your face
> against all that is not you.

It is impossible to look on the past few decades of Edinburgh life and not think of Norman MacCaig. One of the most gregarious of men,

MODERN TIMES

MacCaig has never been secretive about his art and when poetry readings became fashionable in the late nineteen-sixties he at once became an accomplished performer, delighting his audiences with his elegant wit.

Literary events had invaded the Festival in 1962 when the publisher John Calder mounted an International Writers Conference in the MacEwan Hall. The foundation of the Gateway Theatre had also encouraged local writers by performing new work and achieving the kind of results prophesied by Robert Kemp. The city council joined in the theatrical business in 1964 when it bought the Royal Lyceum Theatre which became overnight Scotland's first civic theatre. Tom Fleming was appointed artistic director and for two stormy years he struggled to find a repertoire which would be safe enough to please the city fathers and yet bold enough to attract a sophisticated audience. When he resigned in August 1966 the *Scotsman's* leader starkly placed the blame firmly on the shoulders of Tom Fleming who, they claimed, " . . . was over-ambitious and over-anxious to establish international standards from the start and to provide a diet of plays too exotic for the stomachs of Edinburgh citizens".

Luckily for Edinburgh's constitutions the Traverse Theatre, the city's first modern theatre club which was to gain a dazzling reputation for producing new plays, had been founded in 1963. It started its life in a converted doss-house in James Court in the Lawnmarket before moving down the precipitous hill to more spacious accommodation in the Grassmarket. One of its founders was an American, Jim Haynes, who came from New Orleans and who ran the Paperback Shop in Charles Street. In an act of disgraceful vandalism the University purchased the properties in that area of the south side and razed them to the ground, condemning a thriving city community to live in the outer suburbs.

But the business of bookselling in the city is never done and after the Paperback closed its doors for the last time, Bauermeisters opened their new premises in November 1966, on George IV Bridge, within a stone's throw of the National Library and the Central Lending Library. They had started life as importers in Glasgow before setting up shop in Bank Street and their stock to this day shows a leaning towards European art books. As the trade became more competitive and as booksellers found themselves fighting on the mass market for their share of the public's leisure-time spending, so were there changes. Almost a century after it had been founded, Douglas and Foulis in Castle Street was taken over by the John Menzies organisation in 1957. It has since been "rationalised" with the opening of Menzies' super-store in Princes Street, and it no longer exists. Cairns, the medical booksellers in Teviot Place was taken over by Robert Maxwell's Pergamon Press in 1966, and in George Street the Edinburgh Bookshop was opened in 1955 by the merger of two old-established Edinburgh firms, Robert Grant and William Brown.

In the midst of these changes, general publishing in the city was dealt two swift body blows in the early summer of 1962. In May, Nelson was bought by the Thomson Organisation and three months later Oliver and Boyd was sold to the Financial Times for £525,000. Livingstone, the medical publishers, followed later into the same group. Other specialist publishers survived, notably the mapmakers, Bartholomew, who had set up business in 1860 at 4a North Bridge, and Greens, the law publishers, who remained in their splendid offices in the High Street, opposite the Law Courts. Elswhere publishing life flickered briefly. Ian Hamilton Finlay and Jessie McGuffie set up the Wild Hawthorn Press in Fettes Row in 1962, the same year that Giles Gordon took over the editorship of the ill-fated *New Saltire*, but the loss of Nelson and Oliver and Boyd set the seal on Edinburgh's demise as a publishing centre.

Not that the business of writing was stilled — Edinburgh still had its full complement of writers: Alan Bold, a poet born and brought up at the top of Leith Walk, James Allan Ford, a senior civil servant whose novels hold up a far from flattering mirror to Edinburgh's bourgeiosie, George Bruce, a poet at the BBC who encouraged younger writers, playwrights like Stanley Eveling who graced the Traverse with his work. Sadly, there were losses as well as gains. Sir Compton Mackenzie who had returned to Edinburgh to live in a Drummond Place house that became a centre of hospitality to writers the world over died in 1972. In distant Aberdeen Eric Linklater died in 1974. Sydney Goodsir Smith, to universal sorrow, died the following year, and in September 1978 Hugh MacDiarmid died in a city hospital at the age of eighty-six.

During the nineteen-seventies Edinburgh shook off some of the dust of decades and awoke to a new explosion of cultural vigour. Theatre seemed to have gained a firmer foothold than Ramsay could ever have hoped for, there were more galleries with more open ideas, writers found it somewhat easier to make a living, even though the city may have ignored them in much the way it forgot about Fergusson, and publishing started up again with a generation geared to the changing economic conditions of the latter part of the century. Although subsidies from the Scottish Arts Council helped, the deciding factor in most cases was that there were in Edinburgh, as in the rest of Scotland, lively, creative people ready to work hard and to get things done. It was ever the case.

The decade also saw heated debate about a possible devolution of power from London and the shame of a divided vote at the 1979 referendum which matched the failure of the Darien Scheme three hundred years previously. Hamilton's Royal High School was to have housed the Assembly and it still stands in Regent Road, a close runner-up to the "twelve pillars of this failed Parthenon" — known as Scotland's Disgrace — on the Calton Hill above.

As for the city, it has escaped, so far, the worst ravages of inner city industrialisation but it has paid scant attention to John Ruskin's pleas as the gaunt fortress of the St. James Centre gives mute witness. It remains a divided city with differences not only evident area by area but also street by street. Wealth and poverty, spiritual and material, still exist side by side, the demarcation being made more complete by the break-up of the city centre communities and the sprawl of the city to its suburban outposts. But on a misty winter's evening, with a haar off the Forth seeping through the wynds and closes of the High Street, the shades of Dunbar, Fergusson, Burns or Stevenson would find no reason not to enter one of the brightly-lit pubs for an evening's enjoyment. For, whatever its faults, Edinburgh still retains the magic of centuries.

That vision of Edinburgh, at once medieval and yet geared to its modern consciousness, comes alive in Hamish Henderson's poem *Floret silva undique*, from a longer sequence, *Auld Reekie's Roses*. One of the country's best-known folklorists, Henderson conjures up a wondrous selection of characters who play out a dance which lifts the dead hand of Calvin from the city's grey shoulders. For a few

197

PRECIPITOUS CITY

brief moments, the city and its past surprise themselves by becoming as one, and as the title suggests, "the woodlands flourish on all sides".

Floret silva undique
The rockin righteous are makin hay.

Out from their dens, as shair's your life,
Come Knox and poxy and Mac the Knife;

Major Weir o' the twa-faced faith
And Deacon Brodie in gude braid claith.

Seely sunshine and randy mirk
Like Auld Nick's wing ow'r a pairish kirk.

Whae's yon chattin' up Jess Mackay?
It's Bailie Burke, wi' his weet wall-eye.

The kinchin's bara, so clinch the deal:
Gie her a note, son, and hae a feel.

Edina — Reekie — mon amour.
Dae't, or I'll skelp your airse, ye hoor.

The flesh is bruckle, the fiend is slee
Susanna's elders are on the spree.

The bailie beareth the belle away.
The lily, the rose, the rose I lay.

Select Bibliography

Arnot, Hugo, *The History of Edinburgh*, Edinburgh, 1779.
Baird, William, *Annals of Duddingston and Portobello*, Edinburgh, 1898.
Beattie, James, *Scoticisms, Arranged in Alphabetical Order, Designed to Correct Improprieties of Speech and Writing*, Edinburgh 1779
Black, A & C, Ltd, *Adam and Charles Black, 1807—1957*, London, 1957.
Boswell, James, *Journal of a Tour to the Hebrides*, London, 1785.
Brown, P. Hume, *Early Travellers in Scotland*, London, 1891.
Brown, John, *Rab and his Friends*, London, 1906.
Bruce, David, *Sun Pictures, the Hill-Adamson Calotypes*, London, 1973.
Burt, Edward, *Letters from a Gentleman in the North of Scotland to his Friends in London*, Vol.1, London, 1754.
Carlyle, Rev. Dr Alexander, *Autobiography*, ed. J. Hill Burton, Edinburgh and London, 1910.
Carlyle, Thomas, *Reminiscences*, Int. Ian Campbell, London, 1972.
Catford, E.F., *Edinburgh, The Story of a City*, London, 1975.
Chambers, Robert, *Traditions of Edinburgh*, Edinburgh, 1825.
Chitnis, Anand, *The Scottish Enlightenment*, London, 1976.
Cockburn, Lord, *Journey of Henry Cockburn*, 2 vols., Edinburgh, 1874. *Memorials of his Time*, ed. W. Forbes Gray, Edinburgh, 1946.
Creech, William, *Letters, Addressed to Sir John Sinclair, Bart., Respecting the Mode of Living, Arts, Commerce, Literature, Manners &c. of Edinburgh in 1763*, Edinburgh.
Daiches, David, *Edinburgh*, London, 1978. *The Paradox of Scottish Culture*, Oxford, 1964. *The Selected Poems of Robert Burns*, London, 1979.
Davie, George Elder, *The Democratic Intellect*, Edinburgh and London, 1951.
Defoe, Daniel, *A Tour thro' the Whole Island of Great Britain*, Vol. 2, London, 1927.
Dibdin, J.C., *Annals of the Edinburgh Stage*, Edinburgh, 1888.
Drummond, William, of Hawthornden, *Poems and Prose*, ed. R.H. Macdonald, Edinburgh, 1976.
Dunbar, William, *The Poems of William Dunbar*, ed. W. Mackay Mackenzie, Edinburgh, 1932.
Fergusson, Robert, *Poems*, ed. M. McDiarmid, 2 vols., Edinburgh, 1954-56.
Garioch, Robert, *Collected Poems*, Loanhead, 1978.
Grant, Elizabeth, of Rothiemurcus, *Memoirs of a Highland Lady*, London, 1950.
Grant, James, *Old and New Edinburgh*, 3 vols., London, 1883.
Hamilton, Alan, *Essential Edinburgh*, London, 1977.

Harrison, Wilmot, *Memorable Edinburgh Houses*, rev., Oliphant Smeaton, London, 1898.
Harvie, Christopher, *Scotland and Nationalism, Scottish Society and Politics*, London, 1977.
Hogg, James, *Memoirs of the Author's Life, and Familiar Anecdotes of Sir Walter Scott*, ed. D.S. Mack, Edinburgh,1972. *Selected Poems*, ed. D.S. Mack, Oxford, 1970.
Jack, R.D.S., ed., *Scottish Prose, 1550-1700*, London, 1971. *A Choice of Scottish Verse, 1560-1660*, London, 1978.
Lindsay, Maurice, *The Burns' Encyclopaedia*, rev. ed., London, 1970.
Lockhart, John Gibson, *Memoirs of the Life of Sir Walter Scott, Bart.*, 7 vols., Edinburgh, 1837-38. *Peter's Letters to his Kinsfolk*, ed. William Ruddick, Edinburgh, 1977.
MacDiarmid, Hugh, *Contemporary Scottish Studies*, rev. ed., Edinburgh, 1976. *Complete Poems*, London, 1978.
Mackenzie, Henry, *Anecdotes and Egotisms*, London, 1927.
McLaren, Moray, *The Capital of Scotland*, London, 1950.
Masson, David, *Edinburgh Sketches and Memories*, London, 1892.
Masson, Rosaline, *In Praise of Edinburgh*, London, 1912.
Menzies, John, and Co. Ltd., *The House of Menzies*, Edinburgh, 1958.
Miller, Karl, ed., *Memoirs of a Modern Scotland*, London, 1970.
Muir, Edwin, *Scott and Scotland*, London, 1936. *Scottish Journey*, int., T.C. Smout, Edinburgh, 1979.
Oliphant, Margaret, *William Blackwood and his Sons, the Annals of a Publishing House*, vols. 1, 2, Edinburgh, 1897.
Ramsay, Allan, *The Works of Allan Ramsay*, eds. J.W. Oliver, B. Martin, A.M. Kinghorn and A. Law, Edinburgh, 1974.
Ramsay, John, of Ochtertyre, *Scotland and Scotsmen in the Eighteenth Century*, ed. A. Allardyce, Edinburgh, 1888.
Scott, Walter, *The Journal of Sir Walter Scott*, ed. J.G. Tait, 3 vols., London, 1939-46.
Stevenson, Robert Louis, *Edinburgh: Picturesque Notes*, London, 1879. *Memories and Portraits*, London, 1887.
Stuart, Marie W., *Old Edinburgh Taverns*, Edinburgh, 1952.
Topham, Captain Edward, *Letters from Edinburgh Written in the Years, 1774 and 1775*, London, 1776.
Tredrey, Frank, *The House of Blackwood, 1804-1954*, Edinburgh, 1954.
Watt, Francis, *The Book of Edinburgh Anecdote*, Edinburgh and London, 1913.
Wright, Gordon, *MacDiarmid, An Illustrated Biography*, Edinburgh, 1977.
Youngson, A.J., *The Making of Classicial Edinburgh, 1750-1840*, Edinburgh, 1966.

Acknowledgements

Grateful acknowledgements are due to the following copyright holders who allowed their work to appear in this volume.

Robert Garioch and Macdonald Publishers for the extracts from 'Did ye see me?', 'Embro to the Ploy', 'To Robert Fergusson' and 'Glisk of the Great' from *Collected Poems*.

Mrs Valda Grieve and Martin Brian and O'Keeffe Ltd for the extract from 'Edinburgh' from *Complete Poems of Hugh MacDiarmid*.

Hamish Henderson and the Editor of *Broadsheet* for the extract from 'Floret Silva Undique'.

Norman MacCaig and the Hogarth Press for the extracts from 'Inward Bound' from *The White Bird* and 'Drop-out in Edinburgh' from *The World's Room*.

Bruce Marshall and Constable and Company Ltd for the extract from *The Black Oxen*.

Karl Miller and Faber and Faber Ltd for the extract from *Memoirs of a Modern Scotland*.

Gavin Muir and Mainstream Publishing Ltd for the extract from *Scottish Journey* by Edwin Muir.

A.D. Peters and Co Ltd for the extract from *Magnus Merriman* by Eric Linklater.

Mrs Hazel Smith and John Calder Ltd for the extracts from 'To Li Po in the Delectable Mountains of Tien Mu', 'The Black Bull o Norroway', 'Kynd Kittock's Land' and 'Gowdspink in Reekie' from *Collected Poems* by Sydney Goodsir Smith.

Muriel Spark and Macmillan Ltd for the extract from *The Prime of Miss Jean Brodie*.

Muriel Spark and the Editor of the *New Statesman* for the extract from 'What Images Return'.

Grateful acknowledgements are also due to the following owners who allowed original paintings, illustrations and photographs to appear in this volume.

Edinburgh Public Libraries for the calotype of the Scott Monument under construction.

William Blackwood and Sons Ltd for the portraits of William Blackwood and James Hogg.

PRECIPITOUS CITY

Oscar Marzaroli for the photograph of Sydney Goodsir Smith.

The National Gallery of Scotland for the painting of Baxter's Close.

Mrs Patricia Maxwell Scott for the portrait of Sir Walter Scott and the painting of Sciennes Hill House.

The Scottish National Portrait Gallery for the portraits of Robert Burns, Lord Cockburn, Archibald Constable, William Drummond of Hawthornden, Robert Fergusson, Susan Ferrier, Henry Mackenzie and Allan Ramsay.

Mrs Hazel Smith for the photograph of Sydney Goodsir Smith, Hugh MacDiarmid and Norman MacCaig.

The Taft Museum, Cincinnati, Ohio for the portrait of Robert Louis Stevenson.

The photographs of the portraits and paintings were provided by courtesy of the National Galleries of Scotland, Lothian Regional Council, and Tom Scott.

Index

INDEX

Gregory, John: 94
Grenville, Lord: 109
Greyfriars Church: 59, 67
Grierson, Prof. Herbert: 183, 185
Grieve, Christopher Murray: *see*
  MacDiarmid, Hugh
Grindlay Street: 169
Gunn, Neil: 177
Guthrie Street: 117

Ha', Jenny: 81
Haddington: 31
Hall, Capt. Basil: 143
Hamilton, Duke of: 105
Hamilton, Gavin: 111
Hamilton, William, of Bangour: 81,
  84, 85
Hanover Street: 148, 187
Hardress, Lord: 74
Hare, William: 122
Hart, Andro: 60
Hastings, Warren: 109
Hay, George Campbell: 193
Hay, James: 155
Haynes, Jim: 195
Hazlitt, William: 127
Henderson, Hamish: 197-198
Henley, W.E.: 163, 170, 177
Henry VII: 17, 54
Henry VIII: 37
Herd, David: 99
Heriot Row: 137, 157, 160, 163
High Street: 1, 2, 3, 4, 11, 15, 24, 28,
  29, 80, 86-7, 98, 106, 111, 128, 129,
  155-6, 159, 178-9, 196
Hill, Peter: 106
Hind, Archie: 193
Hogg, James: 3, 4, 16, 64, 70, 122,
  131-8, 142, 145
Holyrood: 2, 11, 14, 24, 27, 32, 44,
  56, 71, 76, 82, 86, 116, 170-1
Holy Trinity, Church of: 14
Home, Henry: 97
Home, John: 104
Hope Park: 155
Horner, Francis: 125
Howard Place: 156, 174
Howard, Thomas, Earl of Surrey: 17
Howe Street: 170
Hudson, Robert: 48

Hume, David: 93, 94, 95, 105
Huntly, Earl of: 52

Inverleith Terr.: 157
Irving, Henry: 169
Irving, John: 124

Jacobite: 79, 82-5, 139
James II: 82, 83
James IV: 13, 14, 16-19, 23, 27, 38, 39
James V: 22-27, 29, 30
James VI: 41, 43-45, 47, 49-54, 56
James Court: 93, 195
Jamieson, Morley: 193
Jeffrey, Francis: 7, 125-8, 130, 147
Jeffrey Street: 77
Jenkin, Fleeming: 160
Johnson, Samuel: 115, 125
Johnston, Maggy: 77, 78
Jonson, Ben: 75, 81

Kailyard: 153, 167, 171, 173
Kames, Lord: 84, 94, 97, 98, 106
Keats, John: 127
Kemble, John Philip: 139
Kemp, George Meikle: 146
Kemp, Robert: 191
Killiecrankie, Battle of: 68
King's Park: 82
King's Wark, The: 51
Kirk of Field, House of: 37
Knox, John: 31, 32, 35, 38, 41

Laidlaw, William: 135
Laing, William: 106
Lamb, Charles: 60
Lauder, Harry: 173
Lawnmarket: 4, 11, 111, 168, 195
Leith: 24, 27, 30, 32, 63, 86, 92, 100,
  105, 124, 139, 142, 148, 153, 158,
  161, 162, 182-3, 186
Leith Wynd: 77
Lekprevik, Robert: 36, 41
Leslie, John: 30, 36
Leyden, John: 125
Liberton Wynd: 124
Libraries: 66, 78, 83, 84, 151, 169, 195
Lindsay, David, Bishop of Edinburgh:
  58
Lindsay, Maurice: 187

INDEX

128, 129, 137, 152, 155, 182, 194
Newton, Lord: 124
Nicholson Street: 107
Nicoll, Sir William Robertson: 167,
  168, 173
Niddry's Wynd: 75, 76
Nor Loch: 17, 28, 81, 93, 102
North Bridge: 99, 148, 196
North Castle Street: 125, 143
North, Christopher: 134, 145, 154
Northern Review: 177

Ochil Hills: 81
Ogilby, Colonel: 74
Ogilvie, George: 172
Old College: 86, 117
Oliphant, Margaret: 153, 167
Oliver & Boyd: 155, 196
Orage, A.R.: 183
Orange, William and Mary of: 68, 69,
  79
Osbourne, Fanny: 163
Owen, Wilfred: 175

Paisley Close: 156
Parliament Close: 66, 71
Parliament House: 98, 142
Paterson, William: 69
PEN: 183-4
Pennant, Thomas: 106
Pentland Hills: 6, 116, 122, 154, 164,
  165, 174
People's Journal: 167
Philp, Sir R.W.: 156
Picardy Place: 170
Pitcairne, Archibald: 79, 83
Polwarth: 49
Pope, Alexander: 81, 96, 109
Porpoise Press: 177, 187
Porteous, Capt. John: 88, 89, 116
Portobello: 124, 137, 154, 173
Potter Row: 113
Power, William: 177
Preston, Sir Symoun: 38
Priestley, J.B.: 181
Princes Street: 1, 93, 128, 129, 146,
  153-4, 159, 177, 182-3, 194, 196
Pringle, Thomas: 130-2
Printing: 106, 107, 138, 155, 187
Ptolemy: 7

Quarterly Review: 128, 146
Queensferry: 6
Queen Street: 132

Raeburn, Henry: 141
Ramsay, Allan: 2, 3, 7, 71, 74-83, 85,
  86, 90, 93, 96, 168, 197
Ramsay, Edward Bannerman: 169
Ramsay Gardens: 81, 168
Ramsay of Ochtertyre: 122
Randolph, Thomas: 45
Rankinian Club: 84
Register House: 93
Riccio, David: 44
Richmond, John: 111
Riddell, Alan: 188
Riddell, Maria: 113
Robert I: 11
Robertson, William: 94, 106
Rollock, Robert: 51
Rosebery, Lord: 166
Rose Street: 185-6
Ross, Robert: 128
Royal Exchange: 124
Royal High School: 84, 107, 108,
  117-8, 121, 150, 185, 193-4
Royal Lyceum Theatre: 169, 191, 195
Ruddiman, Thomas: 83, 84
Ruddiman, Walter: 103
Ruskin, John: 149, 197
Rutherford, John: 117
Rutherford's Bar: 160
Ruthven, Lord: 44

Salisbury Crags: 116, 117, 155
Saltire Society: 192
Sandyknowe: 117-118, 122
Sassoon, Siegfried: 175
Scots Literary Renaissance: 174, 184
Scots Magazine: 135
Scotsman, The: 145, 169, 173, 186, 195
Scots Observer: 163, 177
Scots Standard: 184
Scott, Alexander (16th century): 34, 35
Scott, Alexander: 185
Scott, Francis George: 172
Scott, Tom: 70
Scott, Walter: 3, 4, 17, 43, 44, 60, 64,
  69, 88, 108, 116-146, 151, 152, 155,
  158

INDEX